THE WELL READ PLAY

D0685554

THE WELL READ PLAY

Stephen Unwin

OBERON BOOKS
LONDON

First published in 2011 by Oberon Books Ltd
521 Caledonian Road, London N7 9RH
Tel: +44 (0) 20 7607 3637 / Fax: +44 (0) 20 7607 3629
e-mail: info@oberonbooks.com
www.oberonbooks.com

The Publisher is grateful to other Publishers and Agents for granting
permission to reproduce copyright material.

Acknowledgements for use of extracts from plays
can be found on pages 231-2.

ISBN: 978-1-84002-770-9

Cover illustration by Andrzej Klimowski

Printed by CPI Antony Rowe, Chippenham

Contents

To the playwrights

Acknowledgements

Many people have helped with this book: writers, actors, directors, literary managers and others. I am particularly grateful to James Hogan at Oberon for commissioning me, but also for his friendship and support over the years. I would like to thank my father, Peter Unwin, for helping me cut the dead wood, and my partner, Ginny Schiller, for everything else. My two sons, Laurie and Joe, have put up with me through thick and thin and my daughter, Beatrice, was born as I was working on the final edit; I flatter myself that she will want to read it one day.

*

Note on gender

I have used 'he' and 'his' to denote either gender, except when obviously female. I considered using 'his or her' or 's/he' but found them clumsy. My decision shouldn't be interpreted as implying anything other than grammatical convenience.

Note on the quotations from Shakespeare

The quotations from Shakespeare follow the principles I've laid down in my performance editions for Oberon Books. I use the lightest punctuation possible – no exclamation marks, colons or unnecessary commas, and only full stops and question marks at the end of verse lines. This has no pretence at scholarship, but can be useful for reading aloud and in rehearsals.

1. Why read a play?

I HAVE WRITTEN THIS BOOK because I believe in plays. I don't mean that I believe in the theatre – although I do. I mean that I believe in the ability of written drama to entertain and communicate powerful insights about the individual and the world at large.

Many people have said that they find it hard to read a play. They don't know how to hear the different voices in their heads, they can't imagine how the action might unfold on the stage and they find it difficult to follow the story. Above all, they want the writer to step forward and tell them what to think.

The truth is, of course, that reading a play is an unnatural act. The vast majority of plays were not written to be read – or, at least, only by people who are planning to stage them. Thus reading a play can be compared to studying a musical score: the composer and the playwright's efforts only bear fruit when performed by others – and both require the same kind of skills. The aim of this book is to give some sense of what these might be.

Where to start?

The reader of plays has an enormous wealth of material from which to choose. Kenneth Tynan's 'list of prospective plays for the National Theatre'[1] is a good place to start. Tynan drew up his list in the 1960s and the most modern title is John Osborne's *A Patriot for Me* (1965). The last 40 years have produced hundreds of others and if updated today the list might be half as long again. For an art form that is sometimes dismissed, new writing for the theatre is certainly very active.

---

1 This can be found on www.nationaltheatre.org.uk/?lid=7106. See also www. doollee.com, an invaluable website listing thousands of modern playwrights and their plays, with information about the availability of texts, literary agents and so on.

We're lucky that so many playtexts are available. The National Theatre Bookshop stocks a wide range of titles, not just classics but many new plays, often by less well-known writers. And there are four excellent drama publishers – Oberon Books, Faber and Faber, Methuen and Nick Hern Books – who between them publish the vast majority of professionally performed plays and translations. If the breadth of the repertoire is neglected by theatre managers, we can't complain about the availability of the material.

The well read play?

My title alludes to the nineteenth-century notion of the 'well made play' (*la pièce bien faite*). It should, of course, be taken with a pinch of salt: the 'well read play', like the 'well made' one, implies that there's a right way of doing these things. There isn't, and the chapters that follow are intended to provoke thought rather than offer a tried and tested method.

The foundation text of dramatic criticism is Aristotle's *Poetics*. Written in 345 BC (a hundred years after the Athenian golden age), the *Poetics* are, in effect, a set of lecture notes: Aristotle doesn't tell us how to read plays, but he does give a sense of how they're put together. Many have tried something similar and the results are as revealing about the writers themselves as about drama as a whole. Two of the most significant, Philip Sidney's *An Apology for Poetry* (1583) and Ben Jonson's *Timber* (published 1640), explore the application of classical literary models to English Renaissance poetry and drama. The essayist Dr Johnson, the poet Samuel Taylor Coleridge and the critic William Hazlitt combined blunt English empiricism with fine poetic sensibility, especially fruitful in their work on Shakespeare.[2] Their continental contemporaries included the aesthetic philosopher Denis Diderot, the playwright and liter-

---

2   Dr Johnson *The Preface to Shakespeare* (1765); Samuel Taylor Coleridge *Lectures and Notes on Shakspere and Other English Poets* (1883); William Hazlitt *Lectures on the Literature of the Age of Elizabeth and Characters of Shakespeare's Plays* (1817)

ary manager Gotthold Lessing, and the poet, translator and critic August Schlegel.[3]

The naturalist novelist Emile Zola and the critic Georg Brandes wrote about drama's potential to reflect the real world,[4] while the actor-manager William Poel, the dramatist George Bernard Shaw and the all-round theatrical genius Harley Granville Barker provided the intellectual framework for the modern British theatre.[5] Twentieth-century German 'dramaturgy' was particularly rich, with the leading figures of the Frankfurt School (Walter Benjamin, Theodor Adorno and Ernst Bloch) all making powerful contributions.[6] Meanwhile the playwright, poet and director Bertolt Brecht wrote extensively about the theatre and its role in making a better world.[7]

Several modern directors – Ingmar Bergman, Peter Brook and Peter Hall are the most eminent – have tried to describe how drama works,[8] and various playwrights – Arthur Miller, Edward Bond, Alan Ayckbourn and David Mamet – have added their voices.[9] In addition, a handful of modern critics – Harold Hobson, Kenneth

3   Denis Diderot *Entretiens sur le Fils naturel* (1757) and *Discours sur la Poésie Dramatique* (1758); Gotthold Ephraim Lessing *Laocoon: An Essay on the Limits of Poetry and Painting* (1766) and *The Hamburg Dramaturgy* (1767); August Wilhelm Schlegel *Critical Works* (1828).

4   Emile Zola *Naturalism in the Theatre* (1881); Georg Brandes *The Main Currents in the Literature of the Nineteenth Century* (1872-75).

5   William Poel *Essay on Shakespeare* (1913); George Bernard Shaw *The Quintessence of Ibsenism* (1891); Harley Granville Barker *Prefaces to Shakespeare* (1927-47).

6   Walter Benjamin *One Way Street* (1928), *The Origins of German Tragic Drama* (1928) and *Understanding Brecht* (ed. 1973); Theodor Adorno *Aesthetic Theory* (1970) and *Minima Moralia* (1974)

7   Bertolt Brecht *The Messingkauf Dialogues* (1940) and *A Short Organum for the Theatre* (1948)

8   Ingmar Bergman *The Magic Lantern* (1987); Peter Brook *The Empty Space* (1968), *The Shifting Point* (1988), *There Are No Secrets* (1993), *The Threads of Time: Recollections* (1998), *Evoking Shakespeare* (1998); Peter Hall *The Necessary Theatre* (1999), *Diaries* (2000), *Exposed by the Mask: Form and Language in Drama* (2000) and *Shakespeare's Advice to the Players* (2004).

9   Arthur Miller *Timebends: A Life* (1995); Edward Bond *The Hidden Plot* (1999); Alan Ayckbourn *The Crafty Art of Playmaking* (2002); David Mamet *Writing in Restaurants* (1987), *Three Uses of the Knife* (1996) and *True and False: Common Sense and Heresy for the Actor* (1999).

Tynan, John Peter and Michael Billington – have written with knowledge and insight.[10] Recent years have seen a deluge of theoretical academic work that often takes the form of a structuralist analysis of mimesis; sadly, much of it cannot survive outside the groves of academe.

There are dozens of useful guides to drama.[11] Critical opinion can be counter-productive, however. Old plays come with value judgments attached: '*Fuente Ovejuna* is the best play of the Spanish Golden Age'; '*The Entertainer* is what John Osborne wrote after *Look Back in Anger*'; '*The Two Gentlemen of Verona* is only interesting because of what it tells us about *Hamlet*.' It's difficult to stop these received views from affecting your response.

Reading a new play is different. As you turn its fresh, unbound pages – nearly always a typescript, sometimes handwritten – you find yourself looking at something that has never seen the light of day. A common criticism is to compare it with an old play: 'oh, it's about war but not as good as *Mother Courage*'; '*A Midsummer Night's Dream* says more about teenage sexual desire'; or 'if you want a backstage farce, why not stick with *Noises Off*?' Another is to object to the setting: 'Please, not another play set in an office' or 'I'm bored of people on housing estates.' Or maybe its form is challenging: 'Why isn't there a story', 'why do the characters keep talking to the audience?' or 'why does nobody speak in proper sentences?'

---

10   Harold Hobson *Theatre in Britain* (1984); Kenneth Tynan *Profiles* (1989) and *Diaries* (2002); *Theatre Writings* (2007); Michael Billington *One Night Stands* (2001) and *State of the Nation* (2007).

11   Some of the more readily available are: The Cambridge Companions to *Medieval English Theatre, English Renaissance Drama, Shakespeare Studies, Ibsen, Brecht* and *Beckett*; Nicholas Wright *99 Plays* (1992); Dominic Dromgoole *The Full Room* (2002); Paul Allen *A Pocket Guide to Alan Ayckbourn* (2004); Richard Eyre and Nicholas Wright *Changing Stages* (2000); John Burgess *A Pocket Guide to Greek and Roman Drama* (2005); Simon Trussler *A Pocket Guide to Jacobean and Elizabethan Drama* (2006); and Faber's 'About the Playwright' series. I have co-authored several guides: with Kenneth McLeish *A Pocket Guide to Shakespeare's Plays* (1998); with Carole Woddis *A Pocket Guide to Twentieth Century Drama* (2001); with Michael Pennington *A Pocket Guide to Ibsen, Chekhov and Strindberg* (2004); and, as sole author, *A Guide to the Plays of Bertolt Brecht* (2005).

The mistake, of course, is to judge a play by alien criteria. This book argues that we should try to read a play – new or old – on its own terms and according to its own merits.

Why read a play?

Many people in the professional theatre are aware of a contradiction. On the one hand, they know their work is ephemeral: productions come and go and every night is different with a magical performance one evening followed by frustration and disappointment the next. What they do is a manufactured lie: the 'stuff these dreams are made of', indeed.

On the other hand, they realise that they have been given a set of responsibilities. The first is to the writers of the past – who could bear the disapproval of Shakespeare or Ibsen, Arthur Miller or Tennessee Williams, in despair at the travesties of their intentions? The second is to the audiences, who flock to see these plays re-created and deserve the full benefit of their insights. The third is to the playwrights of today: those brave souls determined to use this most ancient of forms to express and reflect on the world in which we live.

Theatre people often say that plays can best be understood when performed. It's a good argument but shouldn't be taken too literally. Many people still read plays and the answer to the question 'why read a play' is a simple one: because there are so many great plays to choose from, and because we can get so much from reading them. *The Oresteia*, *Hamlet*, *The Man of Mode* and *The Cherry Orchard* are among the finest achievements of the human mind and we'd be crazy to ignore them.

The structure of this book

The book follows the kind of questions I ask whenever I approach a play as a theatre director and think about staging it: Where does it come from? Who wrote it? What happens (and the related question what *really* happens)? Who are the characters? What do they say?

How does it work in the theatre? What does it mean? And, hardest of all, is it any good? I've included a speculative chapter on what's next for playwriting and, as an appendix, a catalogue of 250 key playwrights along with their best-known works. Reading lists are very out of fashion, but I hope this gives some sense of the sheer diversity and quality of the existing repertoire.

I make continuous references to a few dozen plays by a handful of geniuses: Aeschylus, Sophocles and Euripides; Marlowe, Middleton and Webster; Molière, Racine and Corneille; Schiller, Goethe and Kleist; Chekhov, Ibsen and Strindberg; and Brecht, Beckett and Arthur Miller. These have been chosen as the playwrights the reader is most likely to encounter. Dozens of others are mentioned, mostly modern, including a handful of young British playwrights. Towering above them all is Shakespeare, to whom I refer more than any other. It's hard to imagine a general book about drama that didn't give him pride of place.

2. Where does it come from?

Aplay has to exist in the here and now if it's worth performing still. However, plays don't descend fully formed from the heavens, and when reading a play we should try to answer the most basic of questions: 'where does it come from?'

History matters. We don't need to be historians in order to read a play, but we should try to remember, with LP Hartley, that 'the past is a foreign country: they do things differently there'. Playwrights react to their times in different ways, but they live in the real world and are subject to its various pressures and limitations. A feel for a playwright's time and place will deepen our appreciation of his achievement and help us avoid what the historian EP Thompson dubbed 'the enormous condescension of posterity'. As Picasso said 'Why do you think I date everything I do? Because it's not sufficient to know an artist's work – it is necessary to know when he did them, why, how, under what circumstances.'

Changing plays for changing times

Even the sketchiest of historical understandings can help. The big events – war, peace, monarchs and revolutions – give us the outline. More useful, however, is a feeling for society as a whole – life expectancy, living conditions, education, standards of health, and so on. Most importantly, we need an understanding of the role of the theatre in the society that produced it. These are all continuously changing and vary across time and social groups, but they play a crucial role in the development of subject and dramatic form.

The Ancient World
The origins of Greek (and European) drama are much disputed. Some claim that Greek tragedy was a natural extension of fertility (*dionysiac*) and funereal (*thanatos*) rites; others see it in modern

7

secular and political terms. However, as John Burgess declares in his useful book,[1] 'any theory involving such things as scapegoats, rituals, initiation, fertility rites, satyrs or ecstatic religion should be treated with scepticism: *there is no evidence.*' Only thirty or so tragedies survive, all by the trio of great Athenian dramatists (Aeschylus, Sophocles and Euripides). These allowed for the most profound philosophical questioning of such universals as birth and death, desire and fear, love and hate. Compulsory attendance at their performances helped bind Athenian society together and create a shared understanding of history and origin.

It is a mistake, however, to think that Greek drama was monolithic: Greek culture celebrated antithesis, and performances of the tragedies were followed by comedies and satyr plays (by Aristophanes and Menander). Furthermore, Greek drama emerged in a time when Athenian power was tenuous. Athens' very existence had been threatened by two Persian invasions: her eventual victory united the Greek city-states and secured hegemony across the Eastern Mediterranean, but the memory of this crisis is fundamental to the mixture of triumph and anxiety that characterises this first great flowering of drama.

The comic playwrights (above all Terence and Plautus) of the late Roman Republic took on many of the features of their Greek forbears, but developed a much more secular, urban tone; their theatre provided – within the strict limits of the social order – a forum for a discussion of the ways of the world and the frequently irrational and unique behaviour of the individual. Later, Seneca's courtly tragedies of Imperial Rome plumbed the meaning of suffering and violent death – often to spectacular effect.

The Renaissance
The largely anonymous dramatists of fourteenth- and fifteenth-century England served a very different role. The Mystery plays dramatised every aspect of the Christian story, from the Creation to the Last Judgment, and provided a comprehensive account of

---

1   John Burgess *A Pocket Guide to Greek and Roman Drama* (2005)

human experience. Performed by amateur actors, these great dramatic cycles fused the religious with the secular, the spiritual with the physical, and the sacred with the profane. Firmly rooted in the everyday realities of medieval life, they both supported and challenged the status quo and gave everybody involved a glimpse of the opposite: the world turned upside down.

Imperial Spain was an even more rigidly hierarchical society than medieval England, but produced the astonishing masterpieces of its Golden Age (above all by Calderon, Lope de Vega and Tirso de Molina), which exposed the injustices, cruelties and absurdities of the time, while also celebrating the robust confidence of the most powerful nation state in Europe.

It was in late sixteenth and early seventeenth century London, however, that Renaissance drama flourished. The traditional view of Early Modern England as a place of good government and social order, with a clear hierarchy in which everyone knew their place, has been challenged in recent years. Nowhere was this more vividly on display than in the capital. By 1600 London's economic strength, international connections, and political power were turning it into the most important city in Europe. But it was bursting at the seams: crowded, filthy and disease-ridden, with an increasingly vocal mob. The countryside was changing too, and the enclosure of common land, and a series of failed harvests, caused widespread upheaval and social change. It's increasingly clear that 'Shakespeare's changing world'[2] – sandwiched between the trauma of the Reformation and the disaster of the Civil War – was the ideal environment for a new kind of drama.

The birth of the modern theatre can be dated to the construction of the first building specifically designed for professional performance: the Theatre in Shoreditch in 1576. Several other theatres sprang up in its wake, which housed a number of competing professional companies performing a broad stream of new plays. Theirs was a commercial drama, financially independent (though benefiting from royal patronage) and catering to a diverse audience. It

---

2   I have borrowed this phrase from Arnold Kettle's outstanding collection of essays: *Shakespeare in a Changing World* (1964)

fulfilled a wide range of roles: as a forum for debate, as a school for rhetoric, but above all as a purveyor of popular entertainment.

The great Elizabethan and Jacobean dramatists (Christopher Marlowe, John Webster, Cyril Tourneur, Thomas Middleton, John Ford and Shakespeare himself) were involved in an ambitious programme. They wanted to create a new kind of drama that could take its place alongside the Greeks and Romans. They attached enormous importance to the classical world, and ransacked it for an understanding of their own society and its political processes. But they also wrote popular English plays, which could thrive in the commercial conditions of Elizabethan London. They drew on other influences too: the English Chronicles, French humanism, a mass of popular and classical Italian literature, travel writing and so on. Renaissance London was a potent artistic melting pot: diverse, contradictory, and impure.

Restoration, Romanticism and Revolution
Following the Puritan revolution of 1642, the London theatres were closed and all attempts to present plays were forbidden. With the Restoration of the Monarchy in 1660, however, an increasingly prosperous middle class demanded new freedoms and the Glorious Revolution of 1688, with its crucially important Bill of Rights, struck an unprecedented understanding between King and Parliament. A group of remarkable comic dramatists (William Wycherley, John Vanburgh, William Congreve, George Farquhar and George Etherege) explored the foibles, vanity and greed of their own society within the limitations of refined and fashionable entertainment; their plays were designed for the much more comfortable theatres that had been built, in which, for the first time, actresses played the female roles.

A more intellectual drama graced the stages of the French court theatres, which explored the clash between passion and decorum, society and the individual, private vice and public virtue. Neo-classical tragedies (by Pierre Corneille and Jean Racine) appeared in the shadow – and patronage – of an absolute monarch, while the ambitions and, indeed, humiliations of the aspiring *bourgeoisie* are the central subject of French comedy (especially Molière). Human nature was subjected to the analytic methods of the Enlightenment (by Pierre de Marivaux), but it was not until the late eighteenth century – the age of Romanticism and Revolution – that drama re-engaged with the great political and social questions of the day (above all, Pierre Beaumarchais).

By the end of the eighteenth century, the German city-states were attracting a new breed of passionately committed poets, artists and playwrights (Johann von Goethe, Friedrich Schiller and Heinrich von Kleist). Nowhere was this more liberally on display than in Weimar, whose court was a magnet for creative geniuses of all kinds. An educated, coterie audience was offered brilliantly theatrical – and highly intellectual – dramas which examined the political, philosophical and psychological issues of the day.

A different kind of drama again emerged in the second half of the nineteenth century. This appealed, above all, to a wealthier and better-educated urban middle-class, and the comfortable theatres of the European *Belle Époque* presented plays that combined moral sentiment with fashionable display, well-modulated wit with dramatic excitement.

The Modern World

The convulsive social changes brought about by the Industrial Revolution in the mid nineteenth century ushered in the naturalist revolution, with its determination to subject every area of human experience, however squalid, to artistic expression. Naturalism came to drama late, but soon challenged the dominance of boulevard theatre, especially following the crisis of 1870-71 (the Franco-Prussian War and the Paris Commune). A number of great playwrights (above all Chekhov, Ibsen and Strindberg) attempted, in their very different ways, a scientific analysis of the material world and an unblushing presentation of the distasteful realities that most dramatists tended to avoid. At the dawn of a brave new century, audiences were eager for such complex truths.

The multiple disasters of what the historian Eric Hobsbawm has called the 'Age of Extremes' – the First World War, the Bolshevik Revolution, the rise of Fascism and the Second World War – threatened to overshadow anything that the theatre could produce. Nevertheless, the comprehensive social changes of the twentieth century produced dozens of remarkable playwrights (Bertolt Brecht, Sean O'Casey, Friedrich Dürrenmatt, Arthur Miller and many others), taking every political and moral position imaginable, and reflecting the explosive contradictions of the time.

New ways of thinking about the individual and society became increasingly important. Influenced by Freud, some playwrights (Arthur Schnitzler, Frank Wedekind, Tennessee Williams and Eugene O'Neill) tried to dramatise the subconscious. Others were keen to produce popular entertainment which challenged even as it entertained (Noël Coward, Terence Rattigan and JB Priestley). While some playwrights (Jean-Paul Sartre, Samuel Beckett and Eugene Ionesco) attempted to reflect post-war feelings of existential despair, the post-1956 generation of English playwrights (such as John Osborne, John Arden, Arnold Wesker, David Storey, Edward Bond and others) echoed a broader dissatisfaction in society as a whole. The black American dramatists of the 1950s and 1960s (August Wilson and Lorraine Hansberry) played an active role in the civil rights movement and feminism shaped many of the most important new dramatists of the 1960s and 1970s (Caryl Churchill and others).

Twentieth century theatre saw a decisive break with classicism. A hundred years of perpetual revolution produced a wholesale transformation in theatrical style and a full-frontal assault on convention. The century produced more playwrights than ever before, but it also confused the role of the theatre. On the one hand, an increasingly affluent bourgeoisie demanded mass entertainment; on the other, revolutionary changes in politics, technology, society and philosophy demanded a drama that could explore the challenges of modern life. This contradiction should lie at the heart of any analysis of the century's drama.

The twenty-first century playwright, largely free of religious and political interference, but often ignored by the society he tries to reflect, struggles to survive in a highly competitive market.

Hundreds of plays are written every year, but many are left on the shelf gathering dust. It is far from clear what role drama will play in future.

Censorship

When reading a play from the past it's important to recognise the limitations in which the dramatist wrote and understand the conditions of censorship – both subtle and explicit – under which he worked.

Shakespeare was forbidden from writing about recognisable figures, and any dramatisation of history that cast doubt on the legitimacy of the monarch, let alone the wisdom of the political and spiritual authorities of his time, would have been banned. Queen Elizabeth was alert to drama's political potential, as shown by her displeasure at the revival of *Richard II* by Shakespeare's company on the eve of the Essex Rebellion in 1601.[3]

Few plays have caused such uproar as Schnitzler's Viennese comedy of sexual manners, *La Ronde* (1897).[4] First released in a limited edition of 200 copies, the author declared that:

> The scenes are totally unprintable, of no great literary value, but if disinterred after a couple of hundred years, may illuminate in a unique way aspects of our culture.

When it was published three years later, Schnitzler insisted that the play should never be performed. He relented when approached by the great impresario Max Reinhardt, and it was finally staged in

---

3   Blair Worden questions whether the play revived was, in fact, Shakespeare's *Richard II*. In 'Which play was performed at the Globe Theatre on 7 February 1601?' in the *London Review of Books* (Vol 25, No 13, 10 July 2003) he argues that in 1599 the Earl of Essex commissioned a dramatisation of Richard II, *The First Part of the Life and Reign of King Henry IV*, and that it might have been this that the Chamberlain's Men revived in 1601. Jonathan Bate forcefully dismisses this argument in *The Soul of the Age* (2009). Whoever dramatised it, the deposition of Richard II was politically explosive and it is indicative that Elizabeth called its dramatisation 'a seditious prelude to put into the people's heads boldness and faction'.

4   I give a more detailed account of this in the Introduction to my translation (with Peter Zombory-Moldovan) of *La Ronde* (2007).

1921. But several court cases had to be fought before an American judge acknowledged that 'a careful scrutiny of the text reveals not a single line, not a single word, that might be regarded as obscene, lewd, lascivious, filthy, indecent, or disgusting.' By this time, however, Schnitzler was so anxious to protect others from the anti-Semitic bullying that he had experienced, that he prohibited any further productions. It was not until 1981, and the fiftieth anniversary of his death, that the play was revived.

While few cultures have been as restrictive about what could appear on stage as Jacobean England or Imperial Spain, censorship has been a fundamental fact-of-life in the theatre until recently. And when the censorship isn't explicit, subtle pressures have been brought to bear. Many gay dramatists have been forced to pretend that their characters were not homosexual: aspects of *The Importance of Being Earnest* (1895) are written in 'gay code' and Terence Rattigan's beautiful young men had to be resolutely heterosexual if *French Without Tears* (1936) was to be acceptable. This was, as Wilde put it, 'the love that dares not speak its name'.

The Lord Chamberlain's power to censor plays was finally curtailed as a result of the row over Edward Bond's *Saved* (1965), with its notorious stoning of a baby in its pram. The author had refused the Lord Chamberlain's demands for cuts and the Royal Court Theatre was turned into a club. Laurence Olivier made a speech at the trial defending the play, and the theatre held a public forum to discuss the issues raised. A debate was held in the House of Lords and the controversy fuelled the fight against censorship that in 1968 finally ended the Lord Chamberlain's powers.

State censorship – in Britain at least – may be a thing of the past, but individuals have often acted independently. Mary Whitehouse attempted to sue the National Theatre for staging Howard Brenton's *The Romans in Britain* (1980); there were protests at the Royal Court against Jim Allen's *Perdition* (about the Holocaust) and Michael Hastings' adaptation of *The Emperor* (about Haile Selassie); the Birmingham Rep was stopped by violent Sikhs from performing Gurpreet Bhatti's *Bezhti* (2005); and the National Theatre attracted demonstrations and a court case from Christian fundamentalists when it toured *Jerry Springer: The Opera* (2003). The struggle for free speech continues, even in that most liberal of environments, the British subsidised theatre. Peter Hall has coined the phrase 'censorship by subsidy' to suggest an unhealthy relationship between the theatre and the funding bodies, and a subsidised theatre would not retain its funding for long if it produced a series of plays that flew in the face of the core values of the mainstream liberal agenda.

The playwright and the *Zeitgeist*

Cultural history is contradictory and resists tidy generalisations. Many of the best writers straddle different artistic movements and create new forms as a result. Shakespeare combined sophisticated Renaissance humanism with popular theatrical forms; Ibsen took on the highly successful formula of the 'well-made play' and adapted it for his own ends; and Brecht, for all his radical modernity, drew on a combination of classical, folk and oriental styles to create his own peculiarly potent brand of political theatre.

Understanding time and place is invaluable, so long as we don't presume that an individual play, however excellent, is a definitive representative of the theatre of its day, let alone of the *Zeitgeist* as a whole. As Roland Barthes said, the literary work is 'at once the sign of a history and resistance to that history'. And so we need to get a feel for where a playwright fits into, but also where he rebels against, his time; to what extent his work accords with the existing forms, but also where it challenges them.

And so we come to the next question: 'Who wrote it?'

3. Who wrote it?

CONFRONTED BY A WORLD-FAMOUS play, it's sometimes hard to remember that an individual human being sat down and wrote it. The biographical details of a playwright's life aren't essential for an understanding of his plays, but when the information is available, we should devour it greedily.

The playwright's life

The obvious place to start is with a biography.

It's sometimes claimed that Shakespeare's life is a mystery. Actually, scholars know as much about Shakespeare as any other successful Elizabethan (outside royal and noble circles), and numerous studies have appeared recently, rich with well-documented evidence.[1] None of them answer the really hard questions – 'why were the plays written? 'what is it that makes them so great?' or 'what do they mean?' – but they do help us set this unique writer within his time and place. And there are dozens of exhaustive biographies of more modern playwrights.

Some people argue that the facts of a dramatist's life are irrelevant, particularly when they concern private matters. Certainly, we don't need to know much about Brecht's colourful sex life in order to appreciate his plays[2] – let alone his politics – and specu-

---

1   One of the best is James Shapiro's *1599: A Year in the Life of William Shakespeare* (2006), which provides a detailed account of Shakespeare's *annus mirabilis,* in which, it is claimed, Shakespeare wrote *Julius Caesar, Henry V, As You Like It* and *Hamlet.* Biographies include Sam Schoenbaum *William Shakespeare: A Compact Documentary Life* (1987); Park Honan *Shakespeare: A Life* (2000); Peter Ackroyd *Shakespeare: The Biography* (2005); Michael Wood *In Search of Shakespeare* (2005); Stephen Greenblatt *Will in the World: How Shakespeare Became Shakespeare* (2005); Bill Bryson *Shakespeare: The World as a Stage* (2007); René Weis *Shakespeare Revealed: A Biography* (2007); and Jonathan Bate *The Soul of the Age* (2009)

2   See, however, John Fuegi's *Life and Lies of Bertolt Brecht* (1994); for a robust response see Michael Hofmann's review, reprinted in *Behind the Lines: Pieces on Writing and Pictures* (2002).

lation, however scholarly, about the precise nature of Ibsen's relationship with his two young muses isn't essential to understanding
The Master Builder. But the fact that Schnitzler kept a record of
every one of his sexual encounters (and, for a while, every orgasm)
provides us with insight into *Anatol* and *La Ronde*, just as acknowledging Marlowe's homosexuality should inform our reading of
Edward II.

More valuable, perhaps, is gaining a sense of the writer's background: what his childhood was like, what his father did for a
living, how he was educated, and so on. It's a stretch to say that
Shakespeare's modest Stratford background provides the clue to
the equanimity so evident in his plays, but the fact that Chekhov
trained as a doctor helps us detect in his work a combination of
clinical objectivity and human empathy. And we can find in Arthur
Miller's childhood on the Lower East Side during the Depression
the roots of his passion for social justice, just as Peter Gill's Welsh
working-class upbringing is the background to his naturalistic
dramas of everyday life.

We don't need to subject the dramatist to elaborate psychoanalysis, but we should develop a feel for a playwright's personality.
Certainly, when I'm preparing a production of a play by a living
playwright I find it useful to meet him and try to understand what
makes him tick.

Where the playwright comes from

A playwright's relationship with his homeland is often
complicated.

Ibsen found Norway asphyxiating and declared that the key
moment in his artistic development was his decision to leave Scan-
dinavia for Southern Europe. 'This', he said:

> Left its mark on all my later work … [It was like] a feeling
> of being released from darkness into the light, escaping
> through a tunnel; from mists into sunshine.[3]

---

3   Quoted in Michael Meyer *Ibsen* (1971)

Remarkably, he then wrote eight of his greatest plays – all set in Norway[4] – in the sunshine of Italy and Southern Germany.

A playwright is sometimes forced to leave his country for political reasons. Brecht fled Nazi Germany the day after the Reichstag Fire and wrote most of his best work abroad; his fifteen years in exile (1933-48) gave him the space to develop his ideas and create his masterpieces; he certainly never wrote anything so impressive once back in Germany. Another great political playwright, Wole Soyinka, has spent most of his adult life away from his native Nigeria and gained a striking moral authority *in absentia*.

In thinking about where a writer comes from, we should avoid national stereotypes. Saying that Marivaux must be stylish because he's French, Kleist humourless because he's German, or Ibsen gloomy because he's Norwegian is absurd: Marivaux' experimental savagery is fundamental to his work, as is Kleist's lively wit and Ibsen's moral optimism. National characteristics affect playwrights, but most react against them as much as they conform.

Unfortunately, such cultural stereotyping has caused an overreaction, especially in discussions about Shakespeare. Insisting that the greatest playwright of all time must be 'universal', commentators often ignore the peculiarly English quality of his work, from his robust descriptions of the natural world to his practical sense of how society works, not to mention the patriotism that his characters sometimes indulge in. The search for universality without borders is as misleading as the hunting down of national stereotypes.

Shakespeare's own attitude is often paradoxical. John of Gaunt's famous speech in *Richard II* is sometimes cited as evidence for the writer's nationalism. But this is the deathbed prophecy of an old English aristocrat, and the emphasis is on betrayal and failure, not hope and glory:

> That England, that was wont to conquer others
> Hath made a shameful conquest of itself. [5]

---

4   From *Pillars of Society* (1877) to *Hedda Gabler* (1890)

5   *Richard II* (2.1)

Shakespeare is writing about the memory of a faded past and the abandoned hopes for the future; but in doing so, he exhibits a deeper love for his homeland than a simple uncritical homily would have done.

Brecht is similarly complex. For all his oft-stated admiration of English empiricism and dislike of the intellectualism of his native tradition, he is a German writer through and through: like Goethe, Schiller and Kleist, his plays consist of a number of dramatised arguments. Indeed, one could argue that his elaborate theory is simply a restatement of the core principles of German Romantic dramaturgy.

Beliefs

It's sometimes useful to develop an understanding of the play-wright's religious beliefs and political affiliations. But here again we need to proceed cautiously.

Ibsen is often hailed as a great liberal progressive. In fact, his views are much more nuanced:

> I believe that none of us can do anything other or anything better than realise ourselves in spirit and in truth.[6]

This offers a much better guide to Ibsen's intentions than the social programmes ascribed to him by Bernard Shaw.[7] By contrast, Shaw's own plays express his views on a wide range of social ills – prostitution in *Mrs Warren's Profession* (1893), the arms trade in *Arms and the Man* (1894) and unhappy marriages in *The Philanderer* (1898) – and they tell us exactly what he thinks.

Brecht is the most explicit of all major political dramatists and the main currents of Marxist thought are central to his work. However, to some people's surprise, Brecht's chief subject is not the desirability of a revolution, it's the obstinacy with which the working class fails to seize the hour. Likewise, although Athol Fugard's plays made an important contribution to the struggle against apartheid,

---

6   Quoted in Michael Meyer *Ibsen* (1971)

7   See Bernard Shaw *Quintessence of Ibsenism* (1891)

just as Dario Fo, who has been at the forefront of political theatre since the 1950s, campaigned for civil rights and economic justice in his work in the theatre, both dramatists are more concerned with the reality of living under a corrupt and immoral regime, than with presenting dreams of freedom or revolution.

Many of the leading contemporary British playwrights started out firmly on the left. David Hare, Howard Brenton, David Edgar and Caryl Churchill all bring an anti-establishment critique to their work and are allied to many of the great liberal causes – pacifism, feminism, racial equality and so on – but their positions tend to be liberally progressive rather than revolutionary. It's the more individualistic writers such as Tom Stoppard, Peter Nichols, Simon Gray and John Osborne – all of whom have been labelled right wing – whose libertarian energies are the more explosive. The Director of the National Theatre recently bewailed the lack of a 'mischievous right-wing play'; an equally potent criticism might be the absence of contemporary plays that address the core left wing issues: health, education and, above all, poverty.

We must be careful not to assume too much. Should Middleton's sympathy for the Puritan cause be taken as evidence of a revolutionary attitude to the monarchy?[8] Should Synge's support for Irish nationalism affect the way that we read *The Playboy of the Western World*? And does the fact that Gorky knew Lenin, and in his last years became an apologist for Stalin (who quite possibly had him murdered), mean that we should read his plays as advocating violent revolution and rule by terror? The relationship between art and politics is too complex for that.

Bad political playwrights see drama as simple propaganda for their cause. Some of the best disguise their beliefs altogether. Ibsen went out of his way to discourage his feminist followers when he told the Norwegian Women's Rights League (twenty years after writing *A Doll's House*) that:

> I am not a member of the Women's Rights League. I have never been deliberately tendentious in anything I have

---

8   See Margot Heinemann *Puritanism and the Theatre* (1980)

written. I have been more of a poet and less of a social
philosopher than people generally seem inclined to believe.
I thank you for your good wishes, but I must decline the
honour of having been said to have worked for the Women's
Rights movement. I am not even very sure what Women's
Rights actually are.[9]

The young Samuel Beckett was an ardent opponent of fascism: his
contribution to Nancy Cunard's compilation *Authors Take Sides on
the Spanish Civil War* (1937) was the witty 'Up the Republic!' and
he joined the French Resistance in the Second World War. But
we know next to nothing about his broader political views, which
hardly make an appearance in his plays. And although Harold Pinter
became one of the most committed of political writers, his best
plays – above all *The Birthday Party* (1957), *The Caretaker* (1959) and
The Homecoming (1964) – are free of explicit political comment.

Despite many attempts, it has proved impossible to ascertain
Shakespeare's political views. Keats spoke about the great playwright's 'negative capability' – his ability to efface himself in his
work – and Hazlitt, the greatest of the English Romantic critics,
wrote:

The striking peculiarity of Shakespeare's mind was its generic
quality, its power of communication with all other minds –
so that it contained a universe of thought and feeling within
itself, and had no one particular bias, or exclusive excellence
more than another.[10]

The Argentinian writer, Jorge Luis Borges, proposed in his essay
Everything and Nothing[11] that Shakespeare achieved a unique kind
of invisibility, and imagines him on his deathbed saying, 'I, who
have been no man, am all men.' In a similar vein the theatre director Peter Brook wrote:

---

9   Quoted in Michael Meyer *Ibsen* (1971)

10 William Hazlitt *Shakespeare's Genius* (1818)

11 Jorge Luis Borges 'Everything and Nothing' in *Labyrinths* (1964)

> If one takes those thirty-seven plays... one comes out with
> a field of incredible density and complexity; and eventually
> one goes a step further, and one finds that what happened...
> is something quite different from any other author's work.
> It's not Shakespeare's view of the world, it's something which
> actually resembles reality. A sign of this is that any single
> word, line, character or event has not only a large number
> of interpretations, but an unlimited number. Which is the
> characteristic of reality ... What he wrote is not interpreta-
> tion. It is the thing itself.[12]

Despite his gnomic style, Brook goes to the heart of the matter.

The problem with such observations, however, is that they lead
to the claim that Shakespeare's plays are free of political or social
content. In fact, of course, the opposite is true: no other dramatist has done more to explain the way that society works, demystify
the mechanisms of power or show the complex network of inter-
dependence in human affairs. Perhaps the best we can say is that
Shakespeare presents social conflict with such scrupulous even-
handed realism that the audience is confronted by a true image of
the complexity of human experience.

One of the main contentions in recent scholarship has been
that Shakespeare was a closet Catholic and that his plays reveal
deep Papist sympathies. This has come from a new generation of
critics[13] who see recusancy in a tradition of dissent against the
status quo; they suggest that Shakespeare spent the famous 'lost
years' (from the age of 21, when he left Stratford, to 28, when we
first hear of him in London) in Hoghton Tower, a country house
in Lancashire which was a centre for Elizabethan Catholics; it's a
potent hypothesis that has never been satisfactorily proven. But it's
surely true that Shakespeare's religious affiliations cannot be definitively established from his plays.

---

12   'What is a Shakespeare?' Peter Brook *The Shifting Point: Forty Years of Theatrical Exploration, 1946-87* (1987).

13   See, for example, Richard Wilson *Secret Shakespeare* (2004)

The writer's other work

It is sometimes useful to understand how the play you are reading fits into the rest of the writer's work.

More than twenty years stand between *The Two Gentlemen of Verona* (possibly written in 1587) and *The Tempest* (1610). In that time almost everything about Shakespeare's writing changed – dramatic skill, poetic style and psychological insight. An even greater gap – and as broad a social, cultural and theatrical revolution – exists between Ibsen's breakthrough work, *Brand* (1865), and his last play, *When We Dead Awaken* (1899). A similar gap of 29 years separates David Hare's Maoist fantasy *Fanshen* (1975) from his mainstream political satire *Stuff Happens* (2004).

A writer's plays are sometimes grouped into categories. Shakespeare's have traditionally been divided into comedies, histories, tragedies and romances, with sub-groups such as problem plays, tetralogies and Roman dramas emerging later on. People speak of Brecht's 'expressionist' early work, the 'learning plays', the 'realistic' dramas and the 'epic' masterpieces; and the best plays of DH Lawrence and Sean O'Casey have been corralled into trilogies.[14] Such groupings help us see the writer's stylistic and thematic developments, but are largely imposed, and we must be careful that academic, even marketing, terms don't limit our understanding of the dramatist's original creation.

In seeing a playwright in relationship to his development as an artist, we shouldn't leap to narrow autobiographical interpretations. The fact that there are so many young people in *Two Gentlemen of Verona* isn't a direct result of it being written by a young man, nor should we take the old men who populate three out of four of Ibsen's last plays as evidence of Ibsen's own age at the time. One of the most common interpretations of *The Tempest* is to see it as

---

14   The phrase 'The Lawrence Trilogy' was first used to describe Peter Gill's Royal Court productions (1965-7) of three plays set in the Nottinghamshire coalfields: *The Daughter in Law*, *A Collier's Friday Night* and *The Widowing of Mrs Holroyd*. Raymond Williams grouped them together in his edition for Penguin Books (1969). And Sean O'Casey's naturalistic plays – *Juno and the Paycock*, *The Plough and the Stars* and *Shadow of a Gunman* – have been labelled 'The 'Dublin Trilogy'.

Shakespeare's farewell to the theatre; there are textual arguments in support of this[15] but the fact that Shakespeare collaborated with John Fletcher on *The Two Noble Kinsmen* and *Henry VIII* soon after shows either that this wasn't his intention or that he changed his mind.

Some writers have provided useful autobiographical material. Schnitzler's memoirs are astonishing,[16] Brecht's *Work Journal*[17] is a revealing record of his life, from exile in 1933 up to his death in Berlin in 1956, John Osborne's two volumes of autobiography[18] are among the finest things he wrote, and Arthur Miller's *Timebends*[19] is a typically wise account of the development of America's greatest dramatist. Even looking at pictures can be helpful: something of Chekhov's humanity can be glimpsed in the photograph of him sitting on the steps of a dacha with a small dog under his arm.

There are various other places to look. The letters of Chekhov,[20] Brecht[21] and Tennessee Williams[22] are treasure troves, rich not just with biographical information, but opinions often expressed more directly than in the plays. Furthermore, many playwrights had talents in other literary forms, be it Shakespeare's Sonnets, Chekhov's short stories, Brecht's poetry or Harold Pinter's journalism, poems and provocations.

As we study this material, however, we should remember that even the most brilliant of playwrights is likely to have little useful to say about his own plays and we should not expect this supple-

15   See Prospero's speech of resignation, 'Our revels now are ended'

16   Arthur Schnitzler *My Youth in Vienna* (1970)

17   Bertolt Brecht *Work Journal* (1993)

18   John Osborne *Looking Back: Never Explain, Never Apologize*: 'Better Class of Person: An Autobiography 1929-56', 'Almost a Gentleman: An Autobiography, 1955-66' (1992, 1993).

19   Arthur Miller *Timebends* (1987)

20   Anton Chekhov *Dear Actress, Dear Writer: The Love Letters of Olga Knipper and Anton Chekhov* (1996); Anton Chekhov *A Life in Letters* (2004).

21   Bertolt Brecht *Letters* (1990)

22   Tennessee Williams *Selected Letters* (2001)

mentary material to provide us with cast-iron interpretations to the work itself. Reading plays is much more difficult than that.

4. What kind of play is it?

THE AMATEUR THEATRE CRITIC Polonius boasts that the travelling players are:

> The best actors in the world, either for tragedy, comedy, history, pastoral, pastoral-comical, historical-pastoral, tragical-historical, tragical-comical-historical-pastoral, scene individable, or poem unlimited... [1]

Of course, drama cannot be so easily categorised and most good plays are a complex mixture of different genres. Nevertheless, when reading the work of a classical playwright, it's worth trying to understand the genres available to him.

Classical Genres

Tragedy
The field of tragedy is vast. Much has been written on the subject, and on the changing meaning of the word. Aristotle's *Poetics* provides a useful start; Friedrich Nietzsche's *The Birth of Tragedy* (1872), Erich Auerbach's *Mimesis* (1946), George Steiner's *Death of Tragedy* (1961) and Raymond Williams' *Modern Tragedy* (1966) take many of its most vexing questions further.

The three great Greek tragedians are very different. Aeschylus' seven surviving plays – especially the great Oresteia trilogy (*Agamemnon*, *The Libation Bearers*, and *The Eumenides*) – are concerned with the remorseless progress of bloody revenge, resolved only by the imposition of justice and right. Sophocles' plays tend to be more philosophical (again, only seven survive) and in the Oedipus plays (*Antigone*, *Oedipus Tyrannos* and *Oedipus at Colonus*) he explores the

---

1   *Hamlet* (2.2)

merciless nature of tragic irony. Euripides is the most psychological of the three and, in masterpieces such as *Medea*, *The Trojan Women* and *The Bacchae*, dramatises the tragic consequences of human passion.

John Burgess has come up with a remarkably cogent analysis of Greek tragedy, which, he says, examines the relationships between:

- Man and his own death and other men
- Man and the immortal gods and things that don't change
- Man and the passions that live inside him.[2]

This clarifies the connection between Antigone, her dead brother Polyneices and King Creon with the forces that drive them on to catastrophe. It also shows how Agamemnon and Clytemnestra are caught between the external powers that they cannot control – their own mortality and the immortal gods – and the passions that consume them from within – their passions and desires.

The chief difference between Greek and Shakespearean tragedy is in the role of 'the immortal gods'. In Shakespeare, they are internalised as the force of tragic inevitability. Thus, in *Hamlet* and *Macbeth*, they're metaphorical phantoms; in *Othello*, *King Lear* and *Antony and Cleopatra* they've largely disappeared and, when in evidence, are almost entirely malign.[3] This is partly a product of Renaissance humanism, which sees Man as the site for all humanity's dramas. It also derives from Christianity itself: in the best Christian art, Man, created in the image of God, is depicted in all his frailty. Indeed, a radical humanizing of the Christian story – the suffering Christ without the comfort of God the Father – is at the heart of Shakespearean tragedy.

Even without Shakespeare's masterpieces, the English Renaissance would be one of the most significant moments in the history of tragic drama. Probably the most remarkable examples are Thomas Kyd's The *Spanish Tragedy* (1582-92), Christopher Marlowe's *Doctor*

---

2   John Burgess *The Faber Pocket Guide to Greek and Roman Drama* (2005)

3   See, for example, 'As flies to wanton boys are we to the gods / They kill us for their sport' *King Lear* (4.1)

Faustus (c 1589), the variously attributed *Revenger's Tragedy* (1606), John Webster's *The White Devil* (1612) and *The Duchess of Malfi* (1613), Thomas Middleton's *Women Beware Women* (1621) and *The Changeling* (1622), and John Ford's *Tis Pity She's a Whore* (1629?). These tend to be more bloodthirsty than Shakespeare's mature tragedies, more concerned with the extremes of human experience than in our common condition, but are written with such skill and poetic power that they retain their power to induce the 'pity and terror' that Aristotle describes as fundamental to tragedy's effect.

Tragedy next flowered in the France of Louis XIV, the Sun King, especially in the intellectual dramas of Pierre Corneille – *Horace* (1640) and *Polyeucte* (1643) – and the great neo-classical and Biblical tragedies of Jean Racine – especially *Britannicus* (1669), *Bérénice* (1670) and *Phèdre* (1677). These exceptionally sophisticated, courtly tragedies focus on the relationship between human passion and the implacable fact of death, while using the gods as a metaphorical expression of the forces of inevitability and catastrophe.

In modern tragedy, God, as Nietzsche put it, is dead. This does not limit its tragic power, as Arthur Miller argued, when asked to comment about the stature of his modern 'tragic hero', Willy Loman in *Death of a Salesman* (1949):

> I had not understood that these matters are measured by Greco-Elizabethan paragraphs which hold no mention of insurance payments, front porches, refrigerator fan belts, steering knuckles, Chevrolets, and visions seen not through the portals of Delphi but in the blue flame of the hot-water heater.[4]

Something similar could be said of Georg Büchner's astonishing tragic fragment about the passionate life and violent death of a common soldier, *Woyzeck* (1836).

One of the key terms in classical tragedy is 'fate'. It's a difficult concept: is your fate predestined or is it the consequence of the actions you were always going to take, and how do we avoid simplis-

---

4   Arthur Miller Introduction to *The Collected Plays* (1967)

tic notions of people being 'doomed'? It's perhaps more useful to think of 'inevitability': the sense that once certain actions have been initiated they will, inevitably, lead to a crisis. Thus, once Iago goads the proud but culturally excluded Othello about his marriage, it's just a matter of time before disaster strikes. However, we have to be careful about inevitability too: Brecht hated it because it suggests that historical phenomena – the rise of Fascism, for example – are in some sense inevitable. Shakespeare, as ever, gets the balance right: his characters are responsible for their actions, but forces exist that are bigger than the individual, however mighty.

Tragedy has a limited role in cultures with a clearly defined sense of redemption; indeed, fundamental to the monotheistic religions is the existence of a god who makes sense of human experience and triumphs over death. Nor can tragedy be reconciled with either Communism[5] or Fascism, both of which attempt to offer an all-embracing meaning to life. Some say that the illusion of happiness that consumer capitalism offers cannot tolerate the tragic either, which today can only be found in the faces of the excluded, 'the wretched of the earth.'[6]

Nevertheless, tragedy triumphs in a place that most human beings recognise all too well: unsure of what life means, scared of death, and trying to advance their families and themselves. It changes shape according to the society in which it appears, but provides us with the most profound reflection of the human condition. Tragedy's role is simple: it reminds us that we all have to die and helps us make sense of this inescapable and terrifying fact.

Comedy

In comedy, the human subject has the same relationship with the gods, other people and the self as tragedy, but instead of these being governed by death, they're in the pursuit of life, and new life in particular.

---

5   Vsevelod Vishnevsky's *The Optimistic Tragedy* (1934) is an attempt at a Communist tragedy.

6   Frantz Fanon *The Wretched of the Earth* (1962)

Comedy places the human being in relationship to the unchanging realities of our physical existence: the vulnerability of the new born baby, the innocence of the child, the awkwardness of the teenager, the appetites of the young adult, the growing fears of the middle aged and the fragility of the old and dying. And it explores the way that transformation runs through life and shows that, while change can cause confusion and pain, it can also lead to the resolution of these discords and the arrival of harmony. In lesser comedies, the status quo is reinstalled; in the greatest, the way human beings live together is changed forever.

Comedy cannot flourish in those societies where the transformative forces – particularly love and sex, but also greed and folly – are so severely restricted, or where there is such a high level of enforced contentment that the troubling forces cannot make any impact. It flowers instead in the cracks that open up when society is changing.

Fundamental to the role of comedy is the fact that it makes us laugh. But there are many different kinds of laughter, from the satirical guffaw of the political cartoon to the indulgent smile of the love story – and many positions in between. Comedy's great gift is that by showing that human beings can learn to live together and work for a better future, it provides the closest we have to a consolation for death.

As we'll see later, there are three main kinds of comic drama: social comedy, romantic comedy and farce. If tragedy is a narrowly focused dramatic form dependent on a few key factors, comedy is the broadest of churches.

Tragicomedy

Few plays are pure examples of either tragedy or comedy. Most mix the two and are all the better for it. Tragicomedy allows the playwright to set out with tragic intention but rescue the situation before disaster strikes. It allows for a shifting of perspective and introduces new ways of thinking.

Measure for Measure is a good example. The first two acts are hard-edged social realism: Isabella is entering a convent when she hears that her brother, Claudio, has been sentenced to death for getting his fiancée pregnant. Isabella pleads with Angelo, the absent Duke's regent, who offers to pardon Claudio – on condition that she has sex with him. She goes to see Claudio and is appalled when he begs her to comply. Soon, however, a friar (the Duke in disguise) tells her of Mariana:

> She should this Angelo have married, was affianced to her by oath, and the nuptial appointed. Between which time of the contract and limit of the solemnity, her brother Frederick was wrecked at sea, having in that perished vessel the dowry of his sister. But mark how heavily this befell to the poor gentlewoman. There she lost a noble and renowned brother, in his love toward her ever most kind and natural. With him, the portion and sinew of her fortune, her marriage dowry. With both, her combinate husband, this well-seeming Angelo. [7]

This takes the play into a new register: we're suddenly in the world of romance, where abandoned women pine away, where even the most heartless of men are capable of redemption and where love, it seems, can solve every problem. However, this intervention is more than mere wish-fulfilment. By shifting perspectives, Shakespeare presents Isabella with the greatest challenge of all: it's only when she has to beg the Duke to forgive Angelo that she can abandon her vocation and enter the world.

A more modern example is Ibsen's *The Lady from the Sea* (1888). Ellida rebels against the claustrophobia of married life and is drawn to the open sea. An old lover arrives by ship and threatens to hold her to her earlier promise of marriage. It's only when her husband gives her the freedom to do whatever she wants that she can turn her back on the past and recommit herself to her marriage. With this, Ibsen provides the answer to the quandary he posed seven years earlier in *A Doll's House*: harmonious relations between men

---

7 *Measure for Measure* (3.1)

and women are possible, but only under conditions of mutual consent.

Tragicomedy is rare in contemporary drama. Difficult situations are sometimes resolved by surprising twists, but the tendency of modern drama to neglect plot in favour of argument and character means that tragicomedy, like tragedy before it, is disappearing fast.

Pastoral

At the heart of pastoral is the image of Greek shepherds and shepherdesses frolicking innocently under a perpetually blue sky in the remote vales of Arcady. This provides the locale for a charming exploration of young love, unencumbered by manners and society. It has a political role too: by implying that people in the country live a life of independent minded decency, pastoral questions the corruption of the city.

Applying pastoral's conventions to drama is complicated. The physical presence of actors on stage makes its artifice difficult to conceal. Shakespeare managed to combine charm with a realistic presentation of country life, especially in *As You Like It* and *The Winter's Tale*. Several Stuart playwrights attempted pastoral but even the most successful read like intellectual games that fail to engage with reality. As one historian wrote: 'The idealized shepherds of the literary idylls so popular in the early seventeenth century bore no relationship to the wage labourers of Stuart England'.[8]

This sense of *de haut en bas* superiority is fundamental to eighteenth-century culture's susceptibility to pastoral's charms and, when encountering it in neo-classical French drama, we should perhaps remember Marie Antoinette dressing up as a shepherdess in the Petit Trianon as the Bastille was being stormed.

Romance

Romance has nothing to do with love, and should not be confused with Romanticism either. It's an artistic form with its roots in the

---

8   Keith Thomas *Man and the Natural World* (1983)

classical epic – above all, Homer's *Odyssey* and Virgil's *Aeneid*. A romance unfolds over many years, and features a family that has been separated, often under the mistaken assumption that a much-loved member is dead. It usually climaxes with a reunion, in which long hidden secrets are finally revealed, and often stages miracles, but rarely in an explicitly Christian form. These are certainly the characteristics of Shakespeare's trio of late romances – *Pericles*, *A Winter's Tale* and *The Tempest*.

Serious modern drama hardly ever strays into the world of romance, leaving its mixture of wish-fulfilment, epic scale and consolation to popular films and novels. And where romance is suggested, it's usually deflated soon after: in the last scene of *A Doll's House* Nora talks longingly of 'the miracle' that she and Torvald could have 'a real marriage'; but the play, set over the three days of Christmas, suggests a deeper miracle: the possibility of a new way of life.

Historical

One of drama's essential roles in societies with limited literacy is to provide accounts of the nation's history. These are often partisan and unencumbered by accuracy, but they help create a shared narrative about the society to which the audience belongs.

Greek tragedy is a form of historical drama: the plays tell the story of the Fall of Troy and the return of the Greek heroes to their homeland and in performance provided – and promoted – an understanding of Athenian supremacy in the Eastern Mediterranean. And in writing his great cycle of history plays Shakespeare provided an all-embracing account of the creation of early modern England – from the expulsion from the Eden of the early middle ages (*Richard II*), through the hell of civil war (*Henry IV* and *Henry VI*), to the Tudor paradise ushered in at Bosworth Field (*Richard III*). In both societies, dramatic cycles provided a comprehensive, if highly partisan, history of the known world.

Influenced by their reading of Shakespeare, the German Romantic dramatists attempted something similar: Goethe's *Götz von Berlichingen* (1773) and Schiller's *Wallenstein* Trilogy (completed

1799) present German national identity as a strange mixture of the pragmatic and the poetic, the pugnacious and the passionate: the qualities from which the best – and the worst – in the German character emerge.

Brecht saw historical drama as fundamental. Two of his greatest plays – *Life of Galileo* (1938-9, 1945-7) and *Mother Courage and her Children* (1939) – dramatise the impact of social, political and economic factors on everyday life. He attempted a modern version of historical drama in his gangster pastiche of *Richard III*, *The Resistible Rise of Arturo Ui* (1941).

Partly influenced by Brecht, but more by the Elizabethans, modern British playwrights have experimented with historical drama: Robert Bolt's *A Man for all Seasons* (1954), John Osborne's *Luther* (1961) and Edward Bond's *The Woman* (1978) are some of the most successful examples. But drama about remote periods has rather gone out of fashion, with modern playwrights concentrating on more recent events, as in Howard Brenton's *The Churchill Play* (1974), David Hare's *Plenty* (1978) or Tom Stoppard's *Rock 'n' Roll* (2006). Moreover, history plays of whatever kind usually require large casts, which only the largest of the subsidised theatres can afford.

The Unities

First translated into Latin in 1498, Aristotle's *The Poetics* transformed the way Renaissance critics thought about mimesis and no passage was more influential than the following:

> Tragedy is the imitation of an action which is whole, complete and substantial...by whole I mean that it has a beginning, a middle and an end...it must imitate a single, unified and complete sequence of action. Its incidents must be organised in such a way that if any is removed or has its position changed, the whole is dislocated and disjointed. If

something can be added or taken away without any obvious effect, it is not intrinsic to the whole.[9]

Aristotle is simply arguing for a unified artistic focus, but this passage was interpreted as insisting that every tragedy should display the following characteristics:

- Unity of action (it should only have one main action)
- Unity of place (it should all happen in one location)
- Unity of time (it should all occur in one day)

This became a commonplace in neo-classical literary theory, and drama came to be judged by the extent to which it accorded with the 'unities'.

The French neo-classical authors (marshalled by the Académie Française) were keen on the unities, and a number of eighteenth-century English poets, above all Pope and Dryden, argued for their continued relevance. Indeed, Dryden favoured Ben Jonson over Shakespeare for his adherence to classical rules:

If you consider the Historical Playes of Shakespeare, they are rather so many Chronicles of Kings, or the business many times of thirty or forty years, crampt into a representation of two hours and a half, which is not to imitate or paint Nature, but rather to draw her in miniature, to take her in little; to look upon her through the wrong end of a Perspective, and receive her Images not onely much less, but infinitely more imperfect then the life: this instead of making a Play delightful, renders it ridiculous.[10]

The more pragmatic Dr Johnson, however, got to the heart of the matter:

Whether Shakespeare knew the unities, and rejected them by design, or deviated from them by happy ignorance, it is, I think, impossible to decide, and useless to inquire... As nothing is essential to the fable, but unity of action, and

---

9   Aristotle *Poetics* translated Kenneth McLeish (1999)

10 John Dryden *Essay of Dramatick Poesie* (1668)

as the unities of time and place arise evidently from false assumptions, and, by circumscribing the extent of the drama, lessen its variety, I cannot think it much to be lamented, that they were not known by him, or not observed: nor, if such another poet could arise, should I very vehemently reproach him, that his first act passed at Venice, and his next in Cyprus. Such violations of rules, merely positive, become the comprehensive genius of Shakespeare.[11]

The Romantics turned their backs on the unities for different reasons: they felt they prevented the development of a style capable of expressing the organic shapes of human experience; the unities were even more forcefully dismissed by Brecht who proposed a kind of 'non-Aristotelian' drama that could reflect on the complexities and contradictions of the modern world. Intriguingly, they have made an unheralded – and almost certainly unconscious – return in the one-set, one-day, one-unit-of-action plays that are the staple of modern British drama.

Three different kinds of comedy

There are three main strands in comic drama: social comedy, romantic comedy and farce.

Social comedy

Social comedy explores the absurdity of the ways of the world, the folly and corruption of those in power, and the greed and amorality of those who serve them. It lays bare the frequently awkward truths of how we live together.

Social comedy relishes a sharp turn of phrase. It plays best to audiences who are sceptical and open-minded but fails to thrive in cultures that are pious or self-regarding. Nor does it succeed in societies that are so fractured that its natural wit and sophistication strikes a false note. It depends, above all, on a balance being struck between biting satire and elementary good manners.

---

11   Dr Johnson *Prefaces to Shakespeare* (1765)

Social comedy has its roots in the four great comic dramatists of the ancient world: the fantastical and often surreal Aristophanes; his successor, the chief exponent of the Greek New Comedy, Menander; and the Roman dramatists Plautus and Terence, whose brilliant comedies satirised the sexual mores of the Republic. In Medieval Europe, social comedy's subversive energy was largely confined to poetry, but a streak of the grotesque acted as a counter-vailing force in English religious drama.

Social comedy thrived in the changing world of Elizabethan and Jacobean London: Thomas Dekker's *The Shoemaker's Holiday* (1599); Ben Jonson's masterpieces – *Volpone* (1606), *The Alchemist* (1610) and *Bartholomew Fair* (1614) – and Thomas Middleton's city comedies – *The Roaring Girl* (1611), *A Chaste Maid in Cheapside* (1613) and *A Fair Quarrel* (1616) – are the most significant examples. The chief characteristics of social comedy can be detected in Shakespeare's more urban plays – *The Comedy of Errors*, *The Merry Wives of Windsor*, *Much Ado About Nothing* and the Eastcheap scenes in *Henry IV Part One and Two* – but are evident in the abundant and acutely observant wit that runs through all his work.

It was with the Restoration, however, that social comedy gained the dominance that it has retained in British drama. Five playwrights were responsible for nine masterpieces: William Wycherley's *The Country Wife* (1672) and *The Plain Dealer* (1676); George Etherege's *The Man of Mode* (1676); John Vanbrugh's *The Relapse* (1696) and *The Provoked Wife* (1697); William Congreve's *Love for Love* (1695) and *The Way of the World* (1700); and George Farquhar's *The Recruiting Officer* (1706) and *The Beaux' Stratagem* (1707). These remarkable plays present a glittering façade of wit and fashionable display – sometimes with a surprising undertow of true feeling – while coming to sophisticated moral judgments through the unblinking presentation of folly and vice.

The later eighteenth century saw a new tenderness – sentiment, but rarely sentimental – in social comedy, and a less narrowly sexual view of women. This is evident in the three popular masterpieces of the period: Oliver Goldsmith's *She Stoops to Conquer* (1773) and two plays by Richard Brinsley Sheridan, *The Rivals* (1775) and *The*

School for Scandal (1777). These are bathed in a warmer light than Restoration Comedy and reflect a more settled and prosperous time.

Social comedy was not a purely British phenomenon. It flowered in seventeenth-century France, where the presiding genius was the actor, impresario and playwright Jean-Baptiste de Molière. His masterpieces are *The School for Wives* (1662), *Tartuffe* (1664), *The Miser* (1668), *Don Juan* (1665) and *The Misanthrope* (1666). These all featured a leading part for Molière to play and, true to the dark humour of his best work, he collapsed (and later died) on stage playing Argan in *The Hypochondriac* (1673); the audience thought he was still acting. The Danish playwright Ludvig Holberg wrote a series of popular comedies a little too firmly under Molière's influence, which are hardly ever performed today.

Molière's eighteenth-century successor was Pierre de Marivaux, whose work is less satirical (and less funny), and explores identity through the lens of a scientific, often experimental analysis. His best plays are *The Game of Love and Chance* (1730), *The Triumph of Love* (1732), and *Indiscretions* (1737). Marivaux was a superb novelist and mastered a particular style – 'marivaudage' – which expressed his characters' psychological life with unique fluency, style and wit.

The great eighteenth-century revolutions – first America (1776), and then France (1789) – changed the world. No dramatist expressed the period more forcefully than Pierre Beaumarchais, whose trilogy of Figaro comedies addresses many of the great social issues of the day. Indeed, at the premiere of *The Marriage of Figaro* in 1784, Louis XVI was so appalled by its revolutionary implications that he declared that this 'detestable' play 'should never be played', adding prophetically that:

> We'd have to tear the Bastille down for a performance of this play to have no dangerous consequences. This man mocks everything that makes people respect their betters.[12]

---

12   I found the French peculiarly hard to translate: 'C'est détestable, cela ne sera jamais joué: il faudrait détruire la Bastille pour que la représentation de cette pièce ne fût pas une inconséquence dangereuse. Cet homme déjoue tout ce qu'il faut respecter dans un gouvernement.'

With Romanticism sweeping across Europe, social comedy was more often found in the novel than in drama, although the finest comedy in the German language, Heinrich von Kleist's *The Broken Jug* (1811), is an honourable exception. Nevertheless, particularly after the bourgeois revolutions of 1848, popular French writers such as Victorien Sardou, Eugène Scribe and Henri Becque dominated the commercial theatre with their carefully constructed 'well-made plays'. Enormously popular at the time, these have not survived the test of time.

Late Victorian England produced two great comic dramatists. The first, Arthur Wing Pinero, was responsible for almost sixty plays, including the beautiful if occasionally sentimental *The Second Mrs Tanqueray* (1893) and *Trelawney of the 'Wells'* (1898). The other was Oscar Wilde, whose *The Importance of Being Earnest* (1895) has earned its place as one of the best loved and most admired comedies in the language.

British social comedy survived the trauma of the First World War and enjoyed an astonishing revival in the 1920s and 1930s. The two finest playwrights were Noël Coward – especially in *Hay Fever* (1924), *Private Lives* (1929), *Present Laughter* (1939) and *Blithe Spirit* (1941) – and Terence Rattigan, whose debut *French Without Tears* (1936) was one of the great theatrical triumphs of the time.

For the last thirty years, five exceptional comic playwrights have dominated the West End. Writing in a period of unprecedented social liberalism and economic prosperity, Tom Stoppard, Alan Ayckbourn, Michael Frayn, Peter Nichols and Alan Bennett have been responsible for some of British comedy's most impressive achievements. It's as yet unclear who will carry the torch into the future and some wonder whether social comedy's inclusive optimism is the prerogative of a gentler time than our own.

Romantic Comedy

Romantic comedy focuses on personal relationships between men and women and usually offers a positive outcome. With its roots in Roman comedy and the *commedia dell'arte*, it largely transcends the cruelty inherent in its origins.

One of the finest features of Shakespearean comedy is its careful examination of the troubles of the heart. Inspired by Ovid, Shakespeare's comedies show the way that love is a highly subversive force that mounts a powerful challenge against convention and hierarchy. Thus, in *The Comedy of Errors*, when Antipholus of Syracuse meets Luciana he's swept up by feelings that he didn't know he had; the shrew Katherine is only 'tamed' by Petruchio when she submits to the feelings of love that she was so determined to avoid; and, in *Much Ado About Nothing*, the irresistible force of Beatrice and Benedick's mutual attraction humiliates them even as it brings the two together. Nowhere is the impact of *eros* more vividly portrayed than in *A Midsummer Night's Dream*, which dramatises unforgettably the bewildering nature of sexual attraction.

If this is true of Shakespeare's most sexually charged work, it is doubly the case with his more explicitly romantic plays: *The Two Gentlemen of Verona*, *As You Like It* and, above all, *Twelfth Night*. One of the curious facts about this play – sometimes hailed the greatest love poem in the English language – is that it's only occasionally funny: the slapstick routines of Toby Belch and Andrew Aguecheek scarcely conceal a much more melancholic prospect, and the humiliation of Malvolio surely entertained an audience faced with the emergence of Puritanism more successfully than it does today. It's the love triangle of Orsino, Olivia and Viola – and Feste's sad songs about the passing of all things – that compel a modern audience. And here Shakespeare goes to the heart of what it is to be in love and to lose: although the play ends happily, nothing, even the appearance of Sebastian, can compensate Olivia for the non-consummation of her love for Viola.

As in so many things, Shakespeare set a standard that few could match. Restoration comedy explored sex and attraction, usually casting doubt on its characters' frequent declarations of love. Sentimental comedies provided romantic solutions to very unromantic problems – above all the wayward sexual appetites of straying husbands. But none could equal Shakespeare's potent mixture of sex and love, feeling and animality, individuality and society.

Although the naturalists turned their backs on romantic comedy, one of Ibsen's first fully achieved pieces was the delightful *Love's Comedy* (1862) and Chekhov's quartet of masterpieces are best read as comedies of unrequited love. An unforeseen consequence of the naturalist revolution was a fatal divide between 'serious' dramatists on the one hand (who didn't write comedy, certainly not romantic comedy) and lightweight, commercial playwrights on the other, happy to entertain their audiences, and untroubled that they weren't digging beneath the surface of human experience.

Romantic comedy is, of course, a hugely successful genre in its own right on television and in film – 'rom-com' as it's often called – and a handful of serious playwrights are still interested in its demands. However, modernism and its many offshoots have, for now, relegated it to the second division.

Farce

In farce the physical and the mechanical are more important than the romantic or the cerebral. The word itself derives from 'farcie' (the French for 'stuffed'), and the dramatic form draws on the *commedia dell'arte*, with its reduction of human beings to character types and its emphasis on the humiliating realities of physical experience. The best farce has a particular wildness about it and produces a kind of laughter that is both desperate and savage.

Farce flourishes in societies with a high degree of sexual repression, but also with a confident and pleasure-seeking middle class. *Belle Époque* France, torn between the pursuit of every comfort and the continued dominance of the Catholic Church, provided fertile soil, as the great farceur Eugène Labiche memorably declared:

> Of all the subjects which offered themselves to me, I have selected the bourgeois. Essentially mediocre in his vices and in his virtues, he stands half-way between the hero and the scoundrel, between the saint and the profligate.

Labiche's many plays include *An Italian Straw Hat* (1851). His even more prolific successor, Georges Feydeau, wrote dozens of farces, including *A Flea in her Ear* (1907), probably the finest example of the genre.

Farce crossed the English Channel with Arthur Wing Pinero, whose *The Magistrate* (1885) and *The Schoolmistress* (1886) stand comparison with the best of the classic French farces. In the prim England of the 1920s and 1930s, Ben Travers wrote a series of successful farces – including *Rookery Nook* (1926), *Thark* (1927), *Plunder* (1928) and *Spotted Dick* (1939) – and Noël Coward's early comedies stray towards the farcical at times.

Post-war English farce has been surprisingly enduring: Anthony Marriott and Alistair Foot's *No Sex, We're British* (1975), Alan Ayckbourn's *Bedroom Farce* (1975), Michael Frayn's *Noises Off* (1982) and Ray Cooney's *Run For Your Wife* (1983) are among the most commercially successful plays of the last half-century. The great iconoclast, Joe Orton, attempted farce in *What the Butler Saw* (1969), perhaps prompting Ben Travers, in his ninetieth year, to come out of retirement and write *The Bed Before Yesterday* (1975).

Naturalism

Émile Zola declared that 'there is more poetry in the little apartment of a bourgeois than in all the empty, worm-eaten palaces of history',[13] and fundamental to naturalism was the attempt at a scientific depiction of real people within modern and entirely recognisable settings.

Henrik Ibsen, Anton Chekhov and August Strindberg are often hailed as the founders of naturalistic drama. But many of naturalism's chief characteristics are evident in mid-century Russian drama, especially Ivan Turgenev – *A Month in the Country* (1855) – and Alexander Ostrovsky – *The Storm* (1860) and *The Forest* (1871). And there were two important German language dramatists: Gerhart Hauptmann, whose masterpiece about industrial strife, *The Weavers* (1892), brought a new level of political involvement to the form, and the satirist Arthur Schnitzler, who shocked

---

13   Émile Zola *Naturalism in the Theatre* (1881)

Viennese bourgeois taste with his dramas of sexual excess, *Anatol* (1893) and *La Ronde* (1897).

It is impossible, however, to exaggerate the impact of Ibsen, Chekhov and Strindberg. 'Ibsenism' described much more than a theatrical form, it was an attitude to life. Henrik Ibsen exposed the illusions under which his characters labour, and showed how revealing them is both essential and dangerous. His plays are the foundation of modern drama and any appreciation of its qualities must return to his dozen masterpieces, especially *A Doll's House* (1879), *Ghosts* (1881), *The Wild Duck* (1884) and *Hedda Gabler* (1890). If Ibsen's plays are profound explorations of the modern condition, Anton Chekhov's quartet of great plays – *The Seagull* (1896), *Uncle Vanya* (1899), *Three Sisters* (1901) and *The Cherry Orchard* (1904) – manage to be both trivial comedies of unrequited love and sensuous expressions of the transience of all human wishes. The great Swedish iconoclast August Strindberg wrote two of the key texts of the naturalist revolution, *The Father* (1887) and *Miss Julie* (1888); brutal and uncompromising, they contain within them the seeds of the form's self-destruction.

At the turn of the century, a trio of remarkable British playwrights, inspired by what they took to be Ibsen's 'issue drama', created a new kind of British drama, naturalistic in form but political in content. John Galsworthy examined the realities of class in *Strife* (1909) and *The Skin Game* (1920); Harley Granville Barker exposed the hypocrisy of those in power in *The Voysey Inheritance* (1903-5) and *Waste* (1907); while George Bernard Shaw cast a critical eye across a wide range of political and social questions, above all in *Mrs Warren's Profession* (1893), *Candida* (1894), *Major Barbara* (1905) and *Pygmalion* (1913).

The influence of naturalism can be felt to this day, especially on writers committed to anatomising society and assembling a coherent argument for its improvement. Perhaps the most enduring is David Hare who, in plays like *Plenty* (1978), *A Map of the World* (1982) and *The Secret Rapture* (1988), as well as his trilogy about English institutions – *Racing Demon* (1990), *Murmuring Judges* (1991) and *The Absence of War* (1993) – wrote what the critic Michael Billington has usefully described as 'state of the nation' plays.[14]

Symbolism, Expressionism and Surrealism

In reaction to naturalism's emphasis on the physical and the material, many turn of the century artists set out to explore what lies beneath the surface. This manifested itself in different ways according to culture and art form: alternative spirituality, Freudian psychoanalysis, nationalist identity, class politics and the landscape of dreams all played their part.

Intriguingly, the naturalists themselves led the way. Ibsen's late plays are often symbolic in their intentions: he conceived of *When We Dead Awaken* (1899) as the first in a new cycle of expressly poetic dramas. Chekhov's *The Seagull* (1896) is often read in symbolic terms and Strindberg, who was responsible in the Preface to *Miss Julie* for one of the defining manifestos of naturalist theatre, wrote some of the most important non-naturalist plays, including *The Dance of Death* (1900), *A Dream Play* (1901) and *The Ghost Sonata* (1907).

A group of talented Irish playwrights were drawn to the newly established Abbey Theatre in Dublin and their work reflected a growing mood of rebellion against British rule, and the empiricism that was its dominant philosophical and artistic mode. The best plays are by JM Synge – *In the Shadow of the Glen* (1903), *Riders to the Sea* (1904) and *The Playboy of The Western World* (1907) – and WB Yeats (often in collaboration with Lady Gregory) – *Cathleen Ní Houlihan* (1902) and *On Baile's Strand* (1903). Other small European countries saw a similar phenomenon: the Belgian Symbolist Maurice Maeterlinck wrote mystical, fatalist dramas and a similar flavour is evident in Hugo von Hofmannstahl's *Everyman* (1911) and Arthur Schnitzler's late plays.

---

14   See Michael Billington's survey of postwar British theatre, *State of the Nation* (2008)

Turn of the century German painting, music and film was dominated by Expressionism, the attempt to use art to convey anxiety, morbidity and sexual passion. Three leading playwrights strived for a similar intensity: Frank Wedekind in his erotic masterpiece *Spring Awakening* (1891) and his 'Lulu' plays (1895-1904); Carl Sternheim with his cycle of five plays, *The Heroic Life of the Bourgeoisie* (1911-22); and Georg Kaiser's tortured visions, *The Burgers of Calais* (1913), *From Morning till Midnight* (1916) and *Gas* (1918).

Inspired by the revolutionary changes brought about by the First World War, a group of radical German and Austrian playwrights used expressionistic techniques to dramatise the new realities: the best known are Karl Kraus' massive *The Last Days of Mankind* (1919) and the Communist visionary Ernst Toller's *Hoppla! We're Alive* (1927). Brecht's early plays – *Baal* (1918), *Drums in the Night* (1918-20) and *In The Jungle of the Cities* (1921-4) – were all written under the influence of this new mechanistic style, as was the Czech playwright Karel Capek's astonishing science fiction drama, *R.U.R.* (1921).

If the First World War drove some writers into political engagement, it led others into the self-conscious embrace of anti-meaning known as Dadaism – a movement that started in Zürich with the *Cabaret Voltaire* and soon spread to all the capitals of Europe. Dadaism in turn gave birth to Surrealism. There are few genuinely surreal plays – with the possible exceptions of Pablo Picasso's *Desire Caught by a Tail* (1941) and Eugene Ionesco's *The Chairs* (1951) – but the avant-garde Austrian playwright Peter Handke has attempted his own brand of poetic surrealism.

In recent years, the British theatre has been eager to embrace alternative forms and writers have dabbled with symbolism, surrealism, expressionism and so on. However, the demand for this has come from directors and designers more than actors or the audience, and confronts the theatre with a real problem: by replacing the dialectic with a single viewpoint it drains the theatre of its content. It will be interesting to see if the current vogue results in plays that last.

The Theatre of the Absurd

The critic Martin Esslin coined the title 'The Theatre of the Absurd'[15] to describe the work of a group of playwrights whose plays reflect existentialism – the philosophy that life has no meaning beyond itself and is fundamentally absurd. Existentialism had its roots in nineteenth century pessimism and drew on Wittgenstein's insights into the limitations of language. It flourished in the intellectual and artistic *demi-monde* of post-war Paris where it reflected disillusionment with the fanatical idealism that led to two world wars.

The father of existentialism was Jean-Paul Sartre, whose philosophical drama *Huis Clos* (1944) concludes that 'Hell is other people'. Undoubtedly, the greatest existentialist playwright was Samuel Beckett, whose *Waiting for Godot* (1953), *Endgame* (1957), *Krapp's Last Tape* (1958) and *Happy Days* (1961) articulate profound feelings of philosophical despair: 'We are born aside a grave and a difficult birth. Down in the grave, lingeringly, the gravedigger puts on the forceps', says Vladimir in *Waiting for Godot*. Paradoxically, the purity of Beckett's vision and the stripped-down perfection of his language render even this bleakest of dramatic styles astonishingly beautiful. Beckett's natural successor was Harold Pinter whose best plays are probably *The Birthday Party* (1958), *The Caretaker* (1960), *The Homecoming* (1965), *No Man's Land* (1975) and *Betrayal* (1978).

The Theatre of the Absurd was not invented in post-war Paris, however, and its characteristics can be detected earlier, in the cynical materialism of Wedekind, Schnitzler and early Brecht. Chekhov, too, dramatised the underlying absurdity of the human condition: the image of the old retainer Firs left alone in the house at the end of *The Cherry Orchard* is exactly this.

Some critics have even argued for an early version of the Theatre of the Absurd in Shakespeare, especially those late tragedies in which there is no chance of divine intervention. They point to Macbeth declaring that life 'is a tale / Told by an idiot, full of sound and fury / Signifying nothing[16]' and argue that this

---

15   Martin Esslin *The Theatre of the Absurd* (1962)

16   18 *Macbeth* (5.5)

demonstrates the pessimism of Shakespeare's vision. The action of the play, however, shows that such despair is a result of Macbeth's actions and isn't shared by his many victims. What's more, Macbeth is defeated by an army carrying freshly cut trees, and is killed by Macduff, a man born by Caesarean section, the 'naked new-born babe' he imagines earlier. The heretical nihilism of Shakespeare's characters may show a world in which, as Yeats said, 'things fall apart, the centre cannot hold',[17] but they're part of a broader moral scheme, in which amorality is countered by goodness and hope.[18]

For the real birth of the Theatre of the Absurd we should instead turn to the French dramatist Alfred Jarry (1873-1907) whose trilogy of 'Ubu' plays are among the defining texts of modern drama. They are an astonishing collage of scatology, black humour, political satire and atheism, expressed in language singularly lacking in literary finesse: a riot broke out at the premiere of *Ubu the King* (1896) as soon as the first word – 'Pschitt!'[19] – was spoken.

Plays about plays

Central to modernism was a deconstruction of illusion and a fearless exploration of *mimesis* itself. In the theatre, this took the form of plays about plays, of which the greatest is almost certainly Luigi Pirandello's *Six Characters in Search of an Author* (1921): this combines dazzling shifts of theatrical perspective with a realistic dramatisation of the hell of family life. The American playwright Thornton Wilder played with similar meta-theatrical trickery in *Our Town* (1938). More recently, Tom Stoppard's *Rosencrantz and Guildenstern are Dead*'s (1966) remorseless theatricality presents the audience with a sophisticated examination of existentialism;

---

17   WB Yeats 'The Second Coming' (1920)

18   See Stephen Greenblatt's critical review of a much-hailed recent production of *Macbeth*: 'The Stalinist setting does something more than provide an instance of modern tyranny; it closes off the vistas of hope that might otherwise have been glimpsed'. *The New York Review of Books*, July 17, 2008.

19   The original French is 'merdre'. The French for 'shit' is 'merde' – without a second 'r' – so this is sometimes translated as 'shitr'. Others prefer the more guttural 'pschitt!'

many of his later plays – especially *The Real Thing* (1982) – do much the same.

Of course, plays about plays have pedigree. Shakespeare explored the theatrical metaphor extensively – 'All the world's a stage' declares Jacques – and his plays continually evoked the realities of the theatre. Some – *Love's Labour's Lost*, *A Midsummer Night's Dream*, *Hamlet* and *The Tempest* – even include elaborate plays within plays. Shakespeare, however, uses the theatrical metaphor as much to explore the real world as to reflect on the nature of art. By imitating majesty so effortlessly, he shows that a king is no different from 'a poor player' and the result is a demystification of power.

Brecht used the theatrical metaphor extensively and his most popular work, *The Caucasian Chalk Circle* (1944), takes the form of a play within a play. Brecht saw the self-conscious use of the physical realities of the theatre as a way of encouraging his audience to engage with the substance of the play itself; ironically, his famous 'alienation effect' may have made his audiences think more about the plastic nature of the theatre itself than about the political and social implications of the action described.

Issue drama

Brecht declared that 'hitherto the playwright has interpreted the world, the point is to change it'.[20] He wanted to create a kind of theatre that could help spark the revolution that would, he hoped, improve the position of those at the bottom. Turning his back on 'timeless truths', he committed himself to 'plays for the decade', which could concern themselves with the social and political challenges of the day. But, with the notable exceptions of *Fear and Misery in the Third Reich* (1935-8) and *Señora Carrar's Rifles* (1937), few of his plays are concerned with contemporary events, and he preferred to use historical parables as a way of talking about the present.

---

20   In *The Eighteenth Brumaire of Louis Bonaparte* (1852) Karl Marx wrote 'Hitherto the philosophers have interpreted the world, the point is to change it.'

Of course, Brecht was not as original as his admirers sometimes claim. The Danish nineteenth-century critic George Brandes declared that 'What shows a literature to be a living thing today is the fact of it subjecting problems to debate', and Ibsen was widely perceived by his contemporaries as a writer of 'issue drama'. His British followers, Bernard Shaw, Galsworthy and Granville Barker, were all committed to the fight for peace and justice, and wrote plays that campaigned on these issues, as did JB Priestley in *An Inspector Calls* (1945) and Terence Rattigan in *The Winslow Boy* (1946).

Several American playwrights – Clifford Odets, Arthur Miller, Lorraine Hansberry and August Wilson – have argued that America needed to change if it was to live up to the ideals of its founding fathers. In the late 1960s and early 1970s a group of British playwrights emerged – David Edgar, David Hare, Howard Brenton and Caryl Churchill among others – who wanted their plays to help change society. Athol Fugard wrote some of the greatest political plays as his contribution to the struggle against apartheid and, in many societies, drama is still seen as an appropriate artform for political protest.

Drama is used in developing countries as a way of spreading awareness about important health issues: AIDS, women's rights, the danger of land mines and so on. It's particularly valuable in addressing questions that are seen as taboo: the anonymity of a play – these events are happening to someone else – allows the spectators to draw their own conclusions, without being personally confronted. But a word of warning: even the most didactic of Brecht's learning plays (the *Lehrstücke*) do much more than tell us what to think. Drama is a sophisticated activity, as the cigar-chomping movie mogul Samuel Goldwyn declared: 'Pictures are for entertainment, messages should be delivered by Western Union'.

Kitchen sink drama

The phrase 'kitchen sink drama' emerged in the 1960s to describe a kind of play that expressed the ordinary and the unsavoury, using the particular idiom of English poetic realism.

The premiere of John Osborne's debut *Look Back in Anger* (1956) is often regarded as a watershed in post-war British theatre. The naturalists had argued almost a hundred years earlier that everyday experience could be a valid subject for art, but Osborne's combination of bedsit squalor with excoriating wit offered theatregoers a new image of youthful heroism. It also provided a template for many of the best plays of the late 1950s and 1960s: Arnold Wesker's *Roots* (1959), *The Kitchen* (1959), *I'm Talking About Jerusalem* (1960) and *Chips With Everything* (1962); Edward Bond's *The Pope's Wedding* (1962) and *Saved* (1965); and David Storey's *The Contractor* (1969) and *The Changing Room* (1972). Kitchen sink drama was dominant in the British theatre of the 1970s and early 1980s, even if a younger generation of playwrights – Trevor Griffiths, Howard Brenton, David Hare and others – brought a new political passion to the form.

Kitchen sink drama had its roots in the English theatrical tradition. This is first evident in the medieval Mystery plays (see, for example, *The Second Shepherds' Play* from the Wakefield cycle), which powerfully combine the colloquial with the liturgical, the sacred with the profane and the material with the spiritual. It can also be detected in the Elizabethan 'domestic tragedies' – the anonymous *Arden of Faversham* (printed 1592), *The Yorkshire Tragedy* (printed 1608) and Thomas Heywood's masterpiece *A Woman Killed with Kindness* (1603) – and in those marvellous moments in Shakespeare when we can hear the voice of the working man rubbing up against the grand cadences of his social 'betters'.

The most remarkable modern exemplars of this tradition were DH Lawrence, whose realistic plays are set in the Nottinghamshire coalfields – *The Collier's Friday Night* (1909), *The Daughter-in-Law* (1912) and *The Widowing of Mrs Holroyd* (1914) – and Sean O'Casey whose three plays about the Dublin working class – *The Shadow of a Gunman* (1923), *Juno and The Paycock* (1924) and *The Plough and the Stars* (1926) – invented tragedy for the slums.

The British theatre has in recent years reacted against the kitchen sink, because of what is felt to be its restrictive form and its class-based content. Part of the problem is that kitchen sink drama has become mainstream in television soap opera. More importantly, the diversity and contradictions of the modern world demand new forms. One of the surprising successes in recent years was Peter Gill's *The York Realist* (2001): Gill's own production – which featured a fully operational kitchen sink – bore witness to the form's enduring power.

New Modernity

The twenty-first century demands a new kind of drama. Three German language playwrights – Franz Xaver Kroetz, Heiner Müller and Botho Strauß – have been at the forefront of the search for new theatrical styles. Meanwhile, two remarkable female British playwrights have combined formal innovation with a remorseless exploration of new content: Caryl Churchill and Sarah Kane. These could be called the 'new modernists'.

Younger playwrights are struggling to find an appropriate form to describe the very particular features of our times: changing sexual relationships, the role and limits of religion, and widespread feelings of post-modern *anomie*. Three of the most interesting are the British playwright Martin Crimp – *Dealing with Clair* (1988), *Attempts on Her Life* (1991) and *The City* (2008) – and two Americans: Phyllis Nagy – *Disappeared* (1992), *Butterfly Kiss* (1994) and *The Strip* (1995) – and Neil Labute – *Bash: Latter-Day Plays* (1999), *The Shape of Things* (2001) and *Some Girl(s)* (2005). There are dozens of others appearing all the time.

As I will argue, the future belongs to these 'new modernists' – so long as they can balance the demands of rigorous modernity with commercial viability and entertainment.

Now it's time to turn the title page and start to read the text itself.

5. Who's in it?

REPRESENTATIONS OF HUMAN BEINGS lie at the heart of drama and, when reading a play, one of the first questions we need to ask is 'who's in it?'

'Dramatis Personae'

The best place to start is with the list of characters that appears at the beginning of most published plays. This provides core information about the characters, and sometimes more.

Every modern edition of Shakespeare provides different *dramatis personae*. Only two plays in the First Folio (*The Tempest* and *The Two Gentlemen of Verona*) include the 'Names of the Actors'. These appear on the last page of the text and it is unlikely that Shakespeare had a hand in them, but they are instructive nonetheless:

Alonso, K of Naples.

Sebastian his Brother.

Prospero, the right Duke of Millaine.

Anthonio his brother, the usurping Duke of Millaine.

Ferdinand, Son to the King of Naples.

Gonzalo, an honest old councellor.

Adrian, & Francisco, Lords

Caliban, a savage and deformed slave

Trinculo, a jester.

Stephano, a drunkard Butler.

Master of a Ship.

Boat-Swaine

Marriners.

Miranda, daughter to Prospero.

Ariell, an ayrie spirit.

Iris

Ceres

Iuno
Nymphs
Reapers

The K after Alonso's name indicates that he's a king, justifying, in the context of the time, his position at the top of the list. It also alerts us to the play's political content, as do the value judgments further down (e.g. 'the right' and 'the usurping Duke of Millaine'). The positioning of Miranda (the only female character in the play) beside the sexless spirits reminds us of the gender hierarchies of the Jacobean world.

Every period has a different approach. In naturalism, the list attempts a more objective summary. In *The Cherry Orchard* we read:

RANYEVSKAYA, Liubov Andryeevna (Liuba), a landowner
ANIA (Anichka), her daughter, aged 17
VARIA (Varvara Mihailovna), her adopted daughter, aged 24
GAYEV, Leonid Andryeevich (Lionia), brother of Mme
     Ranyevskaya
LOPAKHIN, Yermolai Aleksyeevich, a businessman
TROFIMOV, Piotr Serghyeevich (Pyetia), a student
SIMEONOV-PISHCHIK, Boris Borisovich, a landowner
CHARLOTTA IVANOVNA, a German governess
YEPIHODOV, Semion Pantelyeevich, a clerk on Ranyevskaya's
     estate
DOONIASHA (Andotyia Fiodorovna), a parlour maid
FEERS (Feers Nikolayevich), a manservant, aged 87
YASHA, a young manservant
A TRAMP
STATION-MASTER
POST-OFFICE CLERK
GUESTS, SERVANTS[1]

---

1   Chekhov *Plays* translated by Elisabeta Fen (1954). Because of the Russian system of patronymics, as well as the frequent use of terms of endearment, it's helpful to have this list open in front of you when you first read the play.

This provides useful information about how the characters are related to each other ('her daughter', 'her adopted daughter' and so on), as well as about class and occupation ('a landowner', 'a businessman', 'a German governor'). Intriguingly, Chekhov provides ages selectively and only when it makes a point. Thus it is important that Ania (Anya, as she's sometimes translated) is only 17 and that her adopted sister Varia is of an age (24) at which she 'should' be married; Feers (or Firs) is 87 – the number has been picked at random but carries the all-important sense of antiquity – but Yasha is just 'young': the precise age isn't important, it's the cockiness of youth that Chekhov wants us to imagine.

The order is significant because of what it says about social hierarchy: Ranyevskaya is first because she's the senior landowner. Her immediate family comes next. The wealthy merchant Lopakhin, the student Trofimov and the impoverished landowner Simeonov-Pishchik follow. Beneath them are the skilled servants (Governess and Clerk, both lettered), the illiterate parlour maid Doonyasha and the manservants. At the bottom are the unnamed 'extras': the tramp (a brief but important presence in Act Two), the Station-Master and the Post-Office Clerk, as well as various servants and party guests.

Modern playwrights usually list their characters in order of appearance, occasionally alphabetically, but never by social rank. Brecht tended to put the leading parts first (Mother Courage, Galileo, Azdak etc), but listed the rest by generic names – 'A Farmer', 'a Peasant', 'the Thin Monk' and so on – and often set them out in a continuous paragraph. Some lists deserve careful attention. A glance at Richard Bean's *Honeymoon Suite* (2003)[2] would lead us to assume that the play is about six different people:

Whitchell
Irene
Eddie
Izzy
Tits

2   Richard Bean *Plays Two* Oberon Books (2007)

Marfleet

It's difficult to tell the gender of these characters, let alone their age or status. The action quickly makes it plain, but it's as if Bean is being wilfully misleading: in fact, the play has just two characters – a husband and wife on their wedding night, and its 25th and 50th anniversaries. It's just that as the years have gone by their nicknames have changed.

Names

Playwrights have different approaches to naming. Shakespeare is typically eclectic. In *A Midsummer Night's Dream* – a play ostensibly set in Ancient Athens – the Duke is the Theseus of legend, about to marry the Amazon Queen, Hippolyta; Lysander is named for a Spartan general and Demetrius after a Macedonian king; both Hermia and Helena have Greek names and Hermia's father, Egeus, bears the same name as Theseus' father in the myth. But these classical figures share the stage with a group of English workers: Nick Bottom, Peter Quince, Francis Flute, Robin Starveling, Tom Snout and Snug the joiner. Meanwhile, the supernatural figures combine the medieval French (Oberon) with the classical (Titania), and set Anglo-Saxon folklore (Puck, or Robin Goodfellow) alongside English domesticity (Mustardseed, Moth, Peaseblossom and Cobweb). The result is an astonishing, multi-cultural kaleidoscope.

Shakespeare took similar pleasure in the naming of the poor recruits in *Henry IV Part Two*: Thomas Wart, Rafe Mouldy, Simon Shadow, Francis Feeble and Peter Bullcalf. They are, as Falstaff contemptuously calls them:

> Good enough to toss, food for powder, food for powder. They'll fill a pit as well as better... mortal men, mortal men.[3]

---

3 *Henry IV Part One* (4.2)

But Falstaff's name has its own satirical meaning. Originally called Sir John Oldcastle (after the fifteenth-century Lollard Martyr), Shakespeare was forced to change the surname, and settled on a graphic image of sexual impotence: a falling staff.

The Restoration dramatists deliberately chose names that speak of their characters' psychological and physiological traits. Thus, in Wycherley's *The Country Wife* (1675) (the title itself is an obscene pun) we meet Mr Horner, Mr Sparkish, the Fidget family – Sir Jasper, My Lady and Mrs Dainty Fidget – Mr and Mrs Pinchwife, Mrs Squeamish and her mother, Old Lady Squeamish, and so on. In Congreve's *Love For Love* (1695) the names have a curious literary quality: Sir Sampson Legend and his two sons, Valentine and Ben, Mr Scandal, Mr Tattle and Mr Foresight, and three women called Mrs Foresight, Mrs Frail and Miss Prue ('a silly, awkward country girl'). When reading this today, we need to reconcile such explicit signalling about character – caricature even – with our own preference for psychological realism.

A different kind of naming is evident in naturalism. Hedda Gabler is named after the Edda of Nordic legend, but she doggedly retains her father's surname in preference to her husband's. Bernard Shaw played with nomenclature with Eliza Doolittle in *Pygmalion* (1912) and Captain Shotover in *Heartbreak House*. Sean O'Casey evoked the classical world in naming his embattled mother after the goddess Juno (along with her peacock). Schnitzler mischievously called his adulterous married couple, Karl and Emma, in homage to Flaubert's *Madame Bovary*. Samuel Beckett signalled his universal ambitions through the naming of his characters in *Waiting for Godot* – Vladimir (Russian), Estragon (French), Pozzo (Italian) and Lucky (English). And Arthur Miller chose the punning surname, Loman, for his modern tragedy of the common man, *Death of A Salesman*.

Modern dramatists often use names to generate atmosphere. Think of Edward Bond's *The Pope's Wedding* – Scopey, Bill, Len and Lorry – or Petey, Meg, Stanley, Lulu, Goldberg and McCann in Harold Pinter's *The Birthday Party*: they brilliantly conjure up a sinister English underworld.

Then, of course, we have to watch out for the playwright for whom names are entirely arbitrary: Margaret instead of Elizabeth, John instead of Thomas – for no good reason at all.

Age

Nowadays, we have an almost cavalier attitude to age. Modern life expectancy – in the western world, at least – is almost twice that of sixteenth-century England and a good ten years more than in 1900, and we're pretty much guaranteed a level of health and well being unimaginable to our grandparents. So, when we read a classical play and find a reference to age, it's important to make the necessary adjustments.

Shakespeare's Juliet is thirteen ('On Lammas eve at night shall she be fourteen' says the Nurse).[4] Although some modern thirteen year-old girls have had sexual experience they are, strictly speaking, 'under-age'; in Elizabethan England, however, this was an appropriate age to marry – especially for an aristocrat – and Juliet's father is simply doing his paternal duty in trying to find her a husband. By the same reckoning, Juliet's mother could be as young as twenty-eight – she's probably older, but certainly not more than forty – and her father is surely in the prime of life (his forties or fifties) not the doddering patriarch we sometimes see on stage.

When Othello says that he's 'declined into the vale of years',[5] or Cleopatra admits that she's a 'blown rose',[6] we shouldn't imagine that they are in their sixties: middle age started much earlier for the Jacobeans. And when Justice Shallow in *Henry IV Part Two* remembers things that happened fifty-five years ago, he's talking about a time that is almost impossibly removed. Many people's memories today reach back as far, but Shallow would have struck Shakespeare's audience as much more than an old man: like John of Gaunt in *Richard II* or Queen Margaret in *Richard III*, he's a relic from a forgotten world.

---

4   *Romeo and Juliet* (1.3)

5   *Othello* (1.3)

6   *Antony and Cleopatra* (3.13)

One area where we need to be particularly alert to historical difference is with young women of childbearing years. When we read that Hedda Gabler is twenty-eight we should recognise something particular: she's no longer the fancy-free, beautiful daughter of a dashing general; she's a married woman, and the legitimate expectation from everyone – especially her doting husband – is that she will soon have children. If, as is suggested (but not stated), she's pregnant, then this is her last chance; if not, well, it's probably too late. Similarly, Rita Allmers in *Little Eyolf* is thirty and, despite being the mother of a nine year-old, quite capable of seducing Borgheim. The age of young women matters for another reason too. When Nora leaves her husband at the end of *A Doll's House* and goes out into the world, she's unlikely to have the luck of her friend Mrs Linde in finding a new husband; an unmarried woman past thirty is 'on the shelf' in almost every culture except our own, and Ibsen's audience would have been aware of the fact.

Class

We tend to be uncomfortable about class. Despite the growing gap between rich and poor, we are less class-conscious than our grandparents, and often approach the literature of the past with insufficient attention to social distinctions.

Elizabethan and Jacobean England was exceptionally hierarchical and its drama reflected the fact. Look at the finale of *As You Like It* where the four couples represent four different classes. The union of Celia and Oliver resolves the old rivalry between their two aristocratic families; the marriage of Rosalind and the second son, Orlando, reflects the new middle class belief in the romantic meeting of minds; the yearning of the love-sick, lower middle-class shepherds, Phoebe and Silvius, is out of pastoral; while the force that brings the clown Touchstone and the goatherd Audrey together is little more than peasant lust. This quartet of very different couplings heals the damage done to the entire society.

Or look at the hierarchy in *King Lear*. At the top stands Lear himself. Just beneath him is the youthful King of France (whose marriage to the rejected Cordelia has geopolitical implications). Standing outside the royal circle are the two Dukes, Albany and Cornwall, married to Lear's daughters, Goneril and Regan. Below them come two Earls, Kent and Gloucester, whose two sons, Edmund and Edgar are strictly segregated by virtue of Edmund's illegitimacy. At the bottom are the ambitious manservant Oswald, the rootless Fool, and a large number of anonymous soldiers, servants and retainers. The disruption of this carefully structured hierarchy is the central action of the play.

We need to understand class in precise terms, and not rely on simplistic divisions between rich and poor, worker and toff. Those in the middle deserve particularly close reading. Deflores in *The Changeling* is an interesting case. He's a servant in 'the noble Vermandero's' household and, one might presume, motivated by class-envy. But his position is more complex:

> Though my hard fate has thrust me out to servitude
> I tumbled into the world a gentleman.[7]

This suggests someone whose family has landed on bad times; or perhaps he was disinherited for unsuitable or even criminal behaviour. Unlike the upwardly-mobile steward Malvolio in *Twelfth Night*, however, who dreams of marrying above himself, Deflores has no worse claim to the aristocratic Beatrice-Joanna than her other suitors and refuses to acknowledge the social distance between them; in other words, he's much more than her 'bit of rough'.

Because *The Cherry Orchard* (1904) was written just thirteen years before the Bolshevik Revolution, it's sometimes assumed that Lopakhin must be a representative of the revolutionary movement. In fact, he's a member of the newly rich peasant class who did so well in the rapidly modernising Russia of the turn of the century.[8] He's one of Lenin's hated 'Kulaks', and, as such, one of the first to be persecuted after 1917. If we are searching for a Bolshevik we should turn to Trofimov, the eternal student, or his idealistic girlfriend, the aristocratic young Anya.

---

7   Thomas Middleton and William Rowley *The Changeling* (1622)

8   See Orlando Figes *The People's Tragedy* (1997)

It is easier to be sure about class in modern drama, because the signs – at least to the English – are so much clearer. We can tell an enormous amount about a person's social background the moment he opens his mouth. We quickly recognise the insecure bourgeoisie who populate the plays of Alan Ayckbourn and Mike Leigh, the respectable working class characters in Alan Bennett's Yorkshire and Peter Gill's Cardiff, or the fashionable metropolitan types in the plays of Doug Lucie, Patrick Marber and Mark Ravenhill. These are our contemporaries and we know them well.

But, as usual, we need to be careful since social conditions keep changing. In Edward Bond's *Saved* (1965) we can hear the genuine voice of the South London working class. But Bond is dramatising the breakdown of working class solidarity that was such a feature of the 1960s, and it's easy to forget just how different is its modern equivalent. A recent double bill of Andrea Dunbar's *Rita, Sue and Bob Too* (1982) and Robin Soans' *A State Affair* (2000) revealed the catastrophic impact in recent years of heroin addiction on poverty-stricken housing estates.

Even the most apparently rigid of hierarchies is shifting in subtle ways, and the cracks that we see opening up eventually bring about a landslide. Shakespeare and his contemporaries flourished in the years leading up to the English Civil War; Ibsen and Chekhov emerged in the years before the Russian Revolution; and the explosion of English drama after 1956 reflected the social and sexual revolution of the 1960s. In other words, the times are constantly changing and the best dramatists embrace the fact.

The individual and society

The great ambition of the naturalist pioneers was to bring a new level of scientific objectivity to artistic depictions of the human being. The naturalists argued that the material conditions in which a person lives – the 'given circumstances' in Stanislavsky's phrase – are the key forces in shaping his personality and behaviour. And so one of the striking features of naturalism is the way that characters are placed within a set of physical realities – food, money, living conditions, time of day, weather and so on – and their behaviour is seen as the result.

The opening moments of *The Cherry Orchard* demonstrate this vividly:

> It is daybreak, the sun is just coming up, a fine May morning with the cherry trees in blossom, but a little chilly yet, and all the windows are closed.[9]

Lopahkin has fallen asleep on a chair. He's holding a book that he's not read and has walked all the way from town to welcome Madame Ranyevskaya back to her country estate after her many years in France. He tells Doonyasha that he remembers his father hitting him so hard that his nose started to bleed, and he would go up to 'the big house' where Ranyevskaya – 'she was just a slip of a girl' – cleaned him up. But now he's rich: 'I've pots of money, but when you get right down to it, I'm a peasant through and through'. The train is running late and Doonyasha is nervous of what will happen; Lopahkin tells her off for dressing 'like a young lady': 'you've got to remember your place', he says. Then Yepihodov enters, dressed for the occasion but with squeaking shoes, and he soon drops his flowers. These details contribute to a palpable sense of reality. But this isn't realism for the sake of it; the return of Ranyevskaya to her decaying country estate in Imperial Russia after her years abroad is the catalyst for the action. The contrast between her sentimental attachment to her cherry orchard and the unappealing realities on the ground is where the meaning of the play is to be found.

The naturalists showed that a character's social background is an essential part of his makeup. Thus, Hedda Gabler is a general's daughter as well as a young wife; Madame Arkadina wields considerable power (as a Russian landowner, as a leading actress, as the lover of a famous writer and as Konstantin's mother); and Strindberg's Miss Julie is a Swedish aristocrat who defies convention and takes her father's manservant, Jean, as her lover. The best English dramatists of the time – above all, Galsworthy, Granville Barker,

---

9   *The Cherry Orchard* translated by Stephen Mulrine (1998)

Githa Sowerby and DH Lawrence – likewise shape their characters in relation to their work, social position and financial means.

It is wrong, however, to imagine that the connection between character and environment was first grasped in the 1870s. The great classical playwrights understood that personality is a product of environment as much as of inheritance, and placed their characters within the culture and society that made them. Thus, Brutus and Cassius in *Julius Caesar* may be rebels, but they're patrician rebels, motivated by aristocratic, not plebeian, grievance – even if ordinary human frailties such as jealousy, anger and greed play their part. Likewise, Arnolphe in Molière's *The School for Wives* (1662) is a middle-class husband, with all the anxieties of the *nouveau riche*, just as Judge Adam in Kleist's *The Broken Jug* (1811) finds himself caught between the power of the visiting inspector, Walter, and his own ambitious young clerk, Licht.

A realistic understanding of the impact of society is particularly important in reading the young aristocratic women of Jacobean and Elizabethan drama. Hermia, Juliet, Beatrice-Joanna and Ophelia are defined in relation to their fathers who want to ensure that their line is continued and carefully police their daughters' virginities as a result. It's anachronistic to dismiss their attitudes as pathological, and it's unfair to criticise their writers as male fantasists: the combination of obedience and rebellion makes these portraits of young women from a particular class and at a particular time strikingly realistic.

We should avoid a narrowly determinist notion of character and environment, however. And so, while all these young women do something exceptional in going against their fathers' wishes, they are also voicing the growing belief that young women should be able to choose their marriage partners.[10] Similarly, Brutus and Cassius may be rebelling against the established order, but they also characterise the growing interest in republicanism amongst some sectors of the Elizabethan aristocracy. And Williams in *Henry V* may be challenging the deference that was so fundamental to his time,

---

10   See Lawrence Stone *The Family, Sex and Marriage in England, 1500-1800* (1977)

but he's also an emerging English type: the common soldier who fights ferociously for King and Country, but expects a modicum of respect in return.

Romantic drama presents the individual's attempts to stand free of the conventions and restraints of his society. There are two key stories, whose various manifestations explore different aspects of rebellion and examine its consequences in ways that range from cheerful approval to downright condemnation. The first is the Faust legend: this emerged in Germany in the 1580s, was quickly taken up by Marlowe in *Doctor Faustus* (1590) and reached its fullest expression in Goethe's sprawling dramatic poem *Faust, Parts One* (1806) and *Two* (1832). The second is the great seducer, Don Juan: this first appeared in dramatic form in Tirso de Molina's *Trickster of Seville* (1620) and was the subject of two masterpieces a hundred years apart: Molière's *Dom Juan* (1665) and Mozart's opera *Don Giovanni* (1787).

The story of an individual standing up against society sometimes takes on a specifically political character, particularly in German Romanticism. Schiller's first play *The Robbers* (1781) features a group of young students who drop out of society and set up a Robin Hood-like community in the forest; Goethe's *Torquato Tasso* (1790) dramatises the artist's rebellion against (and eventual submission to) his patron; and in Kleist's *Prince of Homburg* (1811) the hero endangers the life of the ruler as a result of the subversive power of his subconscious and is sentenced to death as a result.[11]

In Brecht, society exerts a very real impact on the individual. In his early plays we watch people alienated from their environment – see, for example, *Baal* (1918) or *Drums in the Night* (1918-20). In his transitional work, especially *Man Equals Man* (1924-6), society is the key to the construction – and destruction – of character; in his mature masterpieces the social order creates profound contradictions within the individual: Mother Courage sacrifices her own children on the altar of her business while Galileo suppresses his knowledge of the truth in order to survive.

---

11   *The Prince of Homburg* was one of Hitler's favourite plays – presumably because the reluctant hero eventually submits to the power of the leader.

Stock characters

Theorists of dramatic writing sometimes claim that there are only a limited number of character types. Popular theatre has always been unashamed to draw on stock characters, and the most sophisticated of great playwrights often use them to provide the basis for their innovations.

One of the key sources is the *commedia dell'arte*. This form of popular theatre emerged in fifteenth-century Italy, and had its roots deep in Roman comedy. Performances were improvised out of a series of simple scenarios, nearly always about the trials and tribulations of young love in the face of concerted opposition from the old and powerful. The classical *commedia* troupe had eleven stock characters: three senior men – Pantalone (the decrepit Pantaloon), the powerful but tyrannical Doctor and the boastful captain; four servants (or *zanni*) – Arlecchino (the Harlequin), his older and more unpleasant brother Brighella, and the two clowns, La Pulcinella (Punch) and Pierrot; the young girl's intelligent and sexually experienced maid, Columbina ('the little dove'), and her husband, Pagliaccio. These buzz around the young couple obsessively, making it impossible for them to enjoy their healthy and passionate appetites.

The distinctive shapes of the *commedia* can be found in Elizabethan and Jacobean drama. Thus, Brabantio in *Othello*, Gloucester in *King Lear* and Alibius in *The Changeling* are versions of Pantalone; Columbina can be glimpsed in the character of Maria in *Twelfth Night* and the Nurse in *Romeo and Juliet*; many of Shakespeare's clowns and servants, particularly in the early Italian comedies, are related to the four servants;[12] and Verona's most famous couple are direct descendents of the young lovers, blocked by the adult world from enjoying their love freely.

---

12   In *The Taming of the Shrew* (5.1) Vincentio claims that Tranio's father is a 'sailmaker in Bergamo'. This is more than simply a social putdown: the landlocked town of Bergamo was hailed as the home of the *commedia dell'arte* and Tranio would have immediately been identified as the son of a harlequin.

The *commedia dell'arte* had an even bigger influence on the French and Italian dramatists of the seventeenth and eighteenth centuries. Molière toured with a *commedia* company and his characters are often taken straight from the tradition; Marivaux wrote for the Comédie-Italienne in Paris and his plays include the black masked Harlequin and other features; and Goldoni and Gozzi used the *commedia* as the chief source for their popular farces and philosophical comedies.

There are many other sources for character types. The Bible and classical mythology offer a seemingly endless supply: the 'foolish king', the 'long-suffering mother', the 'noble hero' (who, like Christ, will lay down his life for others), the 'all-loving, all-forgiving virgin', and so on. The Renaissance ushered in new stock types, including the 'femme fatale' (Gertrude, The Duchess of Malfi and Madame Arkadina), the 'angry young man' (Hamlet, Konstantin and Jimmy Porter), and the harassed and apparently cuckolded husband (Leontes, Othello and Torvald). But such characters often have an ancient lineage: thus the Joseph of the New Testament is the original cuckold (like the Greek Amphitryon, his wife has been seduced by God himself) and subsequent dramatisations of cuckoldry draw on the same combination of laughter and sympathy.

The modern theatre has reacted against stock characters because they simplify psychology and reduce human beings to types. They are often thought to be reactionary in their formation: young women are either pure, upper class virgins or sexually active servants; old men are always impotent, mean and domineering; and the servants of the *commedia* are mere grotesques, denied any dignity or reality of their own.

Such objections are certainly valid, but fail to acknowledge the popular roots of so much great theatre, and the way that stock characters create complicity with the audience: 'ah, he's one of those kind of guys, is he?'; 'I think she might be in trouble if she goes on like that'; 'I'm sure he's going to sacrifice himself for his friends' and so on. The reaction against stock characters is predicated on a romantic belief in the individual and modern notions of psychological complexity and human dignity. But the fact is we often judge our friends and families through the filter of stock characteristics and it's an illusion to imagine that a play can be entirely free of their controlling shapes.

Stanislavsky

Central to nineteenth-century theories of artistic realism was the determination to get beyond stereotypes and explore psychological complexity. The Russian actor and director Konstantin Stanislavsky (1863-1958) was the key figure in pursuing this in the theatre. At the heart of his famous system[13] was an analytical approach to character. Three of his key terms – objectives, obstacles and super-objectives – can help us read a play.

Objective
The first thing to establish is what the character wants: this is his 'objective'. It may change according to circumstances and the extent to which he has achieved his previous objectives, but his individual desires – mostly for money, sex and status, but sometimes for more noble ambitions – provide the energy that drives the character onwards. Stanislavsky argued that it was more useful to look at individual wishes than to make generalised value judgments about character, such as 'he's ambitious', 'she's sex-starved' or 'he's jealous', let alone 'he's good' or 'she's evil'. Understanding what a character does to achieve his objectives is the key to understanding who he is.

Obstacle
Having worked out what a character's objectives are, we should understand what stops him from achieving them. In other words, what are the 'obstacles'? An obstacle can take many forms: another character in the play, historical circumstances, or the character's own psychological blocks – his 'super-ego', according to Freud, his conscience according to others. But answering this question begs

13   For a useful introduction see Bella Merlin *The Complete Stanislavsky Toolkit* (2007)

an all-important follow-up question: how does the character negotiate his way past these obstacles? And if we can answer that, Stanislavsky claimed, we can really begin to understand what makes him tick.

Superobjective

The third of Stanislavsky's terms is the 'superobjective'. This is what *really* drives the character. It's sometimes subconscious and often difficult to define. Thus, does Lopahkin just want to buy the cherry orchard or does he want to be taken seriously and command respect? The fact that both are clear objectives suggests that his superobjective is to 'do well in the world'. And what about Nora in *A Doll's House*? Her initial objective – to prevent her husband from discovering that he owes his restored health to her fraudulent borrowing – changes when she realises that she's caught in a trap in which she cannot achieve her potential; at which point she decides to leave her husband and children and pursue her own truth. Put together, we can see that Nora's superobjective is to become an independent woman and that her deception of her husband is simply a way of denying that truth. By the end of the play it's clear that the only way she can achieve this is to go out into the world on her own. Thus defining the superobjective sheds light on the character's deepest motivation.

The value of Stanislavsky

The great strength of Stanislavsky's system is that it conceives of character as something expressed in action, and not as an unchangeable, simplistic moral judgment. It gives precision to an analysis of the text and roots our reading in the real world. It lends us tools with which we can explore the complex web of motivation and behaviour that makes up the individual.

But we need to be careful. Not every play is written with an interest in modern psychological explanation, and such terms can be counter-productive. Thus, Greek tragedy is much more interested in the issues that are raised by conflict – between Antigone's determination to provide a proper funeral for her brother and Creon's wish to maintain the supremacy of the law at all costs – than in the psychology of individual motivation. Both Antigone and Creon *can* be analysed in Stanislavskyan terms, but the mistake is to imagine that Sophocles set out to write psychological case studies. Much the same could be said of Shakespeare and other Renaissance playwrights.

Perhaps the most significant legacy of Stanislavsky's approach is the 'method' school. The American actor and director Lee Strasberg established the Actors Studio in New York in 1949, where he developed an approach to characterisation that depended on a profound exploration of the actor's own psychological make-up. This has had a huge influence on American theatre and film acting – and, by extension, on American playwriting.

Actors owe an enormous debt to Stanislavsky and Strasberg; playwrights, however, have frequently found their approaches irrelevant. Chekhov, whose plays were central to the early success of Stanislavsky's Moscow Art Theatre, felt the system ran contrary to the free-flowing spirit of his writing; Brecht wrote his plays in defiance of Stanislavsky's analysis;[14] and David Mamet has written about acting in terms that run quite contrary to Lee Strasberg's core precepts.

Search the text for the clues

A technique that actors sometimes use for getting a 'fix' on a role is to write down three different lists:

- What the playwright says about the character
- What the other characters say about him
- What the character says about himself

Although the casual reader is unlikely to do the same, understanding this technique can be useful.

---

14   As usual, Brecht was contradictory. See 'Things that can be learnt from Stanislavsky' in *Brecht on Theatre* (1965) and a letter to Lee Strasberg from 1936 in which Brecht says that they 'worked very well together' on *The Decision*.

What the playwright says about the character
Playwrights sometimes offer insights into their characters beyond the confines of the script. Thus, Brecht in his *Work Journal* described Grusha in *The Caucasian Chalk Circle* as a 'sucker' (he used the American term of friendly abuse) and, in a letter to an actress playing Rebecca West in *Rosmersholm*, Ibsen was clear about how he saw his central character:

> Rebecca's manner must on no account carry any hint of imperiousness or masculinity. She does not force Rosmer forward. She lures him. A controlled power, a quiet determination, are of the essence to her character.[15]

Such authorial commentary is fairly rare, however, and only found in modern dramatists. (Although we'd be grateful for Shakespeare's own insights into the character of Hamlet, I suspect the startled Bard would redirect us to the words of the play).

It's useful to scour the stage directions. There are various different kinds of character directions (see *How Does It Work in the Theatre?* below). The best are brief and to the point, but give a sense of the physical presence of the character, as well as important information about age, job and so on. The more elaborate ones are intended for the reader, not the actor or director, and descriptions of one character's 'sandy hair' or another's 'flamboyant waistcoat' shouldn't be regarded as definitive, merely as a prompt for the imagination. Character directions are a nineteenth- and early twentieth-century invention to help the reader imagine what happens on stage. Classical dramatists are silent on the subject.

What the other characters say about the character
A more fruitful line of enquiry is what the other characters say about the character. If we read carefully we will often come across a crucial adjective, a profound insight, a telling image or a revealing slip of the tongue.

---

15   Quoted in Michael Meyer *Ibsen* (1971)

In the best plays these views are often contradictory. Thus, in *Hamlet*, Laertes tells his sister, Ophelia, that the Prince is not to be trusted while their father, Polonius, insists that his 'lunacy' derives from his love for her.[16] Claudius comes to fear Hamlet's 'liberty' which, he says, is 'full of threats to all',[17] but his mother is more indulgent, declaring that his madness 'like some ore / among a mineral of metals base / shows itself pure.'[18] Ophelia laments the overthrow of Hamlet's 'noble mind' (a quality we hardly ever see) but the Gravedigger irreverently describes him as 'he that is mad and is sent into England'.[19] This variety of perspectives creates the illusion of an entire society at a loss as to what to make of its extraordinary Prince – and of a living and three-dimensional character at the heart of the play.

Of course, one character's judgments about another are often unreliable. A notorious example is the first scene of *King Lear* where Goneril and Regan's extravagant and hollow protestations of love are believed, while Cordelia's 'nothing' startles everyone with its truthful opacity. Most of Lear's subsequent views are based on similarly disastrous misjudgments and by the time he realises the truth it's too late. Shakespeare uses this blindness to devastating effect when Duncan realises that he has failed to grasp a nobleman's rebellious intentions:

> There's no art
> To find the mind's construction in the face.
> He was a gentleman on whom I built
> An absolute trust.[20]

But he repeats the mistake, putting himself into the hands of his 'peerless kinsman', Macbeth, whom he immediately creates Thane of Cawdor. It's a terrible misjudgment that costs him his life.

---

16   *Hamlet* (2.2)

17   Ibid (4.1)

18   Ibid (4.1)

19   Ibid (5.1)

20   *Macbeth* (1.4)

What the characters say about themselves

Characters in plays often talk about themselves and we should scour the text for such self-revelation.

This can be complicated. Brecht's Mother Courage says a great deal in the first scene of the play and through the smokescreen of jokes, self-promotion and commercial patter we are given important information about her and her family. But we need to be careful: much of what she says is exaggeration and should be heard with the same scepticism that the Sergeant and the Recruiter apply. Indeed, part of the point of the scene is to encourage us to listen critically. It's not enough to hear what is being said; we must understand why the character is saying it.

Iago is one of the most inveterate self-revealers in drama:

> Thus do I ever make my fool my purse.
> For I mine own gained knowledge should profane
> If I would time expend with such a snipe
> But for my sport and profit. I hate the Moor
> And it is thought abroad that twixt my sheets
> He has done my office. I know not if it be true
> But I, for mere suspicion in that kind
> Will do as if for surety. He holds me well.
> The better shall my purpose work on him.
> Cassio's a proper man. Let me see now
> To get his place and to plume up my will
> In double knavery.[21]

At first sight, this speech offers a straightforward explanation of Iago's motives. But we quickly discover that Iago isn't to be trusted, even in what he tells us, and that Shakespeare has endowed him with so many different motives for bringing about Othello's downfall – resentment that he's been passed over, racist anger, sexual jealousy, even an excess of love – that we soon agree with Coleridge that Iago is, in fact, a study in 'motiveless malignancy'.[22]

---

21   *Othello* (1.4)

22   This phrase appears jotted in the margin of Coleridge's copy of *Othello*

So long as we read such self-revelation with a clear sense of why the character is saying it, we can discover a great deal about what makes him tick.

The key drives

The most complex of dramatic characters can often be understood with reference to the simplest and most powerful of human motives.

Sex and money
Freud identified sex as the chief motivator in human affairs and Marx saw the pursuit of money as fundamental. We know that these two forces are extraordinarily powerful and it is hardly surprising that they are fundamental in many well-drawn dramatic characters.

Look at Shakespeare's early comedy, *The Taming of the Shrew.* Modern critics have become so exercised by the sexual politics of the play's final scene that they tend to overlook the rest, above all the importance of money. Within moments of his first appearance Petruchio declares his ambition:

> I come to wive it wealthily in Padua.
> If wealthily then happily in Padua.[23]

And when one of Katherine's wooers tries to dissuade him he replies:

> Hortensio, peace. Thou know'st not gold's effect.
> Tell me her father's name and tis enough.
> For I will board her though she chide as loud
> As thunder when the clouds in autumn crack.[24]

At the end, Petruchio is rewarded for his diligence: not only does he marry the rich Kate, she wins for him the 'twenty thousand crowns' that her father has staked:

---

23   *The Taming of the Shrew* (2.2)

24   Ibid (2.2)

Twas I won the wager, though you hit the white.
And being a winner, God give you good night.[25]

Reading the play without understanding the centrality of what Thomas Carlyle called the 'cash nexus'[26] fails to do justice to Shakespeare's realism – worse, it misunderstands the wellspring of the play's comic energy.

If the presence of money surprises us in an early Shakespeare comedy, it's equally intriguing to see sexuality play so central a role in Brecht's *Mother Courage*. Not only is Courage so concerned about her daughter Kattrin's sexual appeal that she smudges her face with dirt and is pleased when she is badly scarred, but Courage's cart acts as a magnet for the rivalry between two homeless, middle-aged men, the Cook and the Chaplain. In all this, Brecht is drawing on his source, Grimmelshausen's picaresque novel, *Simplicissimus* (1667), in which Courage is a camp follower and her different children are the result of her prostitution; but it's perhaps surprising to find such a focus in a writer often lambasted for his narrow political interests.

Sex and money are such fundamental forces that they can be easily overlooked. But they are essential if we are to imagine a three-dimensional character.

Love and power
The desire for sex and money is often linked to more lofty ambitions: for love and power.

The young people who populate many of Shakespeare's plays – Romeo and Juliet; Viola, Olivia and Orsino; the quartet of lovers in *A Midsummer Night's Dream* and dozens of others – are, like Plato's divided soul, scouring the world looking for their other half. This search for love appears in more mature form in the great tragedies, from Hamlet's affection for his mother, to Cleopatra's love for Antony and, even, to Macbeth's love for his 'dearest chuck'.[27]

---

25   Ibid (5.2)

26   Thomas Carlyle *Chartism* (1839)

27   *Macbeth* (3.2)

Many of Chekhov's characters are heartbreakingly in love with the wrong person, and love drives people in Noël Coward, Tennessee Williams and dozens of others. The search for love, for an all-embracing, unconditional love, is the motor for many of drama's greatest characters, and discovering its existence often unlocks the play's deeper meaning.

Worldly power is the other great driving force. The lust for power can be seen at its most naked in the great political dramas: *Richard III* and *Macbeth*, Schiller's *Wallenstein* trilogy or Brecht's *Arturo Ui*. But it's also evident, if on a narrower canvas, in such domestic stories as Lopahkin in *The Cherry Orchard*, Hilde Wangel in *The Master Builder* and Pozzo in *Waiting for Godot*.

Love and power are often closely related, and one of the forces behind many of the most interesting characters is the search for the adulation that the two can bring. The best writers show not only the pleasure of such power but also, critically, its downside. Macbeth realises too late that it's difficult to enjoy both:

> I have lived long enough. My way of life
> Is fallen into the sear, the yellow leaf.
> And that which should accompany old age
> As honour, love, obedience, troops of friends
> I must not look to have. But, in their stead,
> Curses, not loud but deep, mouth-honour, breath,
> Which the poor heart would fain deny, and dare not.[28]

Contradictions

In good drama – as in life – motivation is complex, sometimes incomprehensible, and in trying to understand a character in a play it's a mistake to imagine that he's going to be consistent, or that his actions and responses will follow a fixed pattern.

---

28   Ibid (5.3)

At the beginning of *Much Ado About Nothing* Beatrice and Benedick both declare that they have no interest in marriage and are dedicated to staying single:

BENEDICK

> Then is courtesy a turncoat. But it is certain I am loved of all ladies, only you excepted. And I would I could find it in my heart that I had not a hard heart, for truly I love none.

BEATRICE

> A dear happiness to women, they would else have been troubled with a pernicious suitor. I thank God and my cold blood I am of your humour for that. I had rather hear my dog bark at a crow than a man swear he loves me.[29]

But Shakespeare shows how love and desire transforms and tames this comic jousting. Within a couple of acts they're declaring their love for each other, in language that is all the more touching for its wit and delicious sense of proportion:

BENEDICK

> I do love nothing in the world so well as you. Is not that strange?

BEATRICE

> As strange as the thing I know not. It were as possible for me to say I loved nothing so well as you. But believe me not, and yet I lie not. I confess nothing, nor I deny nothing. I am sorry for my cousin.

BENEDICK

> By my sword, Beatrice, thou lovest me.

BEATRICE

> Do not swear, and eat it.

BENEDICK

> I will swear by it that you love me, and I will make him eat it that says I love not you.

---

29   *Much Ado About Nothing* (1.1)

BEATRICE

Will you not eat your word?

BENEDICK

With no sauce that can be devised to it. I protest I love thee.

BEATRICE

Why, then, God forgive me.

BENEDICK

What offence, sweet Beatrice?

BEATRICE

You have stayed me in a happy hour. I was about to protest I loved you.

BENEDICK

And do it with all thy heart.

BEATRICE

I love you with so much of my heart that none is left to protest.[30]

A similar *volte-face* can be found in *The Changeling*. Beatrice-Joanna starts out by despising the hideous De Flores and, when he kneels to pick up her glove, her reply is savage:

Who bade you stoop? They touch my hand no more.
There, for the other's sake I part with this.
Take them and draw thine own skin with them.[31]

Astonishingly, she ends the play sexually addicted to him and hails him as a 'man worth loving'. It's not consistency that's interesting; inconsistencies reveal much more – above all that opposites attract.

Why does Hamlet delay in killing Claudius? Various explanations have been offered: he lacks the right opportunity; he doesn't want to be tarnished by the same sin; he's a coward; he prefers to think than to act and killing his uncle would commit him to a definite course of action. In fact, all four are true: our actions are driven

---

30   Ibid (4.1)

31   Thomas Middleton and William Rowley *The Changeling* (1622)

by a wide range of forces, both from within and without, and the character of Hamlet is a true reflection of the complex shapes of reality: Shakespeare is holding 'a mirror up to nature' in very deed. Hamlet isn't an idea of a person; he's a picture of life itself.

Brecht claimed that by exposing the contradictions in his characters he was laying bare the contradictions in society. Thus the landowner Puntila is generous when drunk but dangerous when sober; the small tradeswoman Courage lives for her children but loses them to the war that keeps her business going; and Galileo is both a heroic seeker after truth and an all too frail human being, cowed into submission by the threat of torture. Brecht is attempting something more than psychological realism; he's clarifying the contradictions innate in society and helping us understand how they can be resolved.

Actions

'By their deeds shall ye know them' says the Bible, and nothing is more revealing about a character than what he actually does.

One of the most common mistakes is to come to conclusions about character by generalisations, not a careful analysis of actions. The director Max Stafford-Clark has perfected an analytical technique known as 'actioning' as a way of preventing this in rehearsals. He asks his actors to describe an action for everything they say or do. Thus, 'John greets Julia' is what John is doing when he says 'Hello' to Julia. The verb is then tested: maybe it would be truer to say that 'John insults Julia' or that 'John seduces Julia' or even that 'John diverts Julia's attention from his infidelity'. The strength of this approach is that it encourages actors to think about what their character is doing at each moment in very precise terms, and not fall back on generalised emotions or simplistic judgments. 'Actioning' can be useful to the reader too: asking 'what is this character actually doing?' helps us understand the forces that are running through the scene. And this helps us see what's *really* going on.

This approach is particularly valuable with characters we tend to think of as villains. Thus, although we're suspicious of Iago from the outset, Shakespeare insists that we suspend our judgment until he actually starts to deceive Othello. And attending to actions should prevent the sentimental reading of Beatrice-Joanna as a charming young girl, led astray by the 'evil' De Flores; in fact at first he says nothing that should make us suspect his motives. Middleton further confounds simplistic judgment by making Alsemero the first to suggest that her proposed bridegroom, Alonso, should be killed:

> One good service
> Would strike off both your fears, and I'll go near it too
> Since you are so distressed. Remove the cause
> The command ceases. So there's two fears blown out
> With one and the same blast.[32]

In other words, Middleton, like all good dramatists, shows that his characters' actions are, to a large extent, a result of their own free will.

Free will is a complex theological problem and classical tragedies often enact the terms of the debate. Thus, Macbeth is initially torn between the neutral prophesy of the witches and his own conscience: the play shows the way he resolves this problem in his mind and ensures that their predictions come true. Like a Christian granted free will by an omnipotent God, Macbeth makes a series of independent decisions and is accountable for all his actions.

Brecht was particularly keen to stress individual choices and asked his actors to show the processes whereby a character makes a decision, adding that they should also indicate the route that the character has decided *not* to take. And so he devised an exercise in which an actor would say, 'instead of killing Claudius while he's at prayer, Hamlet holds back and declares that he will *only* kill him:

> When he is drunk asleep, or in his rage
> Or in the incestuous pleasure of his bed.
> At gaming, swearing, or about some act

---

32   Ibid

That has no relish of salvation in it.[33]

Such an exercise helps the actor understand the living quality of the writing and see that the outcome isn't necessarily predictable. If drama is to imitate life, it needs to follow what the philosopher Isaiah Berlin has called 'the crooked timbers of humanity'. The reader should be alert to the same sort of intricate questioning of the peculiarities of human behaviour.

Delayed judgement and change

The best playwrights know how to suspend the audience's judgment about character until they do something particular. *King Lear* is full of such objectivity and multiplicity of perspective. Thus Cordelia seems at first rather prim in her adherence to the literal truth and in her refusal to make her father happy; as the play unfolds, however, Shakespeare shows us that such awkwardness is the very quality most needed from a daughter. Similarly, Cornwall starts as an upstanding member of the royal family (through his marriage to Regan); it's not until he blinds the Earl of Gloucester that we realise just how dangerous he is. A reading that showed psychopathic tendencies from the start would undermine Shakespeare's political and social realism, just as a view of Lear which saw him as mad from the outset would make it impossible to track the breakdown of his rational faculties, and make the rule of a mad king seem in some sense normal.[34]

Nina in *The Seagull* is another example of delayed judgement. In Act One we meet a young girl, devoted to Konstantin and his idealistic approach to art and the theatre, and easy prey to the predatory Trigorin. In the first three acts, therefore, she can strike us as rather naïve, even shrill; by Act IV, however, two years later, when she's experienced loss, disappointment and failure, her renewed commitment to the theatre is remarkable:

---

33   *Hamlet* (3.3)

34   See Margot Heinemann '*King Lear* and the World Turned Upside Down' in *Shakespeare and Politics*, edited by Catherine Alexander (2004)

He didn't believe in the theatre, he laughed at my dreams, and gradually I stopped believing too, and lost heart... I became petty and small-minded, I hadn't a clue what to do with my hands, how to stand, I couldn't control my voice. You can't imagine what it feels like, to know you're giving a dreadful performance... What was I saying? Yes I was talking about the stage. I'm not like that now. I'm a real actress. I enjoy performing, I revel in it, I feel intoxicated on stage, I feel wonderful... Kostya, I know now, I understand that's what's important about our work – whether we act on the stage or write – it isn't fame, it isn't glory, it's none of those things I used to dream of, it's simply the capacity to endure. To bear your cross, and have faith. I have faith, and it doesn't hurt so much – when I think of my profession, I'm no longer afraid of life.[35]

Like Nina, the best-written characters change and these changes affect the world in which they live.

Thus, when we read a play we should be careful not to over-freight the characters with early judgments, and allow their individual words and actions to shape and guide our response.

Imaginary casting

An enjoyable way to think about a character is to imagine whom we would like to see playing the part. This needn't be an actor; it could be a friend or a relative, a long-dead film star, a public figure or whoever; it helps give the character a physical presence, a weight and solidity in our mind.

In clarifying your views, it's sometimes worth imagining two very different people: compare Tony Blair with Gordon Brown in the part of Macbeth and you find yourself considering two contrasting Thanes, just as George Bush and Barack Obama would make two very different Hamlets.

---

35   Anton Chekhov *The Seagull* translated by Stephen Mulrine (1997)

6. What do they say?

ONE OF THE HARDEST things about reading a play is to hear the way that the characters speak.

An experienced literary manager once told me that he came to a conclusion about the quality of a play very quickly. You can tell within the first page or so, he said, if the writer has an ear for real speech; occasionally a play with brilliant dialogue will fail for structural reasons, but if it doesn't *sound* right it'll never work. And so when we sit down to read a play we need to listen to the particular nature of the dialogue: its cadences, rhythms, dialect and so on.

But how should we go about it?

Reading aloud

One of the finest Shakespearean actors in Britain (I'm not saying who!) finds it almost impossible to study the plays in silence and always reads them aloud – in bed, in the bath, on the bus even. Try it for yourself. Read this passage from *The Winter's Tale* silently:

> I would there were no age between ten and three-and-twenty, or that youth would sleep out the rest. For there is nothing in the between but getting wenches with child, wronging the ancientry, stealing, fighting. Hark you now. Would any but these boiled-brains of nineteen and two-and-twenty hunt this weather? They have scared away two of my best sheep, which I fear the wolf will sooner find than the master. If anywhere I have them, tis by the seaside, browsing on ivy.[1]

And now read it aloud, savouring the words and relishing the rattling of the consonants, the jaunty shapes of the vowels, the

---

1   *The Winter's Tale* (2.3)

limbs of the language indeed. You can almost hear the roar of the storm in the background.

Gathering a group together to read a play can be richly rewarding. Sadly, many people have been put off this because of the embarrassment felt reading aloud at school. The problem is exacerbated by English courses that treat drama as 'literature', as something not to be spoken, but read in silence. But a friend described a group of young lawyers reading *Twelfth Night* aloud under the stars in an Italian garden and said it was the most powerful experience of the play he'd ever had.

Nothing is more instructive for a dramatist than hearing his words spoken aloud: the woodenness becomes clear within moments, but so also does good dialogue. The reader should listen to them too.

The changing role of language

Speech plays a different role in different periods of drama.

The formal set piece speeches of Greek tragedy, above all the great choruses that interrupt the action, have the most remote relationship to anything one might have heard in the streets of fifth-century Athens:

> Down like a rock from the mountain crest
> He came thundering to earth, the flame
> Dashed from his hand,
> The son of Thebes whose best hope of fame
> Was to conquer his native land
> And who failed in his quest.[2]

Such speeches are highly poetic displays of emotion and thought, massively impressive and powerful, but entirely artificial.

'Stichomythia' by contrast gives a much more immediate sense of dramatic conflict:

---

2   Sophocles *Antigone* translated by Don Taylor (1986)

ANTIGONE

    I love my brother. I honour him dead

    As I loved him living. There's no harm in that.

CREON

    And the one he murdered? Wasn't he your brother?

ANTIGONE

    My mother bore them both, and I loved them both.

CREON

    If you honour one, you insult the other.

ANTIGONE

    Neither of those dead men would say that.

CREON

    Eteocles would. His brother was a traitor.

    Does he merit no greater respect than that?[3]

At first hearing, this feels like quick-fire naturalistic dialogue, but it soon becomes clear that it is built out of carefully constructed paradoxes, counterpoints and crosscurrents. Thus, for all its brilliance, Greek drama never manages to give the illusion that the characters are creating the action and are responsible for what they say; rather, their speeches are a self-conscious articulation of argument, governed throughout by explicit authorial intention.

Shakespeare, by contrast, uses speech to give the illusion of individual human agency: everything you want to know about a character – and everything you *can* know about him – is to be found in the text. But it's a text that seems to be created by the speaker, not the writer. Shakespeare's astonishing style manages to express the inner and the outer, the personal and the political, the subconscious and the conscious in a way no dramatist had achieved previously. Look at Angelo in *Measure for Measure*:

    What's this, what's this? Is this her fault or mine?

    The tempter or the tempted, who sins most, ha?

    Not she nor doth she tempt. Can it be

    That modesty may more betray our sense

---

3   Ibid

Than woman's lightness? Having waste ground enough
Shall we desire to raze the sanctuary
And pitch our evils there? O fie, fie, fie.
What dost thou, or what art thou, Angelo?
Dost thou desire her foully for those things
That make her good? O let her brother live.
Thieves for their robbery have authority
When judges steal themselves. What, do I love her
That I desire to hear her speak again
And feast upon her eyes? What is it I dream on?
O cunning enemy that to catch a saint
With saints dost bait thy hook. Most dangerous
Is that temptation that doth goad us on
To sin in loving virtue. Never could the strumpet
With all her double vigour, art and nature
Once stir my temper, but this virtuous maid
Subdues me quite. Ever till now
When men were fond I smiled and wondered how.[4]

This goes to the heart of Angelo's dilemma and captures the moment when he realises the strength of his lust; it also expresses his overwhelming distaste at his own desire. This isn't mere realism, it's hyperrealism: not content with simply providing a naturalistic description of Angelo's speech at the time, Shakespeare puts into words his characters deepest and mostly repressed thoughts. Harold Bloom claims that Shakespeare invented the human;[5] it's perhaps more accurate to say that he invented the *depiction* of the human, as an independent being living in the world, but capable both of doing good and, as with Angelo, causing hurt and destruction. And it's the words that Shakespeare's characters speak that create this illusion.

Language in Restoration drama operates in a different way again. Its highly polished cadences make it the perfect medium for wit and social repartee: the sexually charged *double entendre*, the ironical put down, the cynical statement of class and power. In the best Restoration writers, however, the prose is also capable of

---

4   *Measure for Measure* (2.2)

5   Harold Bloom *Shakespeare and the Invention of the Human* (1998)

expressing real emotion. Look at the closing moments of Etherege's *The Man of Mode* (1676), as Harriet and Dorimant contemplate the gloomy prospect of life in the country:

LADY WOODVILL

> If his occasions bring him that way, I have now so good an opinion of him he shall be welcome.

HARRIET

> To a great rambling lone house, that looks as it were not inhabited, the family's so small. There you'll find my mother, an old lame aunt, and myself, sir, perched up on chairs at a distance in a large parlour, sitting moping like three or four melancholy birds in a spacious volary – does not this stagger your resolution?

DORIMANT

> Not at all, madam. The first time I saw you, you left me with the pangs of love upon me, and this day my soul has quite given up her liberty.

HARRIET

> This is more dismal than the country! Emilia, pity me, who am going to that sad place. Methinks I hear the hateful noise of rooks already – kaw, kaw, kaw – there's music in the worst cry in London![6]

This extraordinary passage combines social comedy with emotional seriousness, bright optimism with black despair. But Etherege is an exception: the enforced elegance of most Restoration drama prevents such exploration.

The language used in Naturalism is very particular. Both Ibsen and Chekhov reacted against the high-flown rhetoric of Romantic drama and employed the simple language of everyday life. They relied on dramatic situation to provide depth, as the climax of *Hedda Gabler* (1890) makes clear:

HEDDA (*in a low voice*)

> What were you saying about the gun?

---

6   George Etherege *The Man of Mode* (1676)

BRACK (*low*)
> He must have stolen it.

HEDDA
> Why stolen?

BRACK
> There's no other explanation, Mrs Tesman.

HEDDA
> Oh.

BRACK (*looking at her*)
> He came here this morning. Didn't he?

HEDDA
> Yes.

BRACK
> You were alone with him?

HEDDA
> For a while.

BRACK
> While he was here, did you leave the room at all?

HEDDA
> No.[7]

The unfolding of thought and action, driven by backstory and motivation, not the wonders of poetry and prose, provides this brittle dialogue with its exceptional dramatic power.

Such minimalism inevitably triggered a counter-reaction. In much early twentieth-century drama the language became much more self-conscious, further removed from the rhythms of everyday speech. Look at this from Brecht's expressionist debut, *Baal* (1918):

> Brother! Come with me! Give it up! Out to the hard dusty highroad: at night the air grows purple. To bars full of drunks: let the women you've stuffed fall into the black

---

7   Henrik Ibsen *Hedda Gabler* translated by Kenneth McLeish (1995). The Norwegian is just as straightforward and unpoetic.

rivers. To cathedrals with small, pale ladies: you ask, dare a man breathe here? To cowsheds where you bed down with the beasts. It's dark there and the cows moo. And into the forests where axes ring out above and you forget the light of day: God has forgotten you. Do you still remember what the sky looks like?[8]

This has the highly artificial, heightened quality typical of much radical European drama of the time. The fact is, however, that for all its literary ambition, audiences quickly tire of such self-conscious poeticism and the most significant of early twentieth century dramatists restricted their language to an approximation of what could be heard in everyday life.

The best postwar drama tried to distil the cadences of every-day speech and capture its public essence. The result can be both oblique and moving, as in Harold Pinter's strangely affecting *Moon-light* (1993):

I can't sleep. There's no moon. It's so dark, I think I'll go downstairs and walk about. I won't make a noise. I'll be very quiet. Nobody will hear me. It's so dark and I know every-thing is more silent when it's dark. But I don't want anybody to know I'm moving about in the night. I don't want to wake my father and mother. They're so tired. They have given so much of their life for me and for my brothers.[9]

Samuel Beckett is the great master of this style, as can be evident in this astonishing closing speech in *Ohio Impromptu* (1981):

So the sad tale a last time told they sat on as though turned to stone. Through the single window dawn shed no light. From the street no sound of reawakening. Or was it that buried in who knows what thoughts they paid no heed? To light of day. To sound of reawakening. What thoughts who knows. Thoughts, no, not thoughts. Profounds of mind. Buried

8   Bertolt Brecht *Baal* translated by John Willett (1970)

9   Harold Pinter *Moonlight* (1993)

in who knows what profounds of mind. Of mindlessness. Whither no light can reach. No sound. So sat on as though turned to stone. The sad tale a last time told. Nothing is left to tell. Nothing is left to tell.[10]

This is in no sense realistic but nevertheless resonates with the cadences of domestic speech in a way that the expressionists and the symbolists were perhaps too quick to relinquish.

There is, of course, a limit to the compression that Beckett and Pinter pursued. Indeed, the logical next step is to abandon words altogether, as Peter Handke did in *The Hour We Knew Nothing of Each Other* (1992).

Incomprehensibility

Language is in perpetual flux: the English I speak is different from that of my parents, and my children's is different again. And so it's inevitable that some passages in old plays present us with real problems of comprehension. Look, for example, at Feste in *Twelfth Night*:

I did impeticos thy gratility. For Malvolio's nose is no whip-stock. My lady has a white hand and Myrmidons are no bottle alehouses.[11]

The meaning of such a passage is lost in the mists of time, inaccessible to all but the most intrepid of scholars.

It is not just Shakespeare who can be hard to understand. In Wychereley's *The Country Wife* (1675), there is a speech that requires an intimate knowledge of seventeenth century London shop life. Miss Squeamish is shocked to hear Horner say that ladies are bribed for their love, prostituted in fact. He replies to her objections:

With your pardon, ladies, I know, like great men in offices, you seem to exact flattery and attendances only from your followers; but you have receivers about you, and such fees to

---

10   Samuel Beckett *Ohio Impromptu* (1980)

11   *Twelfth Night* (2.3)

pay, a man is afraid to pass your grants. Besides we must let you win at cards, or we lose your hearts; and if you make an assignation, tis at a goldsmith's, jeweller's, or china house, where, for your honour, you deposit to him, he must pawn his to the punctual cit, and so paying for what you take up, pays for what he takes up.[12]

One edition translates the difficult last phrase as 'in paying for what you obtain, the gallant pawns his honour for yours', while another tells us that 'receivers' are 'servants who take bribes'. This edition then explains 'pass your grants' as 'accept your favours' and glosses the last phrase as 'for trusting your honour to the gallant he in his turn must pawn his at the goldsmith's (who will be punctual in asking for redemption) and, paying for your purpose, pays for taking up your skirt.' It's exceptionally difficult and made much worse by the continuous stream of sexual innuendo.

When reading an old play we should not be surprised by such difficulties. What's more, they can be overcome. By comparing different editions,[13] looking words up in a glossary[14] and bringing to your reading a feeling for the dramatic voice of the speaker, it's usually possible to find your way through – although I don't think I'll ever *really* understand that passage from *Twelfth Night*.

The mistake, of course, is to presume that old plays were written in a *deliberately* archaic style; occasionally a playwright will satirise the language and affectations of an older generation, but most difficult passages by good authors are the result of the passage of time, not bad or wilfully obscure writing.

---

12   William Wycherley *The Country Wife* (1675)

13   There are several complete Shakespeare editions: Arden, Penguin, Cambridge and, best of all, Oxford.

14   The most useful is *The Oxford English Dictionary*. CT Onions, one of the compilers of the OED, has produced the excellent *Shakespeare Glossary* (1911), recently supplemented (but not supplanted) by Ben and David Crystal's *Shakespeare's Words* (2002).

Verse

Many plays, especially those from the sixteenth and seventeenth centuries, have extensive passages in verse.

Why verse?

The use of verse in the theatre is a practical solution to a very real problem: the human voice stands a better chance of carrying across a large and acoustically unfriendly environment if it has a clearly defined beat. Vocal energy is required if words are to cast a spell, and verse helps actors speak with strength and confidence.

Verse drama has often played a significant educational role. A talented actor delivering a verbal *tour de force*, with every development clear, every argument in place, every twist and turn registering, all fuelled by emotion and expressed beautifully, makes an important contribution to a society with high levels of functional illiteracy in which the spoken word carries a talismanic force. One of the masters of this was Christopher Marlowe, whose 'mighty line' is abundantly on display in the opening of *Doctor Faustus* (1592?):

> Not marching in the fields of Thrasimene
> Where Mars did mate the Carthagenes
> Nor sporting in the dalliance of love
> In courts of kings where state is overturned
> Nor in the pomp of proud audacious deeds
> Intends our muse to vaunt her heavenly verse.[15]

Anyone hearing this is quickly struck by the power and magnificence of the English language at its ostentatious best.

Finally, dramatic verse provides a concentration of linguistic effect within a limited space. It allows the playwright to both catch the surface of observed speech and express the inner life of the character. Look at this:

> We have scotched the snake, not killed it.
> She'll close and be herself, whilst our poor malice

---

15 Christopher Marlowe *Doctor Faustus* (1592)

> Remains in danger of her former tooth.
> But let the frame of things disjoint
> Both the worlds suffer
> Ere we will eat our meal in fear and sleep
> In the affliction of these terrible dreams
> That shake us nightly. Better be with the dead
> Whom we, to gain our peace, have sent to peace
> Than on the torture of the mind to lie
> In restless ecstasy. Duncan is in his grave.
> After life's fitful fever he sleeps well.
> Treason has done his worst. Nor steel, nor poison
> Malice domestic, foreign levy, nothing
> Can touch him further.[16]

Macbeth's struggle with his subconscious is dramatised with Shakespeare's characteristic economy and imaginative force. The sudden jumps in the imagery, the rapid shifts in register and the increasingly desperate recitation of supposedly logical processes lead Macbeth to a self-imposed hypnosis which allows him to order Banquo and Fleance's murder. In a way that is sadly familiar, Macbeth twists language so as to achieve his ugly ends.

The iambic pentameter
The verse of Elizabethan drama had its roots in the popular, alliterative, liturgical language of the Mystery Cycles. It took its domestic and religious intimacy from Tudor lyric poetry and its grandeur and ambition from the Greek and Roman classics. The dominant form was the iambic pentameter.

People sometimes speak of the iambic pentameter as if Shakespeare invented it; in fact, of course, nearly all the great English poets, from the fifteenth to the nineteenth centuries, have used it. Developing an ear for its rhythms, its grace and its pressure, its forward movement and its rhetorical power, is essential for reading Elizabethan and Jacobean drama. This can be learnt, but it demands

---

16 *Macbeth* (3.2)

careful attention, not just to technical form but also to sound and breath.

The iambic pentameter is the natural rhythm of English speech: 'I **want** a **pot** of **tea** for **two** right **now**' is an iambic pentameter, as is 'The **train** will **leave** at **ten** o'clock to**night**'. Superficially predictable, the pentameter is highly flexible and capable of great subtlety. Its compressed short line and all-important *caesura* (which divides the line into two discrete halves) make it the ideal form for the paradoxical and confrontational style of Elizabethan drama.

A Midsummer Night's Dream has some of the most perfect examples of the form:

> How **happy some** | o'er **other some** can **be**.
> Through **Athens I** | am **thought** as **fair** as **she**.
> But **what of that?** | Demetrius **thinks** not **so**.
> He **will** not **know** | what **all** but **he** do **know**.
> And **as** he **errs** | **dot**ing on **Hermia's eyes**
> So **I**, ad**mir**ing of | **his qualities**.[17]

This consists of three rhyming couplets. The first two are regular, with the strongest stresses being on the first and, above all, last beats of each line. In the fifth line (the third couplet), the second half of the line (after the caesura) starts with a trochee (**dot**ing – the stress is on the first syllable) not an iamb, as does the last line. This irregular final couplet counters the expectations raised by the first two.

Shakespearean verse is sometimes seen as a single style that never developed. In fact, of course, it changed constantly: from the impressive, rough-hewn formality of the early plays to the infinitely more flexible irregularities of the mature dramatist. Compare the opening of two of the Roman plays:

> Noble patricians, patrons of my right
> Defend the justice of my cause with arms.
> And countrymen, my loving followers
> Plead my successive title with your swords.

---

17 *A Midsummer Night's Dream* (1.1)

> I am his first born son that was the last
> That wore the imperial diadem of Rome.
> Then let my father's honours live in me
> Nor wrong mine age with his indignity.[18]

This is from *Titus Andronicus*, one of Shakespeare's earliest plays. Its verse is conventionally impressive, with a steady development and rich with rhetorical flourishes. But now read the opening of *Antony and Cleopatra*:

> Nay, but this dotage of our General's
> Overflows the measure. Those his goodly eyes
> That over the files and musters of the war
> Have glowed like plated Mars, now bend, now turn
> The office and devotion of their view
> Upon a tawny front. His captain's heart
> Which in the scuffles of great fights hath burst
> The buckles on his breast, reneges all temper
> And is become the bellows and the fan
> To cool a gypsy's lust.[19]

It is clear that the iambic pentameter has evolved into something astonishingly sinuous. Its jabbing, seasick rhythm catches the speaker's jealousy, anxiety and anger. It's as if Shakespeare, at the height of his mature style, is on the verge of abandoning the form altogether: like the jazz trumpeter Miles Davis pushing at the boundaries of harmony, rhythm and tonality in search of pure expression.

Shakespeare both created and destroyed the form in which he wrote. The verse of his younger contemporaries – particularly Middleton, Webster and Ford – is either more naturalistic or more artificial, but never achieves the easy, glorious familiarity that Shakespeare mastered in his greatest plays. Look at Deflores in *The Changeling* (1621):

> Here's a favour come with a mischief. Now I know
> She had rather wear my pelt tanned in a pair

---

18   *Titus Andronicus* (1.1)

19   *Antony and Cleopatra* (1.1)

Of dancing pumps than I should thrust my fingers
Into her sockets here. I know she hates me
Yet cannot choose but love her.
No matter if but to vex her I'll haunt her still
Though I get nothing else, I'll have my will.[20]

This has some of the same forward movement as Shakespeare, but is much less mellifluous, less magnificent, in fact – if easier to understand. Or compare the dazzling simplicity of John Ford's 'Tis Pity She's a Whore (1629):

Lost, I am lost. My fates have doomed my death.
The more I strive, I love. The more I love
The less I hope. I see my ruin certain.
What judgment or endeavours could apply
To my incurable and restless wounds
I throughly have examined, but in vain.[21]

Here we see the great tradition of English dramatic verse in its last moments, before the Civil War – and the prose in which it was written – sweeps all before it. In fact, the rose is blown.

Verse drama after the Renaissance

Restoration comedy is written almost exclusively in prose, albeit of a rhythmic and 'sprung' kind. Fragments of verse appear, usually in a Prologue or Epilogue, and occasionally as a heroic parody; thus, in Wycherley's The Country Wife, each act is supplied with a shift into rhyming couplets to bring the curtain down:

How s'e'er the kind wife's belly comes to swell.
The husband breeds for her, and first is ill.[22]

Full-length speeches in verse, however, were reserved for the more formal – and much less popular – tragedies.

---

20   Thomas Middleton and William Rowley The Changeling (1.1)

21   Tis Pity She's a Whore (1.2)

22   The Country Wife (4.4)

Verse drama endured longer in France, where the neo-classical dramatists wrote mostly in alexandrines: these have twelve syllables to the line, not ten, and a *caesura* positioned directly after the sixth. Racine's tragedies are written entirely in lightly inflected couplets: highly structured, with a limited vocabulary and in continuous, but unobtrusive rhymes. Hippolyte's opening speech in *Phèdre* is a good example:

> Le dessein en est pris, je pars, cher Théramène,
> Et quitte le séjour de l'aimable Trézène.
> Dans le doute mortel où je suis agité,
> Je commence à rougir de mon oisiveté.
> Depuis plus de six mois éloigné de mon père,
> J'ignore le destin d'une tête si chère;
> J'ignore jusqu'aux lieux qui le peuvent cacher.[23]

Corneille's plays are written in the same form, as are the more elevated of Molière's comedies. Tony Harrison and Ranjit Bolt have translated several of these into English rhyming couplets, often with great effect – if at the expense of the smooth, rolling surface of the original.

The German Romantic dramatists (above all, Schiller, Goethe and Kleist) used much freer alexandrines, usually unrhyming (it's much harder to rhyme in German) and sometimes with as many as fourteen syllables. Influenced by 'Unser Shakespeare' ('our Shakespeare' as the German theatre sometimes call him), these great playwrights reserved prose for the 'common' characters, or to catch a particularly conversational tone. Kleist is an interesting exception: in his *Katie of Heilbronn* (1808) the Emperor speaks mostly in prose while in his comedy *The Broken Jug* (1811) his peasant characters speak in jaunty verse:

---

23   The standard English translation by John Cairncross (1963) is in iambic pentameters. Ted Hughes' more recent translation (1998) is in free verse: 'I have made my decision / It is six months now /And there hasn't been one word of my father / Somebody somewhere knows what's happened to him. / Life here in Troezen is extremely pleasant/ But I can't hang around doing nothing/With this uncertainty. My idleness makes me sweat./ I must find my father.'

Ei, was zum henker, sagt, gevatter Adam
Was ist euch geschehen, wie seht ihr aus?[24]

The early nineteenth century saw the emergence of Romantic 'closet drama', academic verse plays written designed exclusively for the study: Byron, Shelley and Coleridge dedicated some of their considerable talents to this form, but, frankly, with pretty lame results.[25] And the nationalist dramatists of the later nineteenth century were similarly influenced by Shakespeare: the key figure was Victor Hugo, whose bombastic spectacles provided the basis for a number of important opera libretti, but aren't often performed today. Probably the last great verse drama was Ibsen's early masterpiece, his dramatic poem *Peer Gynt* (1867).

Twentieth-century attempts to write verse drama have been largely unsuccessful. Christopher Fry and T.S. Eliot both made valiant attempts, as did WH Auden, but with distinctly mixed results.[26] Ted Hughes was revealing about the difficulty:

My great drama collapsed disappointingly. My mistake. Too literary… My fault was to attend to the content etc of the verse, rather than simply listen to characters whom I imagined real. That's the dilemma. The moment I begin to ripen up the writing, I lose sight & sound of an actual character speaking. When I simply listen to imagined characters, of course they speak quite natural prose. But whereas the final effect of the former is artificial & literary, the final effect of the latter is real… I think it's probably better to put all the complications into the situation, & let the speech be what you hear.[27]

---

24   My own rough translation of this is: 'Hey what the devil, tell me, old man Adam / What's happened to you? What do you look like?'

25   Byron's plays include *Manfredi* (1817), *Cain* (1821) and *Sardanapalus* (1821). Shelley *The Cenci* (1819) is admired in some circles. Coleridge's best known play is *Remorse* (1813).

26   Christopher Fry's plays include *A Phoenix too Frequent* (1946) and *The Lady's Not for Burning* (1949). T.S. Eliot's most celebrated plays include *Murder in the Cathedral* (1935), *The Family Reunion* (1939) and *The Cocktail Party* (1949). W.H Auden's plays are *The Dog Beneath the Skin* (1935) and *The Ascent of F6* (1936).

27   Ted Hughes *Letters* (2007) 'To Lucas Myers' 10 May 1965

More recently, Tony Harrison has brought welcome muscle to modern verse drama – if not always successfully.[28]

The contemporary German theatre is much more receptive to verse drama. This is partly the legacy of Brecht, who saw verse as fundamental to his 'alienation effect'. Indeed, in *The Resistible Rise of Arturo Ui* (1941), he wrote an entire play in mock-Shakespearean mock-pentameters:

> Friends, countrymen!
> Chicagoans and Ciceronians! When
> A year ago old Dogsborough, God rest
> His honest soul, with tearful eyes
> Appealed to me to protect Chicago's green-
> Goods trade, though moved, I doubted whether
> My powers would be able to justify
> His smiling confidence. Now Dogsborough
> Is dead. He left a will which you're all free
> To read. In simple words therein he calls me
> His son.[29]

It is also a result of the German theatre's warmer embrace of formal experimentation.

The most impressive of Brecht's disciples was Heiner Müller, whose *The Road of Tanks* (1984-8) is written in austere, strictly unpunctuated blank verse:

> Between Moscow and Berlin we lay
> In foxholes made of frozen mud A forest
> At our backs before our eyes a river
> One thousand miles away Berlin
> Less than eighty miles from Moscow
> And waited for the order to attack[30]

---

28   Tony Harrison *The Trackers of Oxyrynchthus* (1988) and *Fram* (2008)

29   Bertolt Brecht *The Resistible Rise of Arturo Ui* translated by Ralph Manheim (1981)

30   Heiner Müller *The Road of Tanks* is from a cycle of plays called *Wolokolamsker Chaussee* (1984-1998) translated by Marc von Henning

It's a kind of writing which, for all its brilliance, is quite alien to the vernacular realism of the British tradition.

Prose

In 1883 Ibsen declared that:

> Verse has done the art of drama irreparable harm. An artist of the theatre, with a repertoire of contemporary dramatic work, should not willingly speak a line of verse. Verse will scarcely find any application worth mentioning in the drama of the near future... In the last seven or eight years I have hardly written a line of verse; instead I have exclusively studied the incomparably more difficult art of writing in the straightforward honest language of reality.[31]

This laid down an important challenge to Ibsen's continental contemporaries who were shocked by his commitment to prose and prosaic subjects.

However, the power of the 'straightforward honest language of reality' has always been integral to the English tradition, as is evident in this extraordinary scene in *Much Ado About Nothing*:

BENEDICK

Lady Beatrice, have you wept all this while?

BEATRICE

Yea, and I will weep a while longer.

BENEDICK

I will not desire that.

BEATRICE

You have no reason. I do it freely.

BENEDICK

Surely I do believe your fair cousin is wronged.

BEATRICE

Ah, how much might the man deserve of me that would right her.

---

31   Quoted in Michael Meyer *Ibsen* (1971)

BENEDICK

    Is there any way to show such friendship?

BEATRICE

    A very even way but no such friend.

BENEDICK

    May a man do it?

BEATRICE

    It is a man's office. But not yours.

BENEDICK

    I do love nothing in the world so well as you. Is not that
    strange?

BEATRICE

    As strange as the thing I know not. It were as possible
    for me to say I loved nothing so well as you, but believe
    me not. And yet I lie not. I confess nothing, nor I deny
    nothing. I am sorry for my cousin.[32]

It's almost as if Shakespeare was looking forward to the moment
when prose would triumph over verse: Beatrice and Benedick,
like Rosalind and Orlando, speak in prose because their emotions
are so strong. Unlike the idealized Romeo and Juliet and Hero and
Claudio, their love cannot be expressed in conventional poetry, and
is all the more profound as a result. As Benedick declares:

    Marry, I cannot show it in rhyme. I have tried. I can find out
    no rhyme to 'lady' but 'baby,' an innocent rhyme, for 'scorn,'
    'horn,' a hard rhyme, for, 'school,' 'fool,' a babbling rhyme.
    Very ominous endings. No, I was not born under a rhyming
    planet, nor I cannot woo in festival terms.[33]

Hamlet, the great versifier, often speaks in prose, as in this explanation to his school friends of why he is unhappy:

    I have of late, but wherefore I know not, lost all my mirth,
    forgone all custom of exercises. And indeed it goes so heavily

---

32   *Much Ado About Nothing* (4.1)

33   Ibid (5.2)

with my disposition that this goodly frame the earth seems to me a sterile promontory. This most excellent canopy the air, look you, this brave overhanging firmament, this majestical roof fretted with golden fire, why it appears no other thing to me than a foul and pestilent congregation of vapours. What a piece of work is a man, how noble in reason, how infinite in faculty, in form and moving how express and admirable, in action how like an angel, in apprehension how like a god, the beauty of the world, the paragon of animals. And yet to me what is this quintessence of dust?[34]

The perfect cadences of this great speech come close to revealing the heart of Hamlet's 'mystery' and it deserves a place alongside his finest verse.

Nevertheless, prose only became dominant in English drama after the Restoration. Listen to Mrs Marwood in William Congreve's difficult masterpiece, *The Way of the World* (1700), which, some say, boasts the finest prose in English drama:

True, tis an unhappy circumstance of life, that love should ever die before us; and that the man so often should outlive the lover. But say what you will, tis better to be left than never to have been loved. To pass our youth in dull indifference, to refuse the sweets of life because they once must leave us, is as preposterous as to wish to have been born old, because we one day must be old. For my part, my youth may wear and waste, but it shall never rust in my possession.[35]

We can hear in the poise, wit and elegance of this passage, the mixture of sentiment and satire, wisdom and laughter, exposure and concealment, that came to dominate the English speaking theatre of Oscar Wilde, Bernard Shaw, Noël Coward and beyond.

Modern English drama is written almost exclusively in prose. At its best, as in this apparently inconsequential passage from Peter Gill's *The York Realist* (2001), it has a glowing, almost physical, presence:

---

34   *Hamlet* (2.2)

35   William Congreve *The Way of the World* (1700)

ARTHUR

Here we are then, Mother. Doreen. Home.

DOREEN

Thank you.

ARTHUR

Well, we're back. What a night, aye?

BARBARA

Are you cold, Mother?

MOTHER

Yes, I am.

BARBARA

I thought it was me.

DOREEN

I got cold, warm as the evening was.

BARBARA

I'm chilled to the bone.

MOTHER

I put a winter vest on and I'm cold.

ARTHUR

Shall I put a match to the fire?

MOTHER

Aye. Go on.
He does.

BARBARA

And it was such a glorious day.

DOREEN

Just get cold sitting, see, summer evenings.

ARTHUR

Still, what a night.

DOREEN

Wasn't it marvellous? I still can't get over it.[36]

---

36 Peter Gill *The York Realist* (2001)

With the notable exceptions of John Osborne and David Storey, few modern British playwrights can write dialogue with such emotional delicacy and luminous feeling. Of course, not all modern dramatists are interested in prose realism and have reacted against its disciplines. Some would say that they abandon its core values at their peril.

Reference

Good playwrights tend to draw on a wide range of cultural references. Academics sometimes call this 'inter-textuality'; others recognise it more simply as 'reference.' At its best, it introduces an electric charge into the language.

Seventeenth- and eighteenth-century dramatists were particularly fond of such referencing and deliberately played with its effect. Thus, in Kleist's *The Broken Jug*, a village judge called Adam (who has a club foot) has fallen from a windowsill and broken a much-valued jug (innocence herself) while trying to climb into the young Eve's bedroom. Then, the clerk who helps discover the truth is called Licht (Light), while a village woman claims that it must have been the Devil. Kleist's play is a reworking of both the Fall of Adam and the Oedipus story, as his short preface makes clear:

> This comedy is based on an historical fact, about which I've not been able to find any more details. I took the inspiration from a copper engraving I saw in Switzerland some years ago. On it was a judge, solemnly sat on the bench. In front of him stood an old woman holding a broken jug, complaining about the wrong that had been done her. The accused was a farmer's lad, pleading his innocence despite the fulminations of the judge, who'd already concluded that he was guilty. A young girl had already testified... and stood there, squirming, between her mother and her bridegroom. She couldn't have looked more pathetic if she'd been giving false evidence. And the court clerk... was looking at the judge suspiciously, just as Creon looked at Oedipus. Below: 'The

Broken Jug'. – The original if I'm not mistaken was by a Dutch master.[37]

Kleist's parable of enlightenment achieves all this and more.

Brecht's *Resistible Rise of Arturo Ui* is thick with cross-cultural references: written in homage to the legendary Chicago gangsters and with copious borrowings from Charlie Chaplin's film *The Great Dictator* (1940), it has explicitly classical roots. Not only is it written in mock Elizabethan blank verse, it deliberately quotes episodes from *Richard III* and *Julius Caesar*; less evident to English readers, perhaps, are the numerous quotations from Goethe's *Faust* and Schiller's *The Maid of Orleans*.

Of course, it is almost impossible for a sophisticated and well-read dramatist to write a play free of 'the anxiety of influence'.[38] Shakespeare cited Plautus and Seneca, Ovid and Virgil, the New Testament and Homer, just as Ibsen quoted Greek myths, Scandinavian folk tales and Bible stories. The challenge is to work out the extent to which such cultural references earn their place. An interesting example is the closing moments of *The York Realist*, when the abandoned farm worker George steps forward and declaims:

> Foxes their dens have they
> Birds have their nests so gay
> But the son of man this day
> Has not where his head he may rest.[39]

The Biblical reference, which originally appears in *The Pinner's Play* in the York Mystery cycle, is a natural conclusion to the domestic drama that has unfolded. It isn't used to impart status: it's tightly woven into the texture of the play and is extraordinarily moving as a result.

---

37   Heinrich von Kleist *The Broken Jug* translated by Stephen Unwin (unpublished)

38   Harold Bloom *The Anxiety of Influence: A Theory of Poetry* (1973)

39   Peter Gill *The York Realist* (2001)

Resonance

A careful distinction should be made between explicit cultural reference and language that subliminally alerts the reader to the existence of something bigger, a shared memory, and a sense of meaning. The word 'resonance', with its suggestion of the vibrations caused by music, is perhaps more appropriate.

Such resonance is evident in much great writing. Indeed I detected three different mythological tropes in one scene (3.1) in *Twelfth Night*: The Fall of Troy, The Expulsion from the Garden of Eden and the Journey into the Underworld. And in one of the darkest scenes of *Measure for Measure*, the language of the Annunciation transforms the situation:

> Look, the unfolding star calls up the shepherd. Put not yourself into amazement how these things should be. All difficulties are but easy when they are known. Call your executioner and off with Barnardine's head. I will give him a present shrift and advise him for a better place. Yet you are amazed, but this shall absolutely resolve you. Come away, it is almost clear dawn.[40]

It's easy to dismiss such claims as intellectual over-reaching, but the more closely I read Shakespeare, the more of this kind of shadow play emerges. Indeed, Ted Hughes has argued that the two myths which provide the subjects for two of Shakespeare's earliest poems, *Venus and Adonis* and *The Rape of Lucrece*, provide a template for all of Shakespeare's mature masterpieces; the result is nothing less than a theory of the complete works.[41]

Classical and biblical resonances can even be detected in Ibsen, that most sophisticated and secular of modern playwrights. It's no accident that the action of *A Doll's House* unfolds over the three days of Christmas: it echoes the Christian and Roman midwinter festivities which clear out the old and dying and celebrate the birth of the new. With its story of Oswald's return to his blood-soaked family

---

40   *Measure for Measure* (4.2)

41   See Ted Hughes *Shakespeare and the Goddess of Complete Being* (1993)

home, *Ghosts* enacts Orestes' *ritorno in patria*. The unforgiving fatalism of Greek Tragedy appears at the end of *Hedda Gabler*: Hedda goes into the alcove, draws the curtain behind her and shoots herself (thus starting her journey down into the underworld). And yet another set of resonances can be detected in *The Lady from the Sea*, a Scandinavian folktale about a mermaid caught between the fjord and the open sea, imprisonment and freedom, blind obedience and individual happiness.

In turn of the century drama – under the influence of Symbolism and Jungian notions of the collective unconscious – such resonance became much more self-consciously pronounced. Behind Schnitzler's Viennese sexual merry-go-round, *La Ronde* (1897), lurks the medieval Dance of Death; Brecht's *Baal* (1918) recasts the Old Testament false god Baal as a dissolute and egocentric drifter in contemporary Germany; and Yeats' densely poetic dramas are self-conscious attempts to reclaim Celtic mythology for the modern world.

While we should recognise the energy released by such prototypes, we must be careful about thinking that they offer us universal artistic criteria: a new play about life on a housing estate that is also a retelling of the Trojan War, or a tale of adultery in North London with knowing allusions to the Tree of Knowledge, should be treated with scepticism. Resonances are only powerful when generated within a culture that finds them potent. In modern life we've become largely deaf to the instruments that in the past created shared meaning and their employment today is sometimes little more than a gesture towards 'universality'.

Soliloquy

One of the chief characteristics of classical theatre is that characters use soliloquies to convey their thoughts directly.

The greatest exponent is, of course, Hamlet, whose tendency to speak alone gives us insights into his frame of mind, the processes of his thoughts, and his lonely position in a world gone wrong. Shakespeare's refinement of the popular tradition of direct address allows for a profound contemplation of life and action, and many believe that it is in these passages that Shakespeare's genius is most liberally on display. Look at this great speech from Act IV:

> How all occasions do inform against me
> And spur my dull revenge. What is a man
> If his chief good and market of his time
> Be but to sleep and feed? A beast, no more.
> Sure he that made us with such large discourse
> Looking before and after, gave us not
> That capability and godlike reason
> To fust in us unused. Now whether it be
> Bestial oblivion or some craven scruple
> Of thinking too precisely on the event
> A thought which quartered hath but one part wisdom
> And ever three parts coward, I do not know
> Why yet I live to say 'This thing's to do'
> Since I have cause and will and strength and means
> To do it. Examples gross as earth exhort me.
> Witness this army of such mass and charge
> Led by a delicate and tender prince
> Whose spirit with divine ambition puffed
> Makes mouths at the invisible event
> Exposing what is mortal and unsure
> To all that fortune, death and danger dare
> Even for an eggshell. Rightly to be great
> Is not to stir without great argument
> But greatly to find quarrel in a straw
> When honour's at the stake. How stand I then
> That have a father killed, a mother stained
> Excitements of my reason and my blood
> And let all sleep? While to my shame I see
> The imminent death of twenty thousand men
> That for a fantasy and trick of fame
> Go to their graves like beds, fight for a plot
> Whereon the numbers cannot try the cause
> Which is not tomb enough and continent
> To hide the slain? O from this time forth

My thoughts be bloody or be nothing worth.[42]

The speech starts with a dry comment about Fortinbras' army. Hamlet then launches into what looks like becoming a long discussion of 'what is a man', but quickly sidesteps into an in-depth examination of his own failings – especially in contrast to the resolution of this 'delicate and tender prince'. Even as he does so, however, his language breaks down and he becomes increasingly persuaded of the logic of his argument and the force of his rhetoric. He ends the speech committed to blind acts of decisive violence. It's a brilliant *tour de force*, around which the second half of *Hamlet* revolves; and the combination of passion and reason, haste and caution, rage and wit, induces in us feelings of unease as much as admiration.

The startling loneliness of Hamlet's soliloquies inspired the Romantic dramatists to attempt something similar. Look at Act V of Kleist's *The Prince of Homburg* (1811):

> Now, immortality, are you fully mine!
> You shine on me through the bandage of my eyes,
> With the blazing light of a thousand suns!
> Wings are growing from both my shoulders,
> My spirit soars through ethereal space;
> And just as a ship driven by the wind
> Sees the bright harbour slipping away,
> So all my life lies setting in the twilight.
> I still glimpse shapes and forms in the distance
> And now all fades away from me in the haze.[43]

The rhetoric is more self-conscious than 'To be or not to be', but Kleist's disgruntled prince is contemplating his own mortality in much the same way as Hamlet – if with a distinctly German idealistic bent.

There are hardly any soliloquies in Racine (which would violate its tightly controlled *vraisemblance*) but Molière used them

---

42 *Hamlet* (4.4)

43 Heinrich von Kleist *The Prince of Homburg* translated by Stephen Unwin (unpublished)

frequently in his comedies. They usually explain what is going on (see *Direct Address*), but they also explore dichotomies, fears and anxieties, as in this breathless speech by Arnolphe in *The School for Wives* (1662):

> I can't hold still a moment, I declare.
> My anxious thoughts keep darting here and there,
> Planning defences, seeking to prevent
> That rascal from achieving his intent.
> How calm the traitress looked when I went in!
> Despite her crimes, she shows no sense of sin.
> And though she's all but sent me to my grave
> How like a little saint she dares behave.[44]

This has much of the emotional and intellectual range of a Shakespeare soliloquy, if it lacks the radical dynamism and interiority that characterises the greatest ones.

The soliloquy is alien to naturalism: characters talking directly to the audience and taking us into their confidence violate the illusion. Of course, Chekhov and Ibsen sometimes leave their characters alone, and give them words to say: Hedda Gabler rushes about the house all by herself, muttering, in a state of some considerable upset, as does Nora, but neither addresses the audience directly. Chekhov, with his roots in the popular Russian vaudeville tradition, is freer: *Uncle Vanya* has three shortish monologues; less integrated, perhaps, is Konstantin's speech in the last act of *The Seagull* just before Nina returns.

Following Brecht's example, many modern writers have written speeches to be spoken directly to the audience. This is particularly prevalent in political drama. Look at the declaration that opens Dario Fo's *Accidental Death of an Anarchist* (1970):

> Good evening. I am Inspector Francesco Batista Giancarlo Bertozzo of the Security Police. This is my office on the first floor of our notorious headquarters here in Milan. Notorious following a sordid little incident a few weeks ago

---

44   *The School for Wives* translated by Kenneth McLeish (1995)

when an anarchist, under interrogation in a similar room a few floors above, fell through the window. Although my colleagues claimed, quite reasonably, that the incident was suicide, the official verdict of the enquiry was 'accidental'. Bit ambiguous you see. So there's been public outrage, accusations, demonstrations and so on flying around this building for weeks. Not the best atmosphere in which a decent nine to five plainclothes policeman like myself can do an honest inconspicuous day's work. I get all types in here. Tea leaves, junkies, pimps, arsonists – this is a sort of clearing house. Next!… I ought to warn you that the author of this sick little play, Dario Fo, has the traditional, irrational hatred of the police common to all narrow minded left wingers and so I shall, no doubt, be the unwilling butt of endless anti-authoritarian jibes.[45]

In the best Brechtian fashion, this speech alerts us to the contradictions of the play that we are about to watch and makes us aware of its key arguments.

In the modern theatre, soliloquies are often used to give the audience direct access to the characters' psychological state. The Canadian dramatist Michel Tremblay has written entire plays built out of carefully intercut monologues.[46] An over-reliance on soliloquies, however, can drain a play of life and energy – as audiences at one-person plays sometimes discover.

Asides

There are hardly any soliloquies in Restoration drama – perhaps the reflection of a culture more interested in the way people live together than in the intricacies of individual psychology. But the playwrights were fascinated by the ways of the world and made much of the comic discrepancy between their characters' often enormous appetites and the restraints imposed by the society in which they lived. The result was the triumph of the 'aside', a

45 Dario Fo *Accidental Death of an Anarchist* (1970) translated by Stuart Hood

46 Michel Tremblay *Sandra/Manon* (1981) and *Albertine in Five Times* (1986)

dramatic device that allows a character caught in a moment of embarrassment to communicate directly with us and let us know what he is feeling without the other characters on stage knowing. Look at this meeting between Dorimant and young Harriet in Act Four of Etherege's *The Man of Mode*:

DORIMANT
> *Aside*
> I love her, and dare not let her know it. I fear she has an ascendant o'er me and may revenge the wrongs I have done her sex.
> *To her*
> Think of making a party, madam; love will engage.

HARRIET
> You make me start! I did not think to have heard of love from you.

DORIMANT
> I never knew what 'twas to have a settled ague yet, but now and then have irregular fits.

HARRIET
> Take heed, sickness after long health is commonly more violent and dangerous.

DORIMANT
> *Aside*
> I have took the infection from her, and feel the disease now spreading in me.
> *To her*
> Is the name of love so frightful that you dare not stand it?[47]

A large part of the pleasure for the audience lies in the distance between the surface and the feelings beneath, in glimpsing the gap between the lie and the truth.

The Restoration did not invent the aside. The Jacobeans used them extensively and the actor's awareness of the audience is fundamental to Renaissance drama. Indeed, one of the most perti-

---

47   William Congreve *The Way of the World* (1700)

nent criticisms of *The Changeling* is that Middleton relied too much on asides to create his much admired sense of psychological 'interiority'. But the aside hardly ever realised its essential wittiness, until the Restoration dramatists grasped its huge psychological – and comic – potential.

The modern theatre tends to avoid the aside. Its stagecraft feels too crude and most modern writers prefer to ensure that the audience knows what a character is thinking through observing his actions, than having him turn out and explain it to us. Where the aside is used extensively, as in Denis Kelly's *Love and Money* (2006), it runs the risk of being self-conscious.

Slang and dialect

Human beings don't usually speak in perfectly formed, fully grammatical sentences, and one of the chief qualities of a good dramatist is that he catches the way that people *really* speak.

Slang and dialect are fundamental to English drama. An early example is this neglected little scene in *Henry IV, Part One*:

FIRST CARRIER

> Heigh ho. And it be not four by the day I'll be hanged. Charles' Wain is over the new chimney and yet our horse not packed. What, ostler.

OSTLER

> Anon, anon.

FIRST CARRIER

> I prithee, Tom, beat Cut's saddle, put a few flocks in the point. Poor jade is wrung in the withers out of all cess.

SECOND CARRIER

> Peas and beans here are as dank as a dog and that is the next way to give poor jades the bots. This house is turned upside down since Robin Ostler died.

FIRST CARRIER

> Poor fellow never joyed since the price of oats rose. It was the death of him.

SECOND CARRIER

> I think this be the most villainous house in all London
> Road for fleas. I am stung like a tench.

FIRST CARRIER

> Like a tench? By the mass, there is never a king Christen
> could be better bit than I have been since the first cock.

SECOND CARRIER

> Why, they will allow us never a Jordan and then we leak
> in your chimney and your chimney lye breeds fleas like
> a loach.

FIRST CARRIER

> What, ostler. Come away and be hanged. Come away.

SECOND CARRIER

> I have a gammon of bacon and two razes of ginger to be
> delivered as far as Charing Cross.

FIRST CARRIER

> God's body, the turkeys in my pannier are quite starved.
> What, ostler. A plague on thee, hast thou never an eye
> in thy head? Canst not hear? And twere as good deed as
> drink to break the pate on thee I am a very villain. Come
> and be hanged. Hast no faith in thee?[48]

This touches on the everyday life of the very poorest in society. It's
bewildering at first; on second reading, however, it reveals itself to
be thick with information. The colloquial language crackles with
alliteration and jokes. The action takes place in Rochester early one
morning. The two carriers have to transport their goods by horse
to the market at Charing Cross. They've spent the night in an inn;
their room was flea-infested and they had to use the chimney as a
chamber pot; they're having problems with Tom, the new ostler,
who, much to their frustration, never appears (he's probably still
in bed); the inn isn't as good as it used to be when Robin Ostler
(Tom's father, surely) was alive: dependent on horses he died when
the price of oats rose – a victim of the great Elizabethan inflations,

---

48   *Henry IV Part One* (2.1)

perhaps. The colloquial language crackles with alliteration and wisecracks and it's a masterpiece of Shakespearean realism.

Slang and dialect appear in the work of several of Shakespeare's contemporaries, especially the city comedies of Thomas Middleton and Ben Jonson, as well as in the working class characters in Restoration comedy. Look at the spirited row between father and daughter that raises the curtain on Farquhar's *The Beaux' Stratagem* (1707):

BONIFACE

Chamberlain! Maid! Cherry! Daughter Cherry! All asleep? All dead?

CHERRY

Here, here! Why d'ye bawl so, father? D'ye think we have no ears?

BONIFACE

You deserve to have none, you young minx! The company of the Warrington coach has stood in the hall this hour, and nobody to show them to their chambers.

CHERRY

And let 'em wait farther: there's neither redcoat in the coach, nor footman behind it.

BONIFACE

But they threaten to go to another inn tonight.

CHERRY

That they dare not, for fear the coachman should overturn them tomorrow – Coming! Coming! – Here's the London coach arrived.[49]

Armed with this, good actors can make the audience feel the squalor and provincialism of an eighteenth-century Midlands inn.

The dialect tradition emerged at full force in twentieth-century Irish drama, especially Sean O'Casey, whose grieving mother declares so memorably:

---

49 George Farquhar *The Beaux' Stratagem* (1707)

Maybe I didn't feel sorry enough for Mrs Tancred when her poor dead son was found as Johnny's been found now – because he was a Diehard! Ah, why didn't I remember that then he wasn't a Diehard or a Stater, but only a poor dead son! It's well I remember all that she said – an' it's my turn to say it now: What was the pain I suffered, Johnny, bringin' you into the world to carry you to your cradle, to the pains I'll suffer carryin' you out o' the world to bring you to your grave! Mother o' God, Mother o' God, have pity on us all! Blessed Virgin, where was you when me darlin' son was riddled with bullets, when me darlin' son was riddled with bullets? Sacred Heart o' Jesus, take away our hearts o' stone, and give us hearts o' flesh! Take away this murdherin' hate, an' give us Thine own eternal love![50]

DH Lawrence wrote a number of dialect plays set in the Nottinghamshire coalfields. *The Daughter-in-Law* (1912) is probably the best:

MRS GASCOIGNE

Well, I s'd ha' thought thy belly 'ud a browt thee whoam afore this.

JOE sits on sofa without answering.

Doesn't ter want no dinner?

JOE looking up

I want it if the' is ony.

MRS GASCOIGNE

An' if the' isna, tha can go be out? Tha talks large, my fine jockey! *She puts a newspaper on the table; on it a plate and his dinner.* Wheer dost reckon ter's bin?

JOE

I've bin ter th' office for my munny.

MRS GASCOIGNE

Tha's niver bin a' this while at th' office.

JOE

They kep' me ower an hour, an' then gen me nowt.

---

50   Sean O'Casey *Juno and the Paycock* (1924)

MRS GASCOIGNE

Gen thee nowt! Why, how do they ma'e that out? It's a wik sin' tha got hurt, an' if a man wi' a broken arm canna ha' his fourteen shillin' a week accident pay, who can, I s'd like to know?

JOE

They'll gie me nowt, whether or not.

MRS GASCOIGNE

An' for why, prithee?

JOE does not answer for some time; then, sullenly:

They reckon I niver got it while I wor at work.

MRS GASCOIGNE

Then where did ter get it, might I ax? I'd think they'd like to lay it onto me.

JOE

Tha talks like a fool, Mother.

MRS GASCOIGNE

Tha looks like one, me lad.[51]

Dialect can be embarrassing, however, especially when the class attitude is condescending – as is sometimes the case in Noël Coward's attempts to write working class characters. Modern dramatists usually avoid such *de haut en bas* condescension and attempt dialogue that is like highly concentrated, flinty, vernacular poetry. An example is the opening of Edward Bond's *Saved* (1965):

LEN

This ain' the bedroom.

PAM

Bed ain' made.

LEN

Oo's bothered?

PAM

It's awful. 'Ere's nice.

---

51 DH Lawrence *The Daughter in Law* (1912)

LEN

> Suit yourself. Yer don't mind if I take me shoes off? *He kicks them off.* No one 'ome?

PAM

> No.

LEN

> Live on yer tod?

PAM

> No.

LEN

> O.[52]

This chatter about casual sex among the South London working class of the 1960s has a real 'crackle', and raises the curtain on an unforgettable drama of poverty and violence.

America has produced an astonishing range of high-quality dialect drama: from the Yiddish and Italian American of Arthur Miller's Lower East Side to the expletive-ridden language of David Mamet's brutal businessmen, con-artists and tramps, and the biblical cadences of August Wilson's great epics of Black American life. Several contemporary British writers – Jonathan Harvey, David Eldridge, Ayub Khan-Din, and Kwame Kwei-Armah – have caught contemporary urban slang with thrilling precision, as can be heard so vividly in Roy Williams' edgy drama of black street life, *Fallout* (2003):

CLINTON

> Kick him in the head, kick him!

DWAYNE

> Yes!

PERRY

> My bowie.

CLINTON

> Kick him.

---

52   Edward Bond *Saved* (1965)

DWAYNE
Tek off him glassers and chuck dem.

CLINTON
Chuck dem now, man.

EMILE
Pass me de phone, you fucker!

CLINTON
Pass him de phone, yu fuck!

EMILE
Pass it now.

PERRY
Do it now.

DWAYNE
My bwoi!

EMILE
Trainers too.

CLINTON
Gwan, Emile!

PERRY
Walk barefott, yu rass.

CLINTON
Like yu do in Africa.

EMILE
Trainers!

CLINTON
Tell him, Emile.

PERRY
Tell the fucker.

DWAYNE
Bus his head.

CLINTON
Bus him up.

EMILE
Trainers!

DWAYNE
Fuck dem over to us.

CLINTON
Before yu dead.

EMILE
Trainers!

DWAYNE
Punch him.

CLINTON
Kick him.

PERRY
Bus him up.

EMILE
Yu see you!
Kicks continuously.[53]

Like all dialect drama this needs a certain amount of 'unpacking' if we are to understand it. But taken at speed by talented young actors it has all the raw energy and violence of a South London gang.

Dialect matters because it gives prominence to a broad range of voices, from frequently ignored classes, regions and ethnicities. By contrasting these with the dominant manner of speaking (the Queen's English) dialect heightens the contradictions – the dialectic of dialect, one could say – of the drama.

Jokes

A distinguished older actor once told me that he finds it odd that so many of his younger colleagues don't know where the jokes are in a play. And as an earnest young director I once criticised a new play because it had 'too many jokes'. Although drama can be unbalanced by unmotivated one-liners, few would argue against the role of humour in the theatre.

---

53   Roy Williams *Fallout* (2003)

Dazzling displays of wit are particularly prevalent in the English and Irish repertoire. The tradition can, as ever, be traced back to Shakespeare, particularly those characters whose lively intelligence cracks jokes whenever they open their mouths: Touchstone always gets a laugh when he assures his new bride, the goatherd Audrey, that 'Sluttishness may come hereafter'[54]; and Rosalind's advice to Phoebe that she should 'Sell now. You're not for all markets' is funny, if in a cruel way.[55] Shakespeare's wittiest play (I don't mean his funniest: that title surely belongs to *The Comedy of Errors*) is *Much Ado About Nothing*: when a messenger observes that Benedick is 'not in your books', Beatrice replies, quick as a flash, is: 'No. And he were, I would burn my study';[56] and when the two of them meet, she assures him that 'I had rather hear my dog bark at a crow than a man swear he loves me'.[57] But he can give as good as he gets and declares: 'If her breath were as terrible as her terminations she would infect to the North Star. There were no living near her.'[58] Their mutual fascination and growing infatuation is a direct result of the pleasure they take in making each other laugh.

The witty put-down, the clever *double-entendre*, the perfectly phrased riposte reached its apogee in Restoration Comedy. These plays combine a genuine exploration of psychological and social truth, with a constant stream of funny – and often filthy – jokes. Three quarters of a century later Sheridan wrote plays which bristle with wit and verbal dexterity. *The Rivals* (1775) is famous for Mrs Malaprop's startling ability to mangle the English language: 'He is the very pineapple of politeness'; 'If I reprehend any thing in this world, it's the use of my oracular tongue, and a nice derangement of epitaphs!' and 'He's as headstrong as an allegory on the banks of the Nile.' Once we know what to listen for, each 'Malapropism' strikes our ear as a delicious, almost forbidden, pleasure. *The School*

---

54 *As You Like It* (3.3)

55 Ibid (3.5)

56 *Much Ado About Nothing* (1.1)

57 Ibid (1.1)

58 Ibid (2.1)

for Scandal (1777) is similarly stuffed full of good jokes which can, when properly delivered, still bring the house down.

Another Irish genius, Oscar Wilde, is defined almost entirely by the power of his wit, which is nowhere more liberally displayed than in *The Importance of Being Earnest* (1895). Miss Cicely tells Prism that 'I never travel without my diary. One should always have something sensational to read in the train'; Mrs Bracknell declares that 'To lose one parent, Mr. Worthing, may be regarded as a misfortune; to lose both looks like carelessness'; and Algernon claims that 'All women become like their mothers. That is their tragedy. No man does. That's his.' The danger with Wilde's masterpiece is that it can feel like an excuse for a string of good jokes; when well done, however, the laughs arise from a particular situation and are all the more enjoyable for it.

A skilful dramatist knows the value of making the audience laugh early; it warms the house up and gets them listening. Noël Coward always managed to get a good joke in within the first minute or so. The first scene of Terence Rattigan's brilliant debut *French Without Tears* (1936) has one of the funniest – and silliest – jokes in twentieth-century drama. Kenneth is learning French and needs to know how to say 'She has ideas above her station'; Brian's answer is 'Elle a des idées au dessus de sa gare'.[59] The joke – which soon entered into common currency even amongst people who never saw the play – lies in a mistranslation of the all-important last word, 'gare', which can only refer to a railway station.

Tom Stoppard is perhaps the wittiest writer of the modern theatre. Having declared that 'the finger nails grow even after death', Rosencrantz says that 'The toenails on the other hand never grow at all'; Guildenstern immediately points out the unintentional comedy: 'The toenails, on the other hand?'[60] Stoppard's comic contemporaries include Alan Ayckbourn, Alan Bennett, Peter Nichols and Michael Frayn who together are responsible for many of the funniest plays of the modern British theatre.

---

59   Terence Rattigan *French Without Tears* (1936)

60   Tom Stoppard *Rosencrantz and Guildenstern Are Dead* (1966)

For many reasons – above all, perhaps, that the theatre is no longer seen as a place for popular entertainment – jokes are less in evidence among younger British playwrights. Richard Bean, Patrick Marber and Alistair Beaton are striking exceptions. American comic drama relies less on turn of phrase than on situation: Ben Hecht and Charles Macarthur's *The Front Page* (1926) and Neil Simon's *Brighton Beach Memoirs* (1983) are perhaps the two greatest American stage comedies, but there are dozens of others. For whatever reason, American humour has flourished more in films and on television than in the theatre.

Modern European theatre has produced few genuinely funny comedies. One can argue that comedy isn't the German theatre's strongest suit, but it's odd that Italy – with the notable exception of Dario Fo – should have produced no dramatist capable of furthering the traditions of Goldoni, or that France – the home of Molière, Marivaux and Feydeau – should boast no major contemporary comic playwrights. It's perhaps indicative that, when given the *Evening Standard*'s 'Best Comedy' Award for her highly successful play *Art* (1995), the French playwright, Yasmina Reza, said she did not realise that she had written a comedy. One would need to explore the high level of respect paid to the serious intellectual in France to explain this.

Translation

In his *Lectures on Russian Translation* the novelist Vladimir Nabokov insisted that:

> The third, and worst degree of turpitude is reached when a masterpiece is planished and patted into such a shape, vilely beautified in such a fashion as to conform to the notions and prejudices of a given public. This is a crime, to be punished by the stocks.[61]

It's a stern warning, especially relevant to drama.

61   Vladimir Nabokov 'The Art of Translation' in *Lectures on Russian Literature* (1981)

A useful distinction can be made between a 'translation' – the attempt to render as accurately as possible the meaning and cadences of the original – and 'a version' – a radical recasting of the play into another cultural context. Of course, these different approaches inevitably overlap. Working on Schnitzler's *La Ronde*[62] my co-translator and I struggled with the characteristically Viennese greeting 'Küß die Hand': the problem is that even in Victorian English, no gentleman would say 'I kiss your hand' (the verbal equivalent of raising one's hat) when meeting a lady. We decided to make the rest of the exchange more formal as compensation.

With the growing internationalisation of the British theatre, we encounter many plays not written in English. If we cannot understand the original we're dependent on translations and need to be careful. Most are reasonably accurate but their theatrical quality is variable. Dozens of translations of the major European dramatists are available, done by both scholars and theatre people. Unfortunately, some great writers are still to find their match: the two chief examples are Brecht[63] and Lorca[64] but there's a strong argument that all good dramatists should be retranslated every ten years or so.

The important thing is to compare and contrast. Look, for example, at the following speech by Mrs Alving in *Ghosts*. She is explaining her attitude towards her (now dead) husband. The first comes from a stuffy if reliable translation by Peter Watts:

> I could never have gone through with it if I hadn't had my work. Yes, I honestly claim to have worked; all the improvements on the estate – all the modern equipment that my husband got so much credit for – do you imagine that he had the energy for anything of the sort – lying all day on the sofa reading an old Court Circular? No, and I'll tell you something else: it was I who was left to manage everything

---

62   Arthur Schnitzler *La Ronde* translated by Stephen Unwin and Peter Zombory-Moldovan (2007)

63   An exception is Michael Hofmann's translation (2006) of *Mother Courage*

64   An exception is Ted Hughes' translation (1997) of *Blood Wedding*.

when he went back to his debauchery, or when he relapsed into whining self-pity.[65]

The second is by the Ibsen scholar Michael Meyer. It's more fluent than Watts, but still rather Victorian:

> I could never have borne it if I had not had my work. Yes, for I think I can say that I have worked! All the additions to the estate, all the improvements, all the useful innovations for which Alving was praised – do you imagine he had the energy to initiate any of them? He, who spent the whole day lying on the sofa reading old court circulars? No; let me tell you this too; I drove him forward when he was in his happier moods; and I had to bear the whole burden when he started again on his dissipations or collapsed in snivelling helplessness.[66]

The third, by Stephen Mulrine, is a great improvement, if we can accept 'lucid intervals' and the coyness of 'debauched ways':

> I'd never have borne it if I hadn't had my work. Yes, I can safely say I've worked hard – all those additions to the property, all the improvements, all the innovations, for which Alving got the credit, of course – do you honestly think he had the initiative for these things? A man who used to lounge around on the sofa the whole day, reading an old Court gazette? No, and I'll tell you something else – it was I who drove him on, during his more lucid intervals. And I had to bear the whole burden when he took to his debauched ways again, or lapsed into abject self-pity.[67]

The last is by the actress and playwright Amelia Bullmore:

> If it hadn't been for work, I wouldn't have survived. My God, I've worked! All the acquisitions, all the charitable initiatives, all the improvements Alving was praised for – you

---

65   Henrik Ibsen *Ghosts* translated by Peter Watts (1964)

66   Ibid translated Michael Meyer (1984)

67   Ibid translated Stephen Mulrine (2002)

> think he was capable? He spent all day flat out on the sofa fumbling through an old almanac! I was the one who galvanised him on his better days and shouldered it all when he was incapacitated with drink or misery or self-pity.[68]

At first glance this is the liveliest – it's certainly the shortest. Unfortunately it misses out on some key details – a 'Court gazette' is grander than an 'almanac'; 'fumbling through' gives an unnecessary gloss to reading; and the last phrase is rhythmically weak.

Whichever we prefer, the crucial point is that every translation is different and reading a range of versions can be bewildering: it sometimes feels as if we're reading a different play. So it's important that we understand the principles at work.

But now it's time to work out what happens in the play.

68   Ibid translated by Amelia Bullmore (2007)

7. What happens?

ARISTOTLE DEFINED DRAMA AS 'an imitation of an action',[1] and declared that the story was more important than anything else.

The impulse for stories runs deep. It can be seen in most forms of child's play and expresses our deep desire to impose order on our lives. We're fascinated by 'what happens next' and want to know more: 'Why does it happen?' 'How does it happen?' and 'Why does it matter that it happens?' It's the story that grabs our attention.

Storytelling has an important philosophical dimension too. The repetition of a well-known tale reminds us of certain established 'truths': the triumph of love, the inevitability of death, the desirability of children and so on. A story speaks of the underlying and unchanging realities of our lives. But it does something else: by showing development, both in the individual and within society, it points to new ways of organising the world. Human beings are more than the sum of their experiences, they're involved in creating the future: stories help us see that change is possible and show us how it can come about.

There are many different ways of telling a story, from the traditional 'once upon a time' to the most oblique, intercut, half-glimpsed, account of a series of events. Some narratives are entirely original, while others conform to well-established patterns. In reading a play we need to identify which kind of storytelling is being used and where the stories we are being told have come from.

---

1   Aristotle *Poetics*

Stock actions

Some theories of narrative claim that there are only a handful of stories available.[2] These provide the playwright with a template from which to work.

In European culture, there are two main sources. The first is the Bible, with its epic tales from the Old Testament (The Flood, The Expulsion from Eden, the Exodus, the Golden Calf etc.) and the more intimate stories of the New Testament (The Annunciation, The Virgin Birth, The Agony in the Garden, The Last Supper, Crucifixion, Death and Resurrection, etc.). The second is the classical world with its vast range of myths and legends (Promethean Fire, the Trojan War, The Descent into the Underworld, The Sirens, The Strange Island, The Epic Journey, etc.). Most classical plays from the European repertoire draw on one or other of these, to a greater or lesser extent.

There are other repositories of less familiar stories: the Norse Sagas, the Hindu epics, the *Arabian Nights* and the Songs of the Niebelung, as well as a myriad of traditional folk tales and legends. Many overlap and later versions often combine elements from diverse sources. Wherever they come from, however, such *tropes* (a literary term perhaps best defined as a poetic unit of action) give the playwright a direct connection with the audience's collective memory.

With the increasing diversity of modern audiences, the voltage of such shared narratives has started to fade; but if we're to read classical plays we need to be alert to the dramatic charge that such stock actions were intended to generate and feel their power.

Popular theatre

From the performance of simple folk tales in an African village to the most elaborate American television series, the telling of the story in popular drama takes precedence over all other concerns

---

2   See Robert McKee *Story: Substance, Structure, Style and the Principles of Screen-writing* (1999); Christopher Booker *The Seven Basic Plots: Why We Tell Stories* (2004)

– not just intellectual enquiry, but metaphor, poetry and character-isation too. Each moment is designed to carry maximum dramatic power and strives to immerse the audience in what is unfolding.

Brecht was a great admirer of all forms of popular entertain-ment and declared that the 'story' (he used the English word) was at the heart of everything he did. He enjoyed the way narrative could be manipulated to make a specific point and tried to encour-age his audiences to see historical and social processes as consist-ing of a number of discrete actions, or 'gests', as he called them. His preparatory notes for his plays often consist of simple narrative actions and his writings on the theatre continually emphasise the importance of storytelling.

The striking thing, however, is that even the most direct kind of popular drama consists of more than mere narrative. *The Comedy of Errors* explores questions of identity, superstition and marriage, even as it makes us laugh out loud at the spiralling confusion. Simi-larly, the great farces of Feydeau and Labiche reveal the hidden depths of nineteenth century Parisian society even as the bedroom doors open and shut with increasingly manic regularity, while Alan Ayckbourn's brilliant comedies are as concerned to anatomise a particular kind of English middle class life as to provide narrative based comic entertainment.

Indeed, it's possible to argue – *pace* the Hollywood action movie – that storytelling always and inevitably raises questions about life and the world; indeed, that the very function of storytelling is to open up a space in which such inquiry is possible.

Direct narration

The simplest form of storytelling is direct address: an actor stands on stage and tells us what is going on.

In Shakespeare, this is usually done 'in character'. Look at Launce (and his infamous dog, Crab) in *The Two Gentlemen of Verona*:

> Nay, twill be this hour ere I have done weeping. All the kind of the Launces have this very fault. I have received my proportion, like the Prodigious Son, and am going with Sir

Proteus to the Imperial's court. I think Crab my dog be the
sourest-natured dog that lives.[3]

Launce maintains this relationship with the audience throughout.
He is highly partial (and much affected by Crab) but gently and
charmingly manages to move the action along.

At other times, Shakespeare provides an apparently neutral
narrator, such as Gower in *Pericles*:

To sing a song that old was sung
From ashes ancient Gower is come
Assuming man's infirmities
To glad your ear and please your eyes.[4]

The Chorus in *Henry V* has much the same function, although
neither of them – or the choruses of Greek tragedy, for that matter
– are as impartial as they pretend.

Eager to break down the boundary between audience and stage,
Brecht often employed his own novel form of direct address. Thus,
in *The Good Person of Szechwan*, but Wang the Water Seller tells the
audience what is happening, his reverence for the Gods shows up
his poverty-stricken passivity and makes us question the authority
of this storyteller. And in *The Caucasian Chalk Circle*, the Singer
attempts an authorial voice throughout:

But you, who have listened to the story of the Chalk Circle
Take note of the meaning of the ancient song:
That what there is shall belong to those who are good for
  it, thus
The children to the maternal, that they thrive;
The carriages to good drivers, that they are driven well;
And the valley to the waterers, that it shall bear fruit.[5]

Of course, this too has been framed: the Singer is one of the farmers
from the Prologue who have just staged the story of 'The Chalk

---

3   *The Two Gentlemen of Verona* (2.3)

4   *Pericles* (1.1)

5   Bertolt Brecht *The Caucasian Chalk Circle* translated by WH Auden and Tanya
Stern (1976)

Circle' to celebrate the peaceful outcome of a property dispute. In other words, Brecht uses direct address as just another element in his dramatic structure, and expects us to listen to his narrators with all the scepticism they deserve.

Classical drama

Mature classical drama usually dispenses with direct address and relies on a more discreet unfolding of the action to tell the story.

While such drama still has narrative at its core, it sees character, thought and expression as equal partners. An interesting example is Egeus' long speech that opens *The Comedy of Errors*:

> Five summers have I spent in farthest Greece
> Roaming clear through the bounds of Asia
> And coasting homewards came to Ephesus
> Hopeless to find yet loath to leave unsought
> Or that or any place that harbours men.
> But here must end the story of my life
> And happy were I in my timely death
> Could all my travels warrant me they live.[6]

This is directed towards the Duke and is motivated by his desire to escape the sentence of death. It is not just essential in terms of narrative, it's thick with philosophical and psychological investigation. Thus, even in this early comedy, Shakespeare is dramatising the epic.

In mature Shakespeare, this integration goes much further, and character, thought and expression emerge more organically. Look, for example, at Hamlet discovering Claudius at prayer. Convinced of his guilt, he's just about to kill him:

> Now might I do it pat, now he is praying.
> And now I'll do it.

When he stops himself and turns out to the audience:

---

6   *The Comedy of Errors* (1.1)

> And so he goes to heaven
> And so am I revenged. That would be scanned.
> A villain kills my father and for that
> I, his sole son, do this same villain send
> To heaven.[7]

Our desire for the story to develop is deliberately frustrated and we're told why things aren't going to progress the way we thought they would. This has a double effect: it draws out the dramatic tension but it also creates a space for Hamlet's exploration of his conscience and his own motives. The hiccup in the storytelling expresses the hiccups in the story itself.

In neo-classical French drama, the storytelling is often slowed right down. The effect is like watching a road crash in slow motion: we see both cars race towards the bend; we get a feel for the drivers and glimpse their psychology; and then we wait, open mouthed, for the collision. And in Racine's *Phèdre* (1677), the author doesn't show us the dramatic conclusion, but gives us a report instead:

> I have seen the best of mortals die,
> And the most innocent, I dare to add.
> Scarce were we issuing from Troezen's gates;
> He drove his chariot; round about him ranged,
> Copying his silence, were his cheerless guards.[8]

And so, for three minutes of highly wrought, classically structured, decorous verse, Théramène's harrowing description of Hippolytus' death brings Racine's slowly developing, psychologically probing, finely counterpointed masterpiece to its shattering conclusion.[9]

---

7   *Hamlet* (3.3)

8   Jean Racine *Phèdre* translated by John Cairncross (1963).

9   After this speech, Phèdre poisons herself – the one time that Racine breaks the neoclassical rules of 'vraisemblance' and has a character die in front of us.

Epic stories

A distinction should be drawn between the epic and the dramatic. Epic tells us that 'this happened and then that happened'; dramatic storytelling says that 'this happened *because* that happened'. The first is an account of actions and events; the second offers us causality.

Christopher Marlowe's *Tamburlaine the Great* (1587) is an example of epic drama at its greatest: written in magnificent, often heroic verse, its two parts cover vast distances and the action unfolds over several years. It has a central, semi-mythical figure who defeats a host of enemies and is driven by the simplest of motives: world conquest. But while the effect is highly impressive the play is often repetitive and benefits from extensive cutting. For all his thunder, Marlowe never adequately explores the deeper questions surrounding his hero's behaviour. And this is indicative of the problem inherent in epic drama.

One of the great strengths of Shakespeare's drama is the way that he manages to combine the epic with the dramatic, the political with the psychological, and the historical with the contemporary. In *As You Like It*, a somewhat obscure dynastic struggle between warring Dukes is partnered with the most sophisticated and intimate of psychological and erotic dramas; in *King Lear*, the disastrous division of the political body is echoed in the private agony of a dysfunctional family. In both plays, the reader is moved effortlessly across the genres and encounters epic stories populated by three-dimensional characters.

In Britain, the dominance of psychologically astute social comedy soon relegated the epic to the academic or the satirical. But it endured in continental Europe and especially in the growing taste for romantic and nationalist drama: thus the Shakespearean-influenced plays of Schiller's maturity, *Don Carlos* (1787), *Wallenstein* (1800) and *Mary Stuart* (1801), are written with an epic sweep, as, even more remarkably, is Goethe's masterpiece *Faust Parts One* (1806) and *Two* (1832). These, to a greater or lesser extent, manage to combine the epic with the dramatic, the personal with the historical. That they are dominated by the working out of certain intellectual ideas is typical of German courtly drama,

Ibsen tried something similar in *Peer Gynt* (1867): a rambling dramatic poem which has little sense of dramatic necessity, but straddles an entire life, travels across continents and mixes the magical with the political, the historical with the contemporary. Ibsen soon abandoned the form and restricted himself to naturalist dramas of everyday life but, paradoxically, in writing epic drama he discovered how to create stories that were psychological convincing.

Brecht was keen to reinstate the epic, as is evident in his three masterpieces, *Mother Courage* (1939), *The Caucasian Chalk Circle* (1944) and *Life of Galileo* (1939-41, 1949). The fragmentary, broken-backed nature of these plays deliberately places contrasting elements side by side, and we are asked to discover within these breaches the meaning of the action. Brecht's British followers tried something similar – Edward Bond in the 1970s, some of David Hare's plays (above all *Fanshen*, 1975), much of Howard Barker, Timberlake Wertenbaker's *Our Country's Good* (1988), and others – and modern directors and theatre-makers have often called for new plays with an epic sweep. Despite this, modern playwrights have usually stuck with the contemporary and the local, and epic theatre may well have had its day.

Naturalistic storytelling

Fundamental to the naturalist revolution was the notion that the characters on stage should never acknowledge that the audience is watching them. This reluctance to violate what has been called 'the fourth wall' makes storytelling in naturalistic drama a complicated business.

The best naturalistic plays carry within them a set of 'back-stories': carefully imagined pasts for the key protagonists and an account of the events that carry them to the moment when we first meet them. Playwrights have to master exposition in the early scenes if they are to establish this backstory successfully.

Ibsen's technique is worth studying. He ensures that everything we need to know about his characters' pasts is sketched out in the first five minutes of the action. But he does this without making us conscious of what he is doing. These backstories then provide the momentum that makes the unfolding of the action feel so unstoppable. This is most in evidence in his great cycle of twelve naturalistic plays.

Chekhov is curious. His great plays can be reduced to a simple number of overarching dramatic actions (as Timothy West has written: 'in Act One the cherry orchard is going to be sold; in Act Two the cherry orchard is about to be sold; in Act Three the cherry sold is being sold; and in Act Four the cherry orchard has been sold'[10]). What's more, most of his characters have relatively clear objectives (Lopahkin wants to buy the cherry orchard and Ranyevskaya doesn't want to sell it) and pursue them to the best of their abilities. They all have individual stories, with a beginning, a middle and an end. But, bizarrely, the cumulative effect, when subjected to Chekhov's objective and counter pointed technique, is of figures caught in an eternal present and incapable of progress: an image, one might add, of the random nature of modern life.

Narrative pace

The best playwrights control the pace of the action carefully and know that changes in rhythm are essential for achieving dramatic suspense and attention.

Shakespeare had a remarkable knack for driving the story on, particularly in the first two acts, with one event leading inevitably to another, and the clashes and contradictions tumbling over each other at a dizzying pace. Thus in the first scene of *A Midsummer Night's Dream* he communicates an enormous amount of information:

- Theseus has returned home to Athens with Hippolyta, whom he is about to marry;

---

10   Timothy West *A Moment Towards the End of the Play* (2001)

- Egeus is furious with his daughter, Hermia, who has refused to marry Demetrius, his choice for her husband, and wants to marry Lysander instead;
- Under pressure from Egeus, Theseus decrees that Hermia must obey her father or, as the law now stands, either be put to death or enter a nunnery;
- Hermia is left alone with Lysander, who suggests that they run off into the woods where 'the sharp Athenian law' cannot restrict them;
- Helena arrives: she's in love with Demetrius who is not in love with her. She decides to tell him about Hermia and Lysander's plan to elope, knowing that he will follow them – and that she will follow all three of them.

This short scene (a mere 260 lines of verse) also succeeds in giving us a sense of the complex psychological forces that drive the story on: political pressure, paternal pride, romantic love, erotic desire, rejection and so on. Shakespeare's dramatic style is thick with such dense layers of storytelling.

Ibsen writes passages of precise and deliberate exposition – two characters sitting side by side talking about the past for as long as ten minutes[11] – and then deliberately interrupts the action just before the crucial information is revealed. He often then follows this with a headlong acceleration in pace: the burning orphanage at the end of Act Two of *Ghosts*, or Hedda playing with her father's pistols just before the end of Act One. In Chekhov, a surprisingly complex story emerges through the apparent inconsequentialities of the dialogue. The four acts progress leisurely but massively: it's difficult to know what exactly has happened – beyond the most obvious – but by the end the shifting of the tectonic plates has changed everything.

---

11   See Hedda and Mrs Elvsted in Act One of *Hedda Gabler* or Nora and Mrs Linde in Act One of *A Doll's House*.

'Deus ex Machina'

In some classical comedies, the situation towards the end is so fraught with danger that the only way for the playwright to avoid unwanted catastrophe is to introduce a *deus ex machina* – a 'god from the machine'.[12] This takes the form of a figure who is often divine, or at least supernatural, but sometimes just a representative of a higher authority. They usually have little dramatic credibility and their role is a simple one: to bring matters to a resolution in which right, wisdom and truth are finally seen to triumph.

There are numerous examples of the *deus ex machina* in Greek and Roman drama. Renaissance playwrights tended to avoid it – because of its lack of plausibility – although versions of it appear in Shakespeare (such as the arrival of the second son of Roland de Boys at the end of *As You Like It*, the appearance of the Abbess in the closing moments of *The Comedy of Errors* and, above all, the descent of Jupiter from the heavens at the end of *Cymbeline*). The revival of intellectual classicism in late seventeenth- and eighteenth-century drama made it much more acceptable and it became a staple in popular nineteenth-century drama.

The naturalists, of course, scoffed at such intervention insisting that the resolutions of their dramas should be the logical conclusion of the preceding action. Brecht, however, was keen to experiment with the *deus ex machina* and his *Threepenny Opera* – based on John Gay's *The Beggar's Opera* – boasts a deeply unconvincing resolution: the arrival of the King's messenger who pardons Macheath at the eleventh hour. But in Brecht's hands the technique is deliberately ironic: it shows that only something as preposterous as a *deus ex machina* can offer hope to the poor.

---

12 The origins of this Latin phrase are in the stage conventions of the Greek theatre: a 'mechane' (a crane) was used to lower actors playing gods down onto the stage.

The modern theatre and the reaction against the story

Narrative retained its primary status in the theatre until well into the twentieth century. Most playwrights of modern drama, however, have tended to downplay the story, seeing intellectual analysis, psychological insight and poetic symbolism as more rewarding. This is certainly the case in Harold Pinter and Samuel Beckett. And even where story is central it plays a different role: *Death of a Salesman* (1949), *Top Girls* (1982) and *Closer* (1997) all have powerful narrative drives, but in none of them is it the most important feature. This reaction against the story is one of the chief characteristics of modern drama.

There are many reasons for this. Perhaps the most important is the argument that a well-organised theatrical narrative implies that real life has similar structure and meaning. Reality, the modern dramatist argues, offers no such consolation. A good story demands a climax and a resolution, but such narrative tidiness is too convenient for the twenty-first century and the modern playwright rejects it.

It's a powerful argument. Calls for plays with 'a good old-fashioned story' usually derive from a lack of thought. They also forget to ask the all-important next question: 'what *really* happens?'

8. What really happens?

Action often conceals as much as it shows. Having discovered what happens in a play, we need to dig beneath the surface and find out what *really* happens.

The subtext

One of the salient features of naturalist drama is that the texts contain not just the words that are spoken but also that which is left unsaid, sometimes called the 'subtext'.

Perhaps the best way of understanding the subtext is with reference to Freud's notion of repression: that is, we all say things which conceal our desires and repress what we feel in deference to what is socially acceptable. The naturalist playwright understands that what people say isn't the sum of what they're thinking, and ensures that what his character *doesn't* say is as important as what he does say.

Ibsen is the master of this. At the beginning of *A Doll's House*, Nora has just come home from Christmas shopping. Her husband, Helmer, is working in his study, and she chatters to him, in seductive baby-language, through the locked door. But her behaviour masks a darker purpose: she's distracting him from questioning her about their household expenses. She has borrowed money illegally to finance their trip to Italy that has saved his life, and is now slowly paying it back.

The tantalising dialogue between Nora and Doctor Rank in Act Two is another example. It reveals the unspoken sexual attraction between a healthy young woman and a much older bachelor. A great deal is said, but more is left unsaid. The pair are sitting together on the sofa and the light is fading:

NORA

> You're my truest, dearest friend. You know you are.
> Doctor, it's something you can help me prevent. You
> know how Torvald loves me... deeply, beyond words...
> he'd give his life...

RANK *leaning forward to her*

> Nora. D'you think he's the only one?

NORA *startling*

> What?

RANK

> The only one who'd give his life for you?

NORA *heavily*

> Ah.

RANK

> I swore I'd tell you before I ... went. Now, Nora, now
> you know. And you know that you can rely on me, as on
> no one else.

NORA *getting up, calmly and evenly*

> Excuse me.

RANK *sitting still, but making room for her to pass*

> Nora –[1]

As soon as Nora realises that Rank is about to declare his love
she asks the maid to bring in the lamps: the subtext was about to
become the text, and in the repressed world of nineteenth century
Norway such feelings must be kept secret. Ibsen is like an iceberg:
the words that are spoken are just a small sign of what is *really*
going on beneath.

Chekhov is equally adept. In *The Seagull*, Trigorin's lofty speeches
to the young Nina about art and fame are motivated by a secret
passion, just as Arkadina's contradictory behaviour to her son – one
moment contempt, the next devotion – is a flamboyant cover for
her failure as a mother. And should we take Ranyevskaya's attachment to her cherry orchard as a simple expression of the purity of

---

1   Henrik Ibsen *A Doll's House* translated by Kenneth McLeish (1994)

her heart? Isn't it rather a harking back to a better time, before she was so bitterly compromised by her experiences in France? What's more, isn't Lopakhin's dedication to Ranyevskaya as much a tactic for ensuring the sale of her estate as a true expression of his admiration? Finally, look how his inability to propose marriage to Varya – his complete silence on the subject, in fact – reveals an ocean of pain:

LOPAKHIN

What are you looking for?

VARYA

I packed these myself, and now I can't remember.

A pause

LOPAKHIN

So where are you off to now, Miss Varvara?

VARYA

Me? I'm going to the Ragulins… I've agreed to look after the house for them… I'll be a sort of housekeeper.

LOPAKHIN

And that's at Yashnevo? That'll be about fifty miles from here.

A pause

So, life in this house is over now.

VARYA *examining the luggage*

Where on earth is it?… Maybe I packed it away in the trunk… Yes, life's finished in this house… There'll be nothing left…

LOPAKHIN

And I'm off to Kharkov now… by the same train. I've a lot of business in hand. I'm leaving Yepihodov here to look after the place. I've taken him on.

VARYA

Not really!

LOPAKHIN

This time last year we already had snow, if you remember, and now it's so cold and sunny. It's cold nonetheless… Three degrees below.

VARYA

> I haven't looked.
> *A pause*
> Our thermometer's broken anyway.
> *A pause*
> *Someone calls through the door from outside 'Mr Lopakhin!'*

LOPAKHIN *As if he'd been waiting for this call*
> Just coming. (*Hurriedly exits*)

> *Varya is sitting on the floor, lays her head on a bundle of dresses and begins quietly sobbing.*[2]

Although the term is modern, the subtext is not confined to naturalistic drama and can be detected in sophisticated classical work. Some say that Falstaff provides Hal with an alternative father figure in *Henry IV Parts One and Two,* to be set against his stern real father, the King. Many see an unspoken Oedipal relationship between Hamlet and his mother, Gertrude, and argue that in the 'closet scene' (3.4) Hamlet's disgust at his mother's marriage ('in the rank sweat of an enseamed bed / Stewed in corruption, honeying and making love / Over the nasty sty'[3]) betrays his own incestuous desires.[4] Others maintain that Macbeth's submission to his wife in their first scene together is a sublimation of his own 'vaulting ambition', and that theirs is an elaborate psychosexual relationship of dominance and enticement. These hypotheses cannot be proven but are fascinating nevertheless.

Actors enjoy playing the subtext, and audiences – and theatre critics – love looking out for it: it gives an illusion of richness and three-dimensionality. But we need to be careful not to invent motivation where there isn't any, or detect secretive passions where the writer has not supplied one. Or rather, if we hunt these out and cannot substantiate them from the overall action of the play, we

---

2   Anton Chekhov *The Cherry Orchard* translated by Stephen Mulrine (1998)

3   *Hamlet* (3.4)

4   See Ernest Jones *The Oedipus Complex as an Explanation of Hamlet's Mystery,* first published in the 'American Journal of Psychology' (January 1910).

should, at least, be prepared to accept that they're the result of creative interpretation.

Lying

Characters in plays often lie. Sometimes they lie to themselves, and sometimes the truth is so well hidden that it's difficult for the audience to establish whether it's a lie or not. But lies are central to much good drama.

The women in Shakespeare are sometimes the bigger liars, perhaps because of their relative powerlessness (a better explanation, I'd argue, than Shakespeare's alleged misogyny). Lear's elder daughters, Goneril and Regan, are good examples. When asked which of them loves their father best, they deliver immaculately phrased statements of loyalty and adoration. Goneril, the oldest, is first:

> Sir, I love you more than words can wield the matter.
> Dearer than eyesight, space and liberty
> Beyond what can be valued, rich or rare
> No less than life, with grace, health, beauty, honour.
> As much as child ever loved, or father found.
> A love that makes breath poor, and speech unable.
> Beyond all manner of so much I love you.[5]

Regan, Lear's second daughter, goes further:

> Sir, I am made
> Of the self-same metal that my sister is
> And prize me at her worth. In my true heart
> I find she names my very deed of love.
> Only she comes too short. That I profess
> Myself an enemy to all other joys
> Which the most precious square of sense possesses
> And find I am alone felicitate

---

5   *King Lear* (1.1)

In your dear highness' love.[6]

It's typical of Shakespeare's paradoxical approach that these lies are so convincing that their father believes them, and that Cordelia's 'nothing' sounds so uncomfortably, even provocatively, truthful, that her father cannot believe it.

Mrs Alving in *Ghosts* isn't a habitual liar, but she's guilty of two enormous lies: hiding the truth of her husband's dissipation from her son, Oswald, and concealing from her maidservant, Regine, the fact that she shares the same father as Oswald. This has allowed all of them some peace, but when she finally tells them the truth – as the sun chases away the rain at the end of Act Three – it's too late: disaster and death are the logical conclusion of a lifetime of lies and concealment.

Irony

Irony is fundamental to the modern English sensibility. The upper class traitor, Hillary, riffs brilliantly on the subject in Alan Bennett's *The Old Country* (1977):

I have to decide. Come down on one side or the other. And without recourse to irony. Which is not to decide at all but have it both ways. The English speciality. I wonder with the new European vogue that we don't have a referendum on it. Irony, is it a good thing? And on the voting paper two boxes, one to read Yes or No. The other Yes *and* No. The whole thing would have to be held under the auspices of an institution impervious to irony... Except there is the problem: no institution you can name but the choice is tinged with irony. Utterly absent, it is never more present. Irony is inescapable. We're conceived in irony. We float in it from the womb. It's the amniotic fluid. It's the silver sea. It's the waters at their priestlike task washing away guilt and purpose and respon-

---

6   Ibid (1.1)

sibility. Joking but not joking. Caring but not caring. Serious but not serious.[7]

Irony, it seems, allows the character to speak from both sides of his face – an appropriate rhetoric for 'Perfidious Albion' perhaps.

Irony is almost entirely absent in classical drama. Yes, Edmund in *King Lear* is being ironical when he says 'fine word, legitimate', as are the aristocratic observers of the play of 'Pyramus and Thisbe' in *A Midsummer Night's Dream* and Berowne and his superior chums watching the Pageant of the Nine Worthies in *Love Labour's Lost*. One of the unfortunate results of Leavisite close reading[8] (especially when allied to pop psychology), is the belief that uncomplicated statements are not a true expression of what the speaker means. But Shakespeare's unique style is both suggestive of tremendous psychological depth and includes everything that the audience needs to know.

Irony, in its political form, is fundamental to Brecht. Mother Courage's refusal to acknowledge the dead body of her son Swiss Cheese is hedged around with irony: surely, we say to ourselves, a mother with real feelings wouldn't be able to keep a dry eye in such a situation, even as we find ourselves smiling knowingly at those who protest that motherhood is a universal constant. And when Galileo publishes his recantation and is roundly condemned by his disciples for failing to live up to their expectations, his answer to the charge 'Unhappy the land that has no heroes' is one of the great ironic putdowns of world drama: 'No, unhappy the land that needs heroes.'[9]

---

7 Alan Bennett *The Old Country* (1977)

8 F.R. Leavis wanted an approach to literary study that placed no barriers between reader and text. Interestingly, despite the fact that many of his students went on to make successful careers in the theatre, he had very little interest in drama and his famous essay on *Othello* in *The Common Pursuit* (1952) has not aged well.

9 Bertolt Brecht *Life of Galileo* translated John Willett (1980)

Dramatic irony

One of the clearest signs of a play's sophistication is the presence of dramatic irony. This is produced by a fundamental discrepancy between what a character knows about his circumstances, and what we, the audience, understand to be the case.

Thus we discover early on that Oedipus killed his father at the crossroads, thinking he was a stranger; we know that Desdemona is innocent, even while Othello is strangling her; and we realise, probably from the beginning, that Cordelia loves her father dearly. In modern drama we know that Nora has borrowed money illegally for Torvald's life-saving trip to Italy even as he accuses her of being extravagant; and we know that Lopakhin wants to buy the cherry orchard even while he listens in awe to Ranyevskaya telling him what it means to her.

Dramatic irony has a double function. On the one hand, it allows us to look at the character's situation with increased objectivity: we know more than he does about what is going on, are interested in seeing how he responds, and can judge his actions accordingly. On the other hand, it grants us a greater degree of empathy: we can see the disaster unfolding and pity the character's suffering as we do so.

Dramatic irony is fundamental to human experience: none of us can predict the hour of our death or what destiny has in store. The religious believe that God knows; non-believers see it as the result of chance and biology. But irony plays around us all the time and such situational irony lends drama the complex three-dimensionality of real life.

Whodunnit?

One of the oldest – and most common – types of narrative is the 'whodunnit?' These are based on a bad deed – often a murder – that took place before the story begins (or sometimes in the first act) and the action shows us where the responsibility lies.

The 'whodunnit' is fundamental to the murder mystery play – most famously, Agatha Christie's *The Mousetrap* (1952). It also appears in a range of classical masterpieces too. Look at *Hamlet* (whose play within a play provided Christie with her title): we start the play ignorant of who killed Hamlet's father, and watch Hamlet's discovery of the truth with growing dismay. The opening scene warns us that there is 'something rotten in the state of Denmark', but we finish the second scene ignorant of the cause of the old King's death: it is not until the end of the first act that we are told the truth. And in Kleist's *The Broken Jug* (1811), we, like Inspector Walter, are offered endless explanations as to who broke Frau Martha's precious jug – in itself a distraction from the question that really matters: who tried to climb into Eve's bedroom that spring night? In *Ghosts*, we, like Oswald, slowly discover the truth about Captain Alving's dissolute behaviour and his wife's complicity in preserving the lie. In JB Priestley's *An Inspector Calls* (1947) the sudden death of a young girl is investigated, with the shocking conclusion that everybody is guilty;[10] in Arthur Miller's *All My Sons* (1947) we discover that Joe Keller is responsible for his own son's death; and, in *Who's Afraid of Virginia Woolf?* (1962), Edward Albee replaces the traditional 'whodunnit?' question with 'who *is* it?' – George and Martha have no child and the whole thing is a pretence to fill the aching hole in their lives.

Audiences watching a 'whodunnit' are encouraged to act as detectives. This has a dual function: we watch everything that happens with extra attention, and the best playwrights are careful in the clues – and red herrings – that they scatter; but we're also expected to come to a set of judgments which reinforce our sense of right and wrong. The 'whodunnit' helps us see the failings of society and the individual, while also provoking us into thinking about how they can be reformed. It is unsurprising that Brecht,

---

10   See JB Priestley *An Inspector Calls* (1945): 'We don't live alone', thunders the Inspector, 'We are members of one body. We are responsible for each other. And I tell you that the time will soon come when, if men will not learn that lesson, then they will be taught it in fire and blood and anguish.'

that most political of playwrights, was a voracious reader of detective stories.

Violence

Since conflict is fundamental to drama, many of the greatest plays feature violence. The critical question is the way that this violence is presented. Shakespeare's goriest play, *Titus Andronicus*, features multiple executions, rape, mutilation and cannibalism. The curious thing is how decorative it all feels: it's almost as if the young dramatist, influenced by Seneca, has written an academic Roman tragedy. The problem isn't that the play is too violent, it's that the violence is unreal.

In the best plays, however, violence is subjected to the most careful moral analysis. The blinding of Gloucester in *King Lear*[11] is a remarkable case in point. The episode is established in detail, charting both Gloucester's incredulity and the growing cruelty of his tormentors:

GLOUCESTER
    What means your graces? Good my friends, consider.
    You are my guests. Do me no foul play, friends.

CORNWALL
    Bind him, I say.

REGAN   Hard. Hard. O filthy traitor.

GLOUCESTER
    Unmerciful lady as you are, I'm none.

CORNWALL
    To this chair bind him. Villain thou shalt find –

GLOUCESTER
    By the kind gods tis most ignobly done
    To pluck me by the beard.

REGAN
    So white and such a traitor.

---

11   *King Lear* (3.7)

GLOUCESTER   Naughty lady
    These hairs which thou dost ravish from my chin
    Will quicken and accuse thee. I am your host.
    With robbers' hands my hospitable favours
    You should not ruffle thus. What will you do?

But Cornwall and Regan are deaf to Gloucester's pleas and behave like common torturers, overlapping and competing with each other for their victim's attention:

CORNWALL
    Where hast thou sent the King?

GLOUCESTER   To Dover.

REGAN
    Wherefore to Dover? Wast thou not charged at peril -

CORNWALL
    Wherefore to Dover? Let him answer that.

GLOUCESTER
    I am tied to the stake and I must stand the course.

REGAN
    Wherefore to Dover?

Tied to a chair, the Earl shows his moral courage and decency:

    If wolves had at thy gate howled that dern time
    Thou shouldst have said 'Good porter turn the key
    All cruels else subscribe'. But I shall see
    The winged Vengeance overtake such children.

Cornwall decides to frustrate Gloucester's intentions, but fatally underestimates his own servants. The First Servant is slow to object – obedience and servility are the norm and he stands passively by until Cornwall has gouged out the first of Gloucester's eyes. He tries to plead with his master to relent, but finally loses patience and attacks him:

FIRST SERVANT
                Hold your hand, my lord.
    I have served you ever since I was a child
    But better service have I never done you

Than now to bid you hold.

REGAN   How now, you dog.

FIRST SERVANT
If you did wear a beard upon your chin
I'd shake it on this quarrel. What do you mean?

CORNWALL
My villain?

FIRST SERVANT
Nay then come on and take the chance of anger.

Regan's response betrays the contemptuous nature of her aristo-cratic logic:

REGAN
Give me thy sword. A peasant stand up thus?

FIRST SERVANT
O, I am slain. My lord, you have one eye left
To see some mischief on him.

CORNWALL
Lest it see more prevent it. Out vile jelly.
Where is thy lustre now?

GLOUCESTER   All dark and comfortless.

But in the process Cornwall has been mortally wounded and this is the last time we see him. The First Servant's rebellion has saved the country from a terrible fate and, in the brief dialogue between the other servants that follows, we see an opposition forming.[12]

The blinding of Gloucester is the turning point in *King Lear*. It brings into the sharpest focus Shakespeare's understanding of the ties that make a society decent, as well as the limits to obedience. It also points out the realities of the class structure: Gloucester is a distinguished Earl and his torturers are a Duke and Duchess. It takes an unnoticed servant to change the course of history. And Shake-speare shows that this violence is something new: Lear's Albion

---

12   In his 1964 RSC production Peter Brook cut this episode wanting to avoid senti-mentality. Shakespeare's aim is much more interesting, however: he provides contradic-tion and dialectic – the stuff of history.

isn't a fascist country in which old men are regularly tortured. Shakespeare is writing a realistic analysis of the way that violence corrupts; he also shows, in the most pertinent way, that occasionally violence is needed to prevent something worse.

Violence has been a constant theme in twentieth century drama. The climax of *Mother Courage* is a good example. Discovering that Catholic soldiers are about to mount a surprise attack on the city of Halle, the dumb Kattrin climbs onto the roof of a hut, pulls the ladder up behind her and starts banging a drum as loud as she can to warn the inhabitants. The soldiers return, try to get her to stop, and eventually shoot her. This is one of the most heartstopping moments in modern drama, but Brecht's intention is that the audience should see that her heroism leads to an early grave: it's not heroics that are needed, it's a wholesale transformation of society. As in *King Lear*, violence is shown in all its reality; but its dramatisation also contributes to a broader investigation of its causes and meaning.

Two other important examples of violence in drama are the stoning of the baby in Edward Bond's *Saved* (1965) and the catalogue of horrors (including anal rape and cannibalism) that runs through Sarah Kane's *Blasted* (1995). Different as they are, the violence in both plays serves to make a broader point about the presence of savagery in the modern world.[13]

Sex

If death and violence are fundamental to tragedy, love and sex are the animating spirit of comedy.

It's difficult to depict sex in the theatre convincingly. This is more than just a question of modesty or censorship, it's because portrayals of copulation – as the pornographer refuses to recognise

---

13   The two plays caused an enormous critical uproar. *The Daily Mail* dismissed *Blasted* as 'this disgusting feast of filth'; more considered opinion has seen it as a visceral reaction to the much televised 'ethnic cleansing' in Bosnia-Herzogovina at the time. *Saved* – which provoked a similar critical uproar – is hailed as one of the defining texts of a particular kind of modern urban helplessness.

– are banal and excluding. The best plays concentrate instead on the build up to – and let down after – the sex act, but divert our gaze when the clothes start to come off.

Schnitzler's *La Ronde* (1897) is an interesting example. The play describes a cycle of sexual coupling that links ten realistically drawn characters from all levels of Viennese society, from a Prostitute to a Count. Schnitzler couldn't portray intercourse on stage and the sex act is indicated by a row of dots – the effect is like Hogarth's 'before' and 'after' in his cycle of drawings, *The Rake's Progress*. But sex isn't the real subject. Instead, Schnitzler shows the truth about the relationship between men and women in all its desperation, fear, and greed – as is evident in this sweetly sentimental but utterly deceptive dialogue between the adulterous young wife, Emma, and her equally unfaithful husband, Karl:

YOUNG WIFE
    Know what tonight reminds me of?

HUSBAND
    What, my darling?

YOUNG WIFE
    Of... of... Venice.

HUSBAND
    Our first... night...

YOUNG WIFE
    Yes... you've...

HUSBAND
    What? Go on, say it.

YOUNG WIFE
    You've been so sweet tonight.

HUSBAND
    Of course.

YOUNG WIFE
    Oh... if only you were always...

HUSBAND *In her arms*
    What?

YOUNG WIFE
Karl! My darling!

HUSBAND
What? If only I were always what?

YOUNG WIFE
You know.

HUSBAND
And what if I were always... ?

YOUNG WIFE
Then I'd always know that you love me.

HUSBAND
Yes, but surely you know that anyway. A man can't always be the loving husband, you know; sometimes he has to go out into the hostile world, he has to fight the good fight. Never forget that, my darling. There's a time for everything in marriage – that's what's so beautiful about it. There aren't many couples, you know, who still, five years on – remember their Venice.

YOUNG WIFE
Absolutely.

HUSBAND
And now... good night... my little darling.

YOUNG WIFE
Good night.[14]

With its revelation not just of the man's adultery but also of his young wife's, this scene would have been just as alarming to Schnitzler's respectable audience as a sexually explicit dramatisation of marital harmony.

When trying to interest young people in Shakespeare, critics and enthusiasts sometimes say that his plays are full of sex.[15] But his approach to sexuality is more complex than the modern celebration of subversive energy suggests. For a start, Shakespeare can

---

14   Arthur Schnitzler *La Ronde* translated by Stephen Unwin and Peter Zombory-Moldovan (2008)

15   See, for example, Stanley Wells *Looking for Sex in Shakespeare* (2004)

be utterly unromantic: Brecht described Romeo as having a 'bursting scrotum' because he's already in love with Rosaline before he meets Juliet.[16] And the results are often dangerous: in *A Midsummer Night's Dream* the sexuality is so extreme – admittedly under the influence of Oberon's 'purple flower' – that one partner can be exchanged for another with hardly a blink. But the anarchic force of youthful sexuality produces, paradoxically, a reformation of adult society and Egeus' antiquated insistence on imposing his will on his daughter's wishes is eventually overruled by a reforming Duke. Similarly, in *Romeo and Juliet*, the feud between the Capulets and the Montagues is finally resolved by the tragic sacrifice of the two young lovers.

Of course, there are limits to how explicit classical dramatists could be. Since all descriptions of sexual activity would have been forbidden, Shakespeare resorts to punning, *double-entendre* and coded language.[17] Like a dramatist in Brezhnev's Russia, Shakespeare's elaborate wordplay allows him to plead innocence: if, as some suggest, the transformed Bottom is an image of an erect phallus, he's also – as the children in the audience know all too well – a funny man with a donkey's head.

Shakespeare's portrayals of commercial sex are astonishingly realistic (and deeply unerotic as a result): look at the Courtesan in *The Comedy of Errors*, Doll Tearsheet and Mistress Quickly in *Henry IV*, Mistress Overdone and Pompey in *Measure for Measure* and, supremely, the denizens of the brothel in *Pericles*. Shakespeare shows that commercial sex has its consequences. Without effective contraception, prostitutes often fell pregnant – as Mistress Overdone, the brothel keeper, protests:

> My lord, this is one Lucio's information against me. Mistress Kate Keepdown was with child by him in the Duke's time. He promised her marriage. His child is a year and a quarter

16   Bertolt Brecht *The Messingkauf Dialogues* (1940)

17   See Eric Partridge *Shakespeare's Bawdy* (1947)

old come Philip and Jacob. I have kept it myself, and see how
he goes about to abuse me.[18]

But there were greater dangers than unwanted children, especially venereal disease. Even before she's heard about the imminent
closure of her brothels, Overdone is worried about the decline in
her business:

Thus what with the war, what with the sweat, what
with the gallows, and what with poverty, I am custom
shrunk.[19]

This is hardly a Rabelaisian celebration of unbridled sexuality, the
carnivalesque challenge to authority that's sometimes claimed
for it.

Shakespeare knows that sexuality is a highly ambivalent force: it
can express love and create new life, but it can also be exploitative
and cruel. Laertes warns his sister Ophelia not to open her 'chaste
treasure / to [Hamlet's] unmastered importunity',[20] while Emilia
tells Desdemona that she might consider being 'unfaithful for the
whole world'.[21] Shakespeare understands that in a Christian society,
where chastity is preferrable to carnality, sexuality is the necessary
compromise if, as Benedick says in *Much Ado About Nothing*, 'the
world must be peopled',[22]but also that it has its dangers. He knows
that sexuality is a fundamental part of everyday life and presents it
in all its complexity.

Modern plays are usually much franker, and in the late 1990s the
British theatre promoted an unabashed appreciation of every form
of sexuality – however recherché – as almost a national style (sometimes dubbed 'In yer face'). Patrick Marber's *Closer* (1997) includes
one of the funniest scenes of sexual excitement and humiliation in

---

18   *Measure for Measure* (5.1). The feast of St Philip and St James (Jacob) was May
Day, a time for sexual license.

19   *Measure for Measure* (1.2)

20   *Hamlet* (1.3)

21   *Othello* (4.3)

22   *Much Ado About Nothing* (2.3)

modern drama. Both men are at home, sitting at their computers.
The typed dialogue appears on a screen above their heads:

DAN
    Hallo

LARRY
    hi

DAN
    Do you come here often?

LARRY
    ?

DAN
    Net

LARRY
    1st time

DAN
    A Virgin. Welcome. What's yout name?

LARRY
    Larry. U?

    Beat

DAN
    Anna

LARRY
    Nice 2 meet U
    Pause
    I love COCK
    Pause

LARRY
    (*Speaking.*) Good evening …
    (*Typing.*) Youre v. forward

DAN
    This web site is called LONDON FUCK. Do you want
    sex?

LARRY
    Yes. Describe u

DAN

   30s dark hair big mouth epic tits.

LARRY

   Define epic

DAN

   36DD

LARRY

   Nice legs?

DAN

   Y.

LARRY

   Becos I want 2 know

DAN *smiles*

   No. 'Y' means 'Yes'.

LARRY

   O

DAN

   I want to suck you senseless

LARRY

   Be my guest

DAN

   Wear my wet knickers

LARRY

   Ok

DAN

   Well hung?

LARRY

   9£
   (*Speaking*) shit.
   9"[23]

Little could demonstrate more vividly the way that sexual relationships vary according to the society in which they are found.

---

23   Patrick Marber *Closer* (1997)

Change

We should ask how characters change and how this change affects the society as a whole. Everything is susceptible to change, and the great dramatist charts the impact of that change. The young aristocrat Alsemero in *The Changeling* is explicit on the subject:

> What an opacous body had that moon
> That last changed on us. Here's beauty changed
> To ugly whoredom. Here, servant obedience
> To a master sin, imperious murder.
> I, a supposed husband, changed embraces
> With wantonness, but that was paid before.
> Your change is come too, from an ignorant wrath
> To knowing friendship.[24]

One of the most important influences on Shakespeare was a Latin poet who never wrote a scene of drama: Ovid's *Metamorphoses*, translated by Arthur Golding (1567), provided him with a template, and a fascination with transformation lies at the heart of Shakespeare's genius. It is most in evidence in his comedies, with their stories of the protean nature of love and pleasure, but is fundamental to the histories and tragedies too, which chart meticulously the social changes brought about by individual actions.

Some have taken this as proof that Shakespeare is arguing for change; others suggest that these stories of transformation are warnings. It is perhaps more useful to see that the playwright understands that birth and death, growth and destruction, rebellion and reaction, innovation and conservation, are fundamental to the contradictory fabric of human life.

This quality of change and development is less evident in modern drama. This may seem paradoxical: the last fifty years have seen some of the most rapid technological and social changes in human history. But a combination of post-war philosophical existentialism with a more recent disillusionment at the very idea of

---

24   Thomas Middleton and William Rowley *The Changeling* (1622)

progress has produced a kind of drama that sometimes denies all possibility of change.

There are some important exceptions. Edward Bond has argued that the last moments of his greatest play, *Saved*, which shows Len fixing a broken chair, provides a positive image of hope. And the most politically engaged of modern playwrights – especially writers like Athol Fugard and Lorraine Hansberry who deal with questions of human rights – have argued unstintingly for the need for root and branch social reform.

Of course, the question of change goes even deeper than political or social reform. There is change even in *Waiting for Godot* (1948). A critic said that in it, 'Nothing happens, twice': actually quite a lot happens, and there are continuous attempts at improvement. The problem is that none of them succeed.

9. How does it work in the theatre?

SINCE A PLAY TEXT can be treated as a blueprint to a set of actions that take place on a stage, we need to think in three-dimensions when we read drama.[1]

The willing suspension of disbelief

Writing about poetry, not drama, Coleridge gave the theatre one of its key concepts: 'the willing suspension of disbelief'.[2] The theatre asks us to set aside our knowledge that we're sitting in a purpose-built hall, watching actors pretending to be other people, and imagine instead that they're real people appearing in front of us.

The Chorus in *Henry V* begs for our indulgence:

> O for a muse of fire that would ascend
> The brightest heaven of invention.
> A kingdom for a stage, princes to act
> And monarchs to behold the swelling scene.
> Then should the warlike Harry like himself
> Assume the port of Mars and at his heels
> Leashed in like hounds, should famine, sword and fire
> Crouch for employment. But pardon, gentles all
> The flat unraised spirit that hath dared
> On this unworthy scaffold to bring forth
> So great an object. Can this cockpit hold
> The vasty fields of France? Or may we crown

---

1   The best books on Shakespeare's theatre are Andrew Gurr's *The Shakespearean Stage* (1970) and *Playgoing in Shakespeare's London* (1996); Peter Thomson's *Shakespeare Theatre* (1992) and *Shakespeare's Professional Career* (1994). Two series published by CUP illuminate more modern theatrical practice: 'Plays in Production' includes volumes on *Death of A Salesman, Mother Courage, Don Juan* and *A Doll's House*, and 'Directors in Perspective' features monographs on André Antoine, Bertolt Brecht, Peter Brook, Ingmar Bergman, Dario Fo, Giorgio Strehler, Andrzej Wajda and Vlesevolod Meyerhold.

2   Coleridge *Biographia Literaria* (1817)

> Within this wooden O the very casques
> That did affright the air at Agincourt?
> O pardon, since a crooked figure may
> Attest in little place a million
> And let us ciphers to this great accompt
> On your imaginary forces work.[3]

This famous speech is sometimes read as evidence of the ease with which the imagination can be employed, and the power of such language on a willing mind is strong indeed: 'Think when we talk of horses', the Chorus goes on to say, 'that you see them / Printing their proud hoofs in the receiving earth'. But it's anachronistic to imagine that the Chorus is liberating us from the narrow conventions of naturalism. Instead, the speech is an apology for the limits of the Globe's technology: 'piece out our imperfections with your thoughts', begs the Chorus. We do so, willingly, but only because we've been asked to do so.

Dr Johnson was merciless in reminding us of the limits of the imagination and of the fact that we're never fully transported:

> The truth is, that the spectators are always in their senses, and know, from the first act to the last, that the stage is only a stage, and that the players are only players. They come to hear a certain number of lines recited with just gesture and elegant modulation. The lines relate to some action, and an action must be in some place; but the different actions that complete a story may be in places very remote from each other; and where is the absurdity of allowing that space to represent first Athens, and then Sicily, which was always known to be neither Sicily nor Athens, but a modern theatre?[4]

Brecht went one step further and drew on both Shakespeare and Oriental theatre to create a dramatic style that deliberately reminds

---

3   *Henry V*

4   Samuel Johnson *Preface to Shakespeare* (1765)

us that what we're watching is just a representation of the reality beyond.[5]

Modern dramatic theory has often played with the question of illusion and anti-illusion. But the experience of going to the theatre and watching a play is usually more straightforward: if the play is well written we become interested in the characters and are affected by what happens; if not – if it's self-conscious, awkward, and lacking a proportionate relationship between content and form – we end up unmoved and not believing a word.

Original theatrical conditions

If we are to understand a classical playwright, we should recognise the physical conditions of the theatre for which he wrote.

A quick glance at the Globe reveals various fundamentals. Everything was centred on the performer and the words that he spoke. The action moved quickly, telling the story in a direct and economical way. There were few changes in scenery, the actors relied on costume and props to make their visual impact, and the building lent itself to metaphorical meanings (the great circle of the globe, Heaven above, Hell below, and so on). Most importantly, it was a popular, all-embracing theatre that lived up its motto: 'Totus mundi agit histrionem' (translated by Shakespeare as 'all the world's a stage').

From 1600, Shakespeare's company used the Blackfriars' Hall for winter seasons. This was candlelit and allowed for some limited 'flying' (Jupiter in *Cymbeline* descends from above). Its smaller capacity meant that higher ticket prices could be charged and it attracted a better-off audience as a result. This subtly changed the dramatists' role: some retreated into courtly escapism, while the best set out to explore the increasingly complex world outside.

Several new theatres were built in London following the Restoration (above all the Theatre Royal, Drury Lane, and the luxurious Duke of York's Theatre in Dorset Gardens). These changed the rela-

---

5   One of my favourite stage directions is in Manfred Karge's post-Brechtian *The Conquest of the South Pole* (1988): 'Bühne als bühne' – 'the stage as a stage'.

tionship between audience and the action that, for the first time, featured scenery, furniture, and specially designed costumes, all framed by the proscenium arch. These theatres were much more comfortable than the Elizabethan amphitheatres, and played a new and important role in the social (and sexual) lives of the middle class audiences who flocked to them. The emphasis on the pictorial and the stylish was echoed by the playwrights' interest in the surface of society.

In the late nineteenth century a new breed of visionary figures – the first theatre directors – led the way in creating a new kind of theatre. The Duke of Saxe-Meiningen founded the Meiningen Players in 1874 and his meticulously crafted productions toured Europe for years; André Antoine founded the tiny Théâtre Libre in Paris in 1887, where he premiered Ibsen's *Ghosts* in 1890; Otto Brahms' Freie Bühne was opened in Berlin in 1889 as a socialist co-operative and JT Grein's Independent Theatre Group was formed in London in 1891, both of them influenced by Antoine (who invented the all-important notion of the 'fourth wall'). Meanwhile, Stanislavsky and Nemirovich-Danchenko founded the Moscow Art Theatre in 1898, and one of their first productions was Chekhov's *The Seagull*; William Archer premiered many of Ibsen's plays in London and the Barker-Vedrenne Management presented influential seasons at the Royal Court and the Savoy Theatres between 1904 and 1907.

Since naturalism is not an absolute, its earliest manifestations would strike theatregoers today as highly artificial, relying on primitive scenic techniques. Functional doors and windows were set into painted canvas scenery. Electric lighting further transformed what was possible (unlike gas lights, electric lamps could be dimmed and focused). Costumes increasingly came to be seen as a way of reflecting 'character'. Make-up had to adjust to the new lighting techniques, and some of the melodramatic excesses of face-painting began to go out of fashion. The hardest task was changing the mentality and style of the actors, which was often stentorian and declamatory, favouring strong emotion over the fine detail that the new theatre demanded. In response Stanislavsky invented his famous System as an attempt to provide a scientific basis for acting and a style of performance rooted in observable reality. It was in these conditions that modern drama was created.

Stage directions

Many of the best playwrights have been practical men of the theatre. Shakespeare and Molière were actors and shareholders in the companies for which they wrote; Ibsen and Brecht were fine directors and understood theatrical realities; Chekhov and Strindberg were married to actresses and were closely involved in productions of their plays; and several modern dramatists have hands-on experience of the theatre as directors in their own right.

Playwrights often provide stage directions. These are the author's attempt to describe what he imagines taking place. Most actors and directors are selective in the way they use them but for the reader they offer important information about the world of the play and offer an invaluable imaginative spark.

Stage directions play different roles according to writer and theatrical context. In naturalism, they act as novelistic scene setting. Ibsen's plays were published simultaneously in various languages and were often read before they were seen in the theatre. Look, for example, at the end of *Ghosts*:

> She walks across to the table and puts out the lamp. Sunrise. The glacier and snow-capped peaks in the background are bathed in dazzling morning light.[6]

This reads more like a film script than a play, and is almost impossible to achieve in the theatre: in the reader's imagination, however, it's magnificent and moving.

Details are telling too. Look at the way Ibsen specifies that Nora and Hedda Gabler move to the stove when they're feeling anxious, engineers the shift from downstairs to upstairs and back again in the first three acts of *John Gabriel Borkman* and insists on the flag

---

6   Henrik Ibsen *Ghosts* translated by Stephen Mulrine (2002)

flying at full mast at the end of *Little Eyolf*. Each of these details is significant, and fundamental to Ibsen's overall composition. Productions can – and often do – dispense with them, but usually at the expense of the play. When we read a play we should be alert to their implications.

The best stage directions aspire to the poetic. Look at Chekhov's sound effect in Act Two of *The Cherry Orchard*:

> They all remain seated, deep in thought. The only sound is that of old Firs, muttering as usual. Suddenly a far-off noise is heard, as if in the heavens – like the sound of a breaking string, dying away, sadly.[7]

Or later in the same act:

> Yepihodov is heard playing his guitar, the same melancholy song. The moon rises. Somewhere beyond the poplars Varya is looking for Anya, calling 'Anya! Where are you?'[8]

These are mysterious and difficult to define – and almost impossible to pull off in the theatre – but as profound as any line of verse.

Some writers treat stage directions as an expression of their controlling voice. Bernard Shaw's are often essays in their own right, replete with exhaustive statements about character, interpretation and mood, as well as clever jokes at the characters' expense. Look at this from *Heartbreak House*:

> The young lady runs and looks at her watch. She rises with an air of one who waits and is almost at the end of her patience. She's a pretty girl, slender, fair, and intelligent looking, nicely but not expensively dressed, evidently not a smart idler.
>
> With a sigh of weary resignation she comes to the draughtsmen's chair; sits down; and begins to read Shakespear. Presently the book sinks to her lap; her eyes close; and she dozes into a slumber.[9]

---

7   Anton Chekhov *The Cherry Orchard* translated by Stephen Mulrine (1998)

8   Ibid

9   Bernard Shaw *Heartbreak House* (1919)

The description isn't merely functional; it's as if Shaw doesn't trust the actress or the words she speaks to convey his intentions and uses stage directions to make his points. Her falling asleep over 'Shakespear' (perversely, Shaw always spelt him without a final 'e') is one of his intellectual jokes: like Tolstoy, Shaw thought 'the Bard' overrated. Shaw's contemporary, Harley Granville Barker – a better playwright, incidentally – wrote some delicious stage directions; this is from the end of his one act play *Farewell to the Theatre*:

> With three fine gestures she puts on her hat again. Time was when one would sit through forty moments of a dull play just to see Dorothy take off her hat and put it on again. Much less expressively he finds his and they go out together. The clerks all stare ecstatically as she passes.[10]

Dorothy used to be a famous actress and Granville Barker's stage direction gives us a flavour of what her quality might be: only an experienced man of the theatre could have written it.

Other writers use stage directions as exercises in psychological or sociological explanation. Look at Sean O'Casey's description of Mary Boyle in *Juno and the Paycock*:

> She is a well-made and good-looking girl of twenty-two. Two forces are working in her mind – one, through the circumstances of her life, pulling her back; the other, through the influence of books she has read, pushing her forward. The opposing forces are apparent in her speech and her manners, both of which are degraded by the environment, and improved by her acquaintance – slight though it be – with literature.[11]

This is much more than stage direction: it is a fully-fledged character description designed to help the reader – and the actress – imagine the character.

Many playwrights keep stage directions to the minimum; others abolish them altogether. Brecht set the vogue and a number

---

10   Harley Granville Barker *Farewell to the Theatre* (1912)

11   Sean O'Casey *Juno and the Paycock* (1924)

of modern dramatists – Manfred Karge, Heiner Müller, Martin Crimp, Peter Gill and others – have followed suit. They are aware of the scale of the director's contribution (some are directors in their own right) and are keen to create a script open to the widest possible range of scenic interpretation.

Stage directions found in modern editions of Shakespeare need to be handled with care; the vast majority don't appear in the Folio and have been invented by editors in an attempt to give the playwright's free-flowing scenic imagination 'a local habitation and a name', as Theseus calls it. The danger is that they encourage the reader to imagine 'the city walls', 'the banqueting hall' and so on, when all Shakespeare himself expected was the stage of the Globe theatre, some decent costumes and, perhaps, a throne. When I read Shakespeare, I pay no attention to the stage directions and, if I'm preparing a new production, remove them entirely.[12]

The theatre publishers, Samuel French, produce 'acting editions' of popular plays. Designed for amateur groups, they include lists of properties, costumes and sound effects, as well as ground plans and additional stage directions. Largely spurned by the professionals, it would be a shame if these editions came to stand between the general reader and the original text.

Setting

Playwrights have not always been able to choose their locations freely. With just one exception, every surviving Greek play takes place in a mythological past.[13] Roman comedy was always set in ancient Greece, and Elizabethan and Jacobean censorship forced playwrights to set their plays in the past, or in remote or fantastical lands. More recently, writers living under repressive governments have chosen abstract locations to speak about their world.

A quick survey of Shakespeare's locations reveals not just a surprising variety, but a profound grasp of the imaginative meaning of each place, rich with metaphorical and literary associations. His

---

12   See Oberon Books: *King Lear, Twelfth Night, Romeo and Juliet* and *Hamlet*.

13   Aeschylus *The Persians*

Venice is a brutal, materialist place, dedicated to money and power, with little mercy, sympathy or warmth; the Athens of *A Midsummer Night's Dream* is, by contrast, a small city, almost a village, a primitive democracy with an essentially benevolent ruler – a sentimental version of the London of 'Good Queen Bess', perhaps; and the Rome of *Julius Caesar, Antony and Cleopatra* and *Coriolanus* is a blood-soaked metropolis, where the mob struggles with the aristocracy for power, and it's unclear who's going to win – a perfect setting for a dramatisation of the growing differences between Parliament and Monarch in pre-revolutionary London, one might add.

Strongly influenced by classical models, seventeenth- and eighteenth-century drama tended to reserve contemporary settings for comedy, and mythological or historical settings for tragedy. Thus, the great comedies of the Restoration take place in modern England, while the much less popular tragedies have classical locations. Similarly, Racine and Corneille almost invariably chose a classical or Biblical past for their tragedies, while Molière's comedies are set in the French society of their time. The German Romantic dramatists, inspired by Shakespeare, resisted this dualism: several of Schiller's best plays are set in the European past while Goethe's are either classical or national. Kleist is especially eclectic with one play set in a Dutch village courthouse (*The Broken Jug*), two classical myths (*Penthesilea* and *Amphitryon*), a Prussian history play (*The Prince of Homburg*) and an epic South German chivalric romance (*Katie of Heilbronn*).

The nationalist plays of the nineteenth century usually had classical settings (as in Ibsen's 'world-historical' drama *Emperor and Galilean*) or took place in the country's mythological, or at least historical, past (as in *Peer Gynt*). In deciding to set his cycle of realistic plays in contemporary Norway, Ibsen made a decisive break,[14] but he was not the first playwright to do so: Turgenev's *A Month in the Country* and Ostrovsky's *The Storm* are both set in Tsarist Russia, while T W Robertson's 'cup and saucer' dramas are played out in

---

14   Several of Ibsen's plays take place in or near the capital, Christiania (now Oslo): *A Doll's House, Hedda Gabler, The Wild Duck* and *John Gabriel Borkman*. Others are set in more remote parts of Norway (*Ghosts, Rosmersholm* and *The Lady from the Sea*).

Victorian England. Ibsen's continental contemporaries, Bjørn-stjerne Bjørnson, Henry Becque and Gerhart Hauptmann, similarly rejected historical and mythical settings while in England Pinero, Galsworthy and Granville Barker all quickly took up Ibsen's challenge and used modern settings for their plays.

The first half of the twentieth century saw sporadic attempts to move beyond contemporary naturalistic settings. Brecht's locations were characteristically eclectic: he used a Kiplingesque India for *Man Equals Man*, a mythical London for *The Threepenny Opera*, a half-modern, half-ancient China for *The Good Person of Szechwan*, Southern Russia for *The Caucasian Chalk Circle*, the Central Europe of the Thirty Years War for *Mother Courage* and the Italian Renaissance for *Life of Galileo*. Dürrenmatt, Lorca, Anouilh, Ionesco and Beckett all rejected naturalism in search of something more universal and, since the early 1980s, British drama has often tried to break free of 'the kitchen sink'.

Nevertheless, especially in the British theatre, naturalism's commitment to contemporary settings has held its own. DH Lawrence's finest plays are set in the Nottinghamshire coalfields, while O'Casey's astonishing naturalist trilogy is located in the tenements and bars of 1920's Dublin. More recently, the successful dramatisation of Edward Bond's South London, Alan Bennett's Yorkshire, Harold Pinter's East End and Richard Bean's Hull suggest that, for the time being at least, a wholesale return to abstract, neoclassical or mythological settings is unlikely.

Spoken locations

Writing for a theatre that made hardly any attempt at physical illusion, Shakespeare managed to create a vivid sense of location with just a few words.

Look at how he indicates the weather: Borachio tells Conrade to 'stand thee then close under this penthouse, for it drizzles rain';[15] Hamlet agrees with Horatio that 'Tis a nipping and an eager air';[16]

---

15 *Much Ado About Nothing* (3.3)

16 *Hamlet* (1.4)

and, as a red sun appears over the fields of Shrewsbury, Henry IV
talks with his son, Hal, about the omens of the natural world:

KING

> How bloodily the sun begins to peer
> Above yon bulky hill. The day looks pale
> At his distemperature.

HAL

>   The southern wind
> Doth play the trumpet to his purposes
> And by the hollow whistling in the leaves
> Foretells a tempest and a blustering day.[17]

Antony and Cleopatra is one of Shakespeare's hardest plays to stage,
not just because of the richness of its characterisations, but also
because of its continuous and lightning quick shifts in location.
Designers sometimes try to bring on stage Rome and Egypt in all
their glory; Shakespeare, meanwhile, uses just a few key phrases to
give the audience everything it needs.

Modern drama often sets the scene with a few carefully chosen
words. The opening of Shelagh Delaney's debut *A Taste of Honey*
(1958) is a good example:

HELEN

> Well! This is the place.

JO

> And I don't like it.

HELEN

> When I find somewhere for us to live I have to consider
> something far more important than your feelings... the
> rent. It's all I can afford.

JO

> You can afford something better than this old ruin.

HELEN

> When you start earning you can start moaning.

---

17   *Henry IV Part One* (5.1)

Jo

> Can't be soon enough for me. I'm cold and my shoes let in water... what a place... and we're supposed to live off her immoral earnings.

HELEN

> I'm careful. Anyway, what's wrong with this place? Everything in it's falling apart, it's true, and we've no heating – but there's a lovely view of the gasworks, we share a bathroom with the community and this wallpaper's contemporary. What more do you want?[18]

Within moments, we've been told everything we need to imagine a 'comfortless flat in Manchester'.

Look at how John Arden conjures up a wintry northern town in the self-consciously poetic opening of *Serjeant's Musgrave's Dance* (1959):

> Brr, oh a cold winter, snow, dark. We wait too long, that's the trouble. Once you've started, keep on travelling. No good sitting to wait in the middle of it. Only makes the cold night colder.[19]

In much of the best drama, the setting is indicated by what is said, as much as by scenery or stage effects.

Act and Scene Numbers

There are various ways of dividing a play into units of action.

Greek drama makes a clear distinction between dialogue and chorus. The dialogue is always between just two characters, and consists of a mixture of set speeches and quick-fire 'stichomythia'. The chorus, by contrast, is written for a large number of voices speaking – or singing – together. Although the two forms are distinct, the overall effect is of a single sweep of action.

---

18   Shelagh Delaney *A Taste of Honey* (1958)

19   John Arden *Serjeant Musgrave's Dance* (1959)

The five-act form is the staple of Elizabethan and Jacobean drama. Where the manuscripts haven't survived, editors have imposed act and scene breaks, which tend to follow the basic action of classical drama. The critic and dramatist Gustav Freytag provided an influential analysis of the various phases of the five-act structure:[20]

1. Exposition
2. Rising action
3. Climax
4. Falling Action
5. Denouement (or catastrophe)

Although this was intended to describe a typical arc of action, it has limited value and should be seen within the context of German nineteenth-century dramaturgy. Many five act plays place the climax in Act Four or even Act Five, and Freytag neglects the phenomenon of the double climax. Shakespeare, especially, wrote with a freedom of movement that defies such limitations.

Until naturalism, however, most dramatists followed these basic divisions of acts and scenes (although sometimes in just three acts). With many writers (Molière, Marivaux, Holberg and others) the entrance of each new character marks a new scene, but each act consists of a continuous movement. There are exceptions: Kleist's *Katie of Heilbronn* and *The Prince of Homburg* have different locations within each act, while in *Amphitryon* and *Penthesilea* the individual acts flow uninterrupted. A continuous act betrays the writer's neo-classical ambitions, while an episodic approach usually results from a self-conscious imitation of Shakespeare.

Nineteenth-century naturalist drama tends to maintain the basic act form but dispenses with individual scenes. Thus, Chekhov's four great comedies are all in four uninterrupted acts while most of Ibsen's plays are in three (although *Hedda Gabler* and *John Gabriel Borkman* have four and *The Lady from the Sea* has five). These acts are not subdivided into smaller units and if a change of

---

20   Gustav Freytag *Die Technik des Dramas* (1863)

location is required a new act is introduced. Strindberg dispensed with these conventions as he moved away from naturalism.

Brecht declared provocatively that 'Petroleum resists the five act structure' and, looking for a theatrical form appropriate for the modern world, gave his epic dramas simply numbered scenes. Only *The Threepenny Opera*, with its conscious pastiche of classical opera, and the early expressionist plays, are written in acts. Some modern writers follow Brecht, or fragment the action into even smaller, less fixed units of action. Most, however, follow the conventions established by the naturalists, and, increasingly, have two acts of roughly equal length.

Act breaks offer the audience the opportunity for a rest. It's thought that the action at the Globe was regularly interrupted for short intervals. Many nineteenth century and early twentieth century plays allowed for two intervals. Nowadays, this causes problems for producers: *A Doll's House*, *French Without Tears* and *Rosencrantz And Guildenstern are Dead* are all written in three acts: one interval divides the evening unequally while two can make it too long. The vast majority of modern plays only allow for one interval, or have no break at all.

The clashes of voices

It's useful to think about a play in musical terms, and hear the sound of the clashing voices, and the headlong energy that it creates.

Listen to the tremendous noise that opens *Julius Caesar:*

FLAVIUS

    Hence, home, you idle creatures get you home.
    Is this a holiday? What, know you not
    Being mechanical, you ought not walk
    Upon a labouring day without the sign
    Of your profession? Speak, what trade art thou?

FIRST COMMONER

    Why, sir, a carpenter.

MARULLUS

    Where is thy leather apron and thy rule?

What dost thou with thy best apparel on?
You, sir, what trade are you?

SECOND COMMONER

Truly, sir, in respect of a fine workman, I am but, as you
would say, a cobbler.

MARULLUS

But what trade art thou? Answer me directly.

SECOND COMMONER

A trade, sir, that, I hope, I may use with a safe conscience.
Which is, indeed, sir, a mender of bad soles.

MARULLUS

What trade, thou knave? Thou naughty knave, what trade?

SECOND COMMONER

Nay, I beseech you, sir, be not out with me. Yet, if you be
out, sir, I can mend you.

MARULLUS

What meanest thou by that? Mend me, thou saucy fellow?

SECOND COMMONER

Why, sir, cobble you?

FLAVIUS

Thou art a cobbler, art thou?

SECOND COMMONER

Truly, sir, all that I live by is with the awl. I meddle
with no tradesman's matters, nor women's matters,
but with awl. I am indeed, sir, a surgeon to old shoes.
When they are in great danger, I recover them.[21]

In Flavius and Marullus' insistent, dismissive interrogations, and
the two commoners' quietly subversive replies, we can hear the
tensions of the Jacobean London street: a ruling class desperately
trying to control a mob that's increasingly determined to stand
up for itself. The result is a clash of dissonant voices, a startling
opening to a play about the slide into civil war.

---

21   *Julius Caesar* (1.1)

Schiller pulls off an astonishing trick in *Mary Stuart* (1800) when Mary first tastes the freedom of the open air. He shifts verse form from unrhyming Alexandrines, to a much more expansive, alternating A-B-A-B structure:

> Liberty! O how I feel it so sweetly!
> Let me be young, be young with me!
> Step like a child so swiftly and fleetly
> Over the green of the meadow and the lea!
> Am I escaped from the prison that bound me?
> Am I no longer to stifle there?
> Oh how I thirst for this freedom around me,
> Let me drink deep of the heavenly air![22]

It's a brilliant moment that crucially changes the balance of sympathy in the play.

Scenic Rhythm

The best classical dramatists keep changing the rhythm of the action.

Ibsen is a master of this, with many of his most settled conversations interrupted by a powerful, dramatic action. No moment is more striking than the end of *Hedda Gabler* where he deliberately settles the action into almost inconsequential stillness before the final catastrophe:

TESMAN *at the writing desk*
> She's upset to see us at such a tragic task. Mrs Elvsted,
> I tell you what: why don't you move in with Aunt Julia?
> I'll come round every evening. We'll sit and work there.
> Work there!

MRS ELVSTED
> It might be best –

---

22   Friedrich Schiller *Mary Stuart* translated by FJ Lamport (1969)

HEDDA *from inner room*
> I hear what you're saying, Tesman. And what will I do, every evening here?

TESMAN *turning over the papers*
> I'm sure His Honour will be kind enough to call.

BRACK *calling cheerfully from the armchair*
> Mrs Tesman, every evening! We'll have such a jolly time…

HEDDA *clearly and audibly*
> You really hope so, Judge Brack. Cock of the walk –

> *We hear a shot inside. Tesman, Mrs Elvsted and Brack jump to their feet.*

TESMAN
> She's playing with those guns again.

> *He pulls the curtains and runs in, followed by Mrs Elvsted. Hedda is lying dead on the sofa. Noise and confusion. Enter Berta right, beside herself. Tesman shrieks at Brack.*

> Shot herself! In the temple! Shot herself!

BRACK *slumping in the chair*
> No one does that. No one.[23]

Ibsen's control of tension is masterful, and the shot, which we've been expecting since we first saw the pistols at the end of Act One, comes as a terrible surprise. With the opening of the alcove curtains we are confronted with the final tragic tableau of the dead Hedda with a smoking pistol in her hand.

Another example is the long and involved conversation between Macduff and Malcolm in the 'England scene' in *Macbeth*. Shakespeare asks us to listen to Malcolm's confessions of his failings as a man and his unsuitability to be king. Having provoked Macduff's righteous rage ('Fit to rule? No, not to live.'), Malcolm finally admits that none of it is true, and we see that his purpose was to test Macduff's integrity. The two are briefly united in their resolu-

---

23   Henrik Ibsen *Hedda Gabler* translated by Kenneth McLeish (1995)

tion to fight Macbeth, but are interrupted by Ross's arrival. But this is elongated too, and Shakespeare ratchets up the dramatic tension. It's a scene rich with misunderstandings, hesitations and one of the most heartbreaking expressions of grief in world drama. It deserves to be quoted in its entirety:

MACDUFF
See, who comes here?

MALCOLM
My countryman, but yet I know him not.

MACDUFF
My ever gentle cousin, welcome hither.

MALCOLM
I know him now. Good God, betimes remove
The means that makes us strangers.

ROSS
                                                          Sir, amen.

MACDUFF
Stands Scotland where it did?

ROSS
                                              Alas, poor country.
Almost afraid to know itself. It cannot
Be called our mother, but our grave. Where nothing
But who knows nothing, is once seen to smile.
Where sighs and groans and shrieks that rend the air
Are made, not marked. Where violent sorrow seems
A modern ecstasy. The dead man's knell
Is there scarce asked for who and good men's lives
Expire before the flowers in their caps
Dying or ere they sicken.

MACDUFF
                                      O relation
Too nice, and yet too true.

MALCOLM
                                          What's the newest grief?

ROSS
That of an hour's age doth hiss the speaker.

Each minute teems a new one.

MACDUFF

How does my wife?

ROSS

Why, well.

MACDUFF

And all my children?

ROSS

Well too.

MACDUFF

The tyrant has not battered at their peace?

ROSS

No, they were well at peace when I did leave em.

MACDUFF

Be not a niggard of your speech. How goes it?

ROSS

When I came hither to transport the tidings
Which I have heavily borne, there ran a rumour
Of many worthy fellows that were out
Which was to my belief witnessed the rather
For that I saw the tyrant's power afoot.
Now is the time of help. Your eye in Scotland
Would create soldiers, make our women fight
To doff their dire distresses.

MALCOLM

Be it their comfort
We are coming thither. Gracious England hath
Lent us good Siward and ten thousand men.
An older and a better soldier none
That Christendom gives out.

ROSS

Would I could answer
This comfort with the like. But I have words
That would be howled out in the desert air
Where hearing should not latch them.

MACDUFF

What concern they?

The general cause? Or is it a fee grief
Due to some single breast?

ROSS

No mind that's honest
But in it shares some woe, though the main part
Pertains to you alone.

MACDUFF

If it be mine
Keep it not from me. Quickly let me have it.

ROSS

Let not your ears despise my tongue for ever
Which shall possess them with the heaviest sound
That ever yet they heard.

MACDUFF

Hum. I guess at it.

ROSS

Your castle is surprised. Your wife and babes
Savagely slaughtered. To relate the manner
Were, on the quarry of these murdered deer
To add the death of you.

MALCOLM

Merciful heaven.
What, man? Never pull your hat upon your brows.
Give sorrow words. The grief that does not speak
Whispers the over-fraught heart and bids it break.

MACDUFF

My children too?

ROSS

Wife, children, servants, all
That could be found.

MACDUFF

And I must be from thence?
My wife killed too?

Ross

        I have said.

Malcolm

               Be comforted.
Let's make us medicines of our great revenge
To cure this deadly grief.

Macduff

He has no children. All my pretty ones?
Did you say all? O hell-kite. All?
What, all my pretty chickens and their dam
At one fell swoop?

Malcolm

         Dispute it like a man.

Macduff

I shall do so.
But I must also feel it as a man.
I cannot but remember such things were
That were most precious to me.[24]

Playwriting of this quality resists all interpretation and deserves to be read and staged with discretion, honesty and deep realism. And it makes it even harder to answer the all-important next question: what does the play mean?

---

24   *Macbeth* (4.3)

10. What does it mean?

IF WE EXPECT WRITTEN drama to tell us truths about life, we will eventually be confronted with the really hard questions: 'What is the point of this play?' 'What does it all add up to?' and 'What does it mean?'

There are easy exam-passing answers: 'Oh, *A Doll's House* is about feminism'; '*Hamlet* is about indecision'; or '*Mother Courage* is about money and war'. But these fail to grasp the contradictory nature of drama and we could counter them with a set of equally valid opposite interpretations: '*A Doll's House* is about patriarchal oppression'; '*Hamlet* is about seizing the moment'; or '*Mother Courage* is about poverty and peace'.

Furthermore, the question is built on a false premise. In most contexts the first function of any play is to entertain, not provide 'meaning'. 'Nothing needs less justification than pleasure', Brecht declared, and not just laughter machines like Ben Travers' *Rookery Nook* or Ray Cooney's *Run For Your Wife* but comic masterpieces like *As You Like It* or *The Importance of Being Earnest*, are fully justified by the pleasure they so successfully generate. Meaning comes second to entertainment, and we shouldn't confuse the two.

What's more, the search for meaning assumes that there is a meaning to be found. There's a counter-argument that drama – and all art – has no meaning at all and that to insist on one puts artistic activity in a straitjacket. The terms of this argument – 'art for art's sake', in fact – are too complex for the purposes of this chapter, but we should temper our celebration of the value of written drama with the reflection that perhaps it has no meaning at all.

Conflict

Good drama depends on conflict: one person wants one thing and another wants the opposite. The result is struggle and it's here,

179

if meaning in drama does exist, that we're most likely to find it. Hegel defined tragedy as 'the collision of mutually exclusive but equally legitimate causes' and in the best plays it's often difficult to know for certain who's right and who's wrong. Indeed, one could say that the more finely balanced the conflict, the more striking its resolution.

Thus in Sophocles' *Antigone* we see the age old struggle between the state – Creon's decree that the body of the traitor Polyneices should lie unburied on the battlefield – and the individual – Antigone's insistence on burying her brother. In bad adaptations (and productions), this balance is broken, usually in favour of Antigone's rebelliousness.[1] Sophocles, however, goes out of his way to show Creon's reasons:

> No one who is an enemy of the State
> Shall ever be any friend of mine.
> The State, the Fatherland, is everything
> To us, the ship we all sail in.
> If she sinks, we all drown,
> And friendship drowns with us. That's my policy:
> A policy of service to the Commonwealth.
> And in pursuance of that policy,
> I have issued an official State decree
> Concerning the sons of Oedipus.
> Eteocles, who died fighting for his country,
> And with exceptional bravery, we shall bury him
> With all the honours and funeral ceremonies
> Customary for a man who died a hero.
> The other, the outcast, the exile
> His brother Polyneices, who retuned here
> At the head of a foreign army, to destroy
> His homeland, to burn down the city
> And reduce the people to a condition of slavery
> Or kill them in the streets – I have ordered
> That he have no grave at all.

---

1   For an account of the many ways that Sophocles' masterpiece has been interpreted see George Steiner *Antigones* (1979)

No one is left to bury him, or mourn for him.
His body is to be left in the open, uncovered,
A stinking feast for the scavengers,
Dogs and crows, a sight to inspire terror.
I intend to make it quite plain
That never, under my administration,
Will people, who commit crimes against the state
Reap any benefits from their actions: and at the expense
Of honest decent citizens too.[2]

Creon isn't just interested in wielding power: his argument is born out of a deep commitment to the wellbeing of the state as a whole. Antigone's act of rebellion is an expression of the individual but not of the broader good. To interpret the play as a celebration of heroic rebellion in the face of tyranny is to underestimate Sophocles: the revolutionary Antigone declares that the law is wrong and should be broken, while the ruler Creon argues – like most of us – that the law is all that stands between order and chaos. The play shows the validity of both positions and dramatises the inevitable crisis when the two come into conflict.

The Cherry Orchard revolves around a similar irreconcilable clash, but this time between different social classes: the decayed aristocracy to which Ranyevskaya and her brother, Gaev, belong on the one hand, and Lopakhin's upwardly mobile peasantry on the other. For all the touching humanity of their private relationship (Lopakhin is besotted with Ranyevskaya while she's wracked by confused feelings of *noblesse oblige* towards him), the conflict embodies the dialectic of the time. Neither is wholly wrong nor completely right and Chekhov's astonishing technique ensures that the play achieves both the ironic objectivity of comedy and the cruel inevitability of true tragedy.

Another example is the triangular relationship between Angelo, Isabella and Claudio in *Measure for Measure*. Isabella would rather die than sleep with Angelo; her brother, Claudio, would rather she slept with Angelo than that he should be executed for sleeping

---

2   Sophocles *Antigone* translated by Don Taylor (1986)

with Juliet; but Angelo, under whose sentence Claudio has been condemned, is determined to sleep with Isabella. The complexity of Shakespeare's multiple perspectives makes Isabella's visit to Claudio in the prison agonising to watch. Claudio is a healthy young man, terrified of death. But he's also the noble brother and only surviving relative of Isabella, and his first duty is to protect her honour. What's more, she's a young woman of impeccable intellectual and religious convictions; she loves and admires her brother, but would be destroyed if she gave in to Angelo's request. Each of these positions is expressed to the full: even the sexual awakening of Angelo, for all its hypocrisy, is a fundamental part of his humanity. The clash of these irreconcilable positions leaves us incapable of drawing a narrow moral: the action provides us with a complex play of moral perspectives, culminating in the all-embracing possibility of forgiveness, marriage and new life. If *Measure for Measure* has a meaning, it's to be glimpsed in the working out of an impossible situation, in an understanding that the world is complex and cannot be seen in simple terms of good and bad, right or wrong.

Counterpointing

Great dramatists often structure their plays in such a way that different plot lines interlink and eventually connect. This has a profound effect on what they mean.

A Doll's House doesn't say that all wives should leave their husbands. What Ibsen shows, instead, is the process whereby one particular wife, Nora, realises that leaving her husband, Torvald, is the best possible outcome to her particular situation. He counterpoints this with the reconciliation of another woman, the divorced Mrs Linde, with her first love, the disgraced moneylender Krogstad. And so the play is concerned with the complexity of relations between men and women and, if it recommends anything, it's the need to pursue your own individual truth, free of the pressures of society and of others. As Ibsen himself wrote: 'I believe that none of us can do anything other or anything better than realise ourselves in spirit and in truth.' The contradictory – dialectical even –

outcome of *A Doll's House* bears out the comprehensive vision of this statement.

Shakespeare employs a similar stereoscopic technique. *King Lear* tells the stories of two families, and each reflects on the other. Gloucester's belief in the illegitimate Edmund's allegation of the legitimate Edgar's patricidal intentions provides a dramatic echo-chamber to the King's own disastrous trusting of his two elder daughters' protestations of love. As the play progresses, the two stories cut across each other, climaxing with Lear in a hovel, contemplating Poor Tom, (the exiled Edgar in disguise) and the 'poor naked wretches' in all their 'bare, forked' reality. When the mad King and the blind Earl finally meet each other on Dover Cliff (4.6), they present an image of old age and fatherhood, performing in an equal but opposite double act. The play's meaning lies in these mutually reinforcing narratives.

Such complex counter pointing requires great dramatic skill, and lesser writers sometimes find it hard to link the subplot to the main plot. *The Changeling*, which was written by two authors, sets Thomas Middleton's story of the aristocrat Beatrice-Joanna's murderous lust against William Rowley's tale of two young men who pretend to be insane in order to seduce the wife of a lunatic asylum keeper, is a good example. Both plots share the same theme (what would you do for love?) and are brought together in the closing movement of the play, but it's a tenuous link, made harder by the very different writing styles of the two playwrights.

Modern drama tends to dispose with subplots. Brecht often used contrasting narratives within one play to make his point and some writers – Edward Bond and Howard Barker, for example – employ an epic, jump cut technique that requires the audience to take in contradictory points of view. Usually, however, the single focus and limited physical means of modern drama prohibit it.

Alien ideologies

One of the most common mistakes in searching for the meaning of a play, is to impose an alien ideology onto a text.

A striking example is E M W Tillyard's appropriation of Ulysses' famous speech about 'degree' in *Troilus and Cressida* (1.3) as evidence for his theory of the primacy of social order in Shakespeare, who, he claims, subscribes to a doctrine which:

> Is primarily political but evidently goes far beyond mere practical politics. First we learn that the order which prevails in the heavens is duplicated on earth, the king corresponding to the sun; then that disorder in the heavens breeds disorder on earth, both in the physical sublunary organisation and in the commonwealth of men. When Shakespeare calls degree the ladder to all high designs he probably has another correspondence in mind; that between the ascending grades of man in his social state and the ladder of creation or chain of being which stretched from the meanest piece of inanimate matter in unbroken ascent to the highest of the archangels.[3]

This view has been frequently lambasted, usually by people who prefer to ignore the reality of civil war and the bloody consequences of a breakdown of social order. But there are real problems with Tillyard's approach, whatever one thinks of his political conclusions.

The first is that he fails to take into account the context in which the speech appears. Agamemnon has asked why it is 'that after seven years siege yet Troy walls stand' and Ulysses' answer is a direct reprimand. When pressed as to the 'remedy', Ulysses explains that 'The Great Achilles upon a lazy bed / The livelong day lies mocking our designs'.[4] In other words, the real threat to order comes from the top: not only is Agamemnon failing to impose his authority, but Achilles is showing insufficient respect for his own class. Ulysses is exploiting a private feud to make a general point: respect for 'degree' may be important, but here it's being deployed as the solution to a ruling class in crisis.

3   EMW Tillyard *Shakespeare's History Plays* (1944)

4   *Troilus and Cressida* (1.3)

Second, *Troilus and Cressida* is a late, dark, scholarly play, probably written for the Inns of Court, set in a world in which social order and hierarchy is breaking down. In such a context, Ulysses is indulging in mere nostalgia. What's more, his views are ignored and the chaos persists – evidence perhaps of the truth of his argument, but also of the futility of making it in those circumstances. In other words, Shakespeare debates war and disorder from several different points of view and Ulysses is presented as just another squabbling Greek. Tillyard's mistake is that he identifies with what a character says and presumes that the writer is speaking through him.

Finally, and most importantly, Tillyard fails to engage with the realities of the time. Although Jacobean society was divided into a number of class categories, these were crumbling. Tillyard proposes Ulysses' opinion as a warning, when the disorder that he's predicting is already the dominant reality. There was, of course, an active debate about how society should be organised and the sense of increasing chaos was answered by calls for a reassertion of the 'natural order', but Shakespeare's plays dramatise the debate, and aren't works of propaganda. The world was being turned upside down and the plays reflect that turmoil as much as they articulate the forces that were trying to prevent it.

There are many other examples of alien ideologies being applied anachronistically – from Hitler's appropriation of *The Merchant of Venice* to the automatic reflexes of the politically correct – and the important thing is to try to recognise the bias that inevitably informs all such interpretations, whether we agree with them or not.

Philosophical insights

One of the key roles of all art is to offer insights into human life and help answer the great philosophical questions of why we're born and why we have to die. Of course, art can never answer these questions definitively, but, by watching a fictional enactment of common human experience with a degree of critical detachment, we may at least find a meaningful way of asking them.

Nowhere is the philosophical role of drama clearer than in the different attitudes to suffering evident in tragedy. Here, there are as many different answers as there are periods of drama. In Greek tragedy, suffering is presented as a necessity that will appease the angry gods. In *King Lear* (perhaps the most potent fusion of humanism with Christianity), the sufferings of the mad King and the blind Earl play a fundamental role in reforming a society that has gone badly wrong. In modern political drama, suffering is presented as a direct result of a disordered world or – as in *Mother Courage* – of our support for the systems that oppress us. And in a time in which religion has lost its power and political change seems impossible, *Waiting for Godot* offers no consolation whatsoever. This is what life is like, Beckett says: cruel, absurd and full of suffering. The best we can do is put one foot in front of the other: 'No matter. Try again. Fail again. Fail better.'[5]

Of course, these various philosophical positions overlap, and the best plays provide contradictory and multiple accounts of human suffering. But however many philosophical systems they draw on, good plays try to help us understand the meaning of life – or, at least, accept its absence.

Emblems and symbols

Drama approaches its subject through metaphor. Metaphor enhances the power of the narrative and lifts the play beyond literalism into a complex web of significance. By listening to the patterns of imagery and metaphor we grasp the writer's insights into life and the world.

Thus the wood outside Athens in *A Midsummer Night's Dream* is both a real destination for people needing to leave the city, and a metaphorical location for the upheavals of love and sexual desire. The storm in *King Lear* is all too real – 'With hey, ho, the wind and

---

5   Samuel Beckett *Worstward Ho* (1983)

the rain', sings the Fool – but it also reflects the tempest in the old man's mind. And the grave being dug for the young suicide, Ophelia, allows for a profound statement about the inevitability of death and the transience of all living things:

HAMLET

> To what base uses we may return, Horatio. Why, may not imagination trace the noble dust of Alexander till he find it stopping a bunghole?

HORATIO

> Twere to consider too curiously to consider so.

HAMLET

> No, faith, not a jot. But to follow him thither with modesty enough, and likelihood to lead it as thus: Alexander died, Alexander was buried, Alexander returneth into dust, the dust is earth, of earth we make loam, and why of that loam, whereto he was converted, might they not stop a beer-barrel?[6]

Metaphor in Shakespeare takes many different forms. When Lear talks of his 'pelican daughters'[7] we see the young carnivorous animals pecking at their father's flesh. When Hamlet speaks of 'the undiscovered country from whose bourn / no traveller returns'[8] we're given a potent image of death as a strange land far across a huge ocean. And when Helena speaks of her and Hermia's friendship as having grown like 'A double cherry seeming parted / But an union in partition'[9] we see fruit in a perfect moment of budding, but also two young women at their most fertile.

Of course, poetic metaphor is not confined to Shakespeare. The sexual intimacy of *The Changeling* is expressed in language rich with images of dark passages, private gardens, and, most importantly, the father's proud and mighty castle. In Racine's *Phèdre* the verse continually returns to images of the sky, the sea and the

---

6   *Hamlet* (5.1)

7   *King Lear* (3.4)

8   *Hamlet* (3.1)

9   *A Midsummer Night's Dream* (3.2)

blood-soaked earth. And in Kleist's *The Broken Jug*, the balmy night in which Adam tried to climb into Eve's bedroom ('this January night as warm / as May') is a potent image of the Garden of Eden before the Fall.

Furthermore, the renunciation of verse by the naturalists did not lead them to ignore metaphor. *A Doll's House* isn't just the story of a marriage; it also explores permanence and change, freedom and society, truth and lies. The Helmers' apartment is a territory thick with metaphor – Torvald's locked study door, the piano in the corner, the daylight outside, and so on. *The Cherry Orchard* is similarly rich with images of innocence – the nursery, the cherry trees and the rural shrine – on the one hand, and the onward march into the future – the telegraph poles, the town in the distance and Lopahkin's men taking axes to the cherry trees – on the other. For Chekhov and Ibsen, the domestic and the everyday is imbued with metaphorical and poetic power.

At the start of the twentieth century a new kind of drama emerged which harked back to classical poetic drama and made the play of symbols and metaphor explicit. This reaction against naturalism arose from the desire to make drama capable of exploring the subconscious and expressing deeper truths about the human condition. Ironically, as a direct result of this search for the transcendent and universal, symbolist drama has not aged well and strikes many as arch and self-conscious. More positively, two of the greatest plays of the period (both with avian titles) contain both symbolism and a self-conscious reaction against it: in *The Seagull*, Nina is forced to deal with the real consequences of a symbolic action – Konstantin's shooting of the seagull – just as in *The Wild Duck* the elevation of a domestic pet into a sacrificial offering leads inexorably to the death of young Hedvig.

Although metaphor and symbol are fundamental to good drama we should be careful not to see them everywhere. Picasso's patron, Gertrude Stein, rightly declared that 'a rose is a rose is a rose' and, pressed by an actor on the meaning of a particular line, Harold Pinter said with his customary saltiness: 'Mind your own fucking business'. The most potent symbols – Desdemona's handkerchief,

Ranyevskaya's cherry orchard, Mother Courage's cart – are embodied in the action of the play, and aren't grafted on to it to give it a false poetic status.

Contemporary relevance

One of the most common ways of approaching plays from the past is to read them in modern terms. Nowhere is this more prevalent than in the discussion of Shakespeare.

Jan Kott was a distinguished Polish critic, whose views were formed during the Nazi occupation and under Communism. He saw Shakespeare as a writer whose plays could provide a mirror image to his own time and preoccupations. His book *Shakespeare Our Contemporary* was one of the most influential works of criticism of the twentieth century. As Peter Brook's *Preface* to the English edition says:

> It is Poland that in our time has come closest to the tumult, the intensity, the imaginativeness and the daily involvement with the social process that made life so horrible, subtle and ecstatic to an Elizabethan. So it is quite naturally up to a Pole to point us the way.[10]

Kott draws fascinating parallels between his society and Shakespeare's: the political murders of mid twentieth-century Eastern Europe and the history plays; the philosophical nihilism of Samuel Beckett and *King Lear*; and the psycho-sexual revolution of the 1960s and *A Midsummer Night's Dream*. He approaches these familiar texts with a directness that provokes the reader to think about them in radically new ways. His book blew the cobwebs off Shakespearean studies and ushered in a new and stimulating way of staging the plays.

But Kott's approach causes as many problems as it solves. The first is that it places an overarching emphasis on the single image – Titania in love with the donkey's head, Lear pulling on his boots,

---

10   Jan Kott *Shakespeare our Contemporary* (1964)

the remorseless cycle of political murder – at the expense of the story. Kott discovers resonance, and even relevance, in isolated moments, but cannot trace it in the arc of the dramatic action: the icon replaces the story and dynamic change is ignored in favour of the static picture.

Furthermore, Kott fails to recognise Shakespeare's interest in history. As the Hungarian Marxist critic Georg Lukács wrote in a (badly translated) letter to Kott:

> Where I disagree with you most deeply is the fact that you interpret the Shakespearean understanding of history from an historical perspective of the Kafka frame of reference of our time. As far as I understand Shakespeare, his central historical problem was the dissolution of feudalism in the form of a self-destruction in the War of the Roses. But he already understood the Tudor period as a separation from these battles... This understanding runs though all the later dramas in which moral-ideological problems of the feudal period are dealt with.[11]

In other words, by denying the particular nature of history and preferring to emphasise the repetitive and cyclical pattern of what he calls the 'Grand Mechanism' of murder, Kott neglects Shakespeare's grasp of historical processes and social change.

The most significant problem is that Kott ignores the particular context in which the action of the plays take place: violence, cruelty, appetite, ambition and greed may recur throughout human history, but their significance is different according to the circumstances in which they appear. Killing a king is very different from betraying your party leader; even sex subtly changes its meaning within a generation. By fusing the past with the present, Kott does an injustice to both.

This notion of contemporary relevance is often cited as the best way of getting young people interested in the great plays from the past: however, laudable as it is to help students grasp the

---

11   Reprinted in *Science and Society*, New York, Spring (1977)

energy of the original, such intellectual sleights of hand can prove counterproductive.

Changing relevance

If contemporaneity is a dead end, most useful in providing striking images in the theatre, it's perhaps more rewarding to consider the changing relevance – or resonance – of an old play.

I remember in 1982 thinking that Fortinbras' Captain must have known about the Falklands War when he explains to Hamlet:

> Truly to speak and with no addition
> We go to gain a little patch of ground
> That hath in it no profit but the name.
> To pay five ducats, five, I would not farm it
> Nor will it yield to Norway or the Pole
> A ranker rate should it be sold in fee.[12]

And I was struck to hear Kate in *The Taming of the Shrew* answering Petruchio's perfectly cordial greeting, 'Good morrow, Kate, for that's your name I hear,' in the language and cadences of the 'bolshie' teenager:

> Well have you heard, but something hard of hearing.
> They call me Katherine that do talk of me.[13]

It's uncanny how often Shakespeare echoes across the centuries. But, of course, such relevance is the result of mere coincidence, inevitable in a writer blessed with the ability to convey such a wide range of human experiences and on whose cadences and wit so much of modern English phraseology is based.

Nineteenth-century writers can surprise us too. Listen to Astrov in *Uncle Vanya* lamenting the destruction of the natural environment:

---

12   *Hamlet* (4.4)

13   *The Taming of the Shrew* (2.1)

I don't mind people cutting wood from necessity, but why destroy the forests? Our Russian forests are groaning under the axe, millions of trees are perishing, the habitats of animals and birds are being laid waste, rivers are shrinking and drying up, the most wonderful landscapes are disappearing, never to return, all because some lazy individual hasn't the wit to bend down and pick up his firewood from the ground… A man would need to be a mindless savage to burn up such beauty in his stove, to destroy what he cannot create. We've been endowed with reason, and creative power, so we can increase what has been given to us, but up to now we've created nothing, only destroyed. There are fewer and fewer forests, the rivers are running dry, wild life is becoming extinct, the climate's ruined, and with each passing day the earth gets poorer and uglier.[14]

It's difficult to read this today without thinking about climate change.

Many other playwrights have the same prophetic knack, be it Sean O'Casey writing about terrorism in *The Shadow of a Gunman* (1923), Bernard Shaw on the sale of weapons in *Arms and the Man* (1894), or Brecht on the close alliance between demagoguery and business interests in *The Resistible Rise of Arturo Ui* (1941). Ironically, if happily, some political playwrights discover that their plays have become irrelevant. Thus, the great early plays of Athol Fugard – above all, *Sizwe Bansi is Dead* (1972), *The Island* (1973) and *Statements after an Arrest Under the Immorality Act* (1974) – are so rooted in their time and place, and so committed to criticising apartheid, that they lost much of their relevance with the election of a black majority government in 1994. Of course, they present a powerful image of the dignity of the human spirit under an immoral regime, and apply metaphorically wherever prejudice and injustice hold sway. But their greatness lies in their specificity, and as the world moves forwards, so they – thankfully – slide into history.

---

14   Anton Chekhov *Uncle Vanya* translated by Stephen Mulrine (1999)

Brecht's highly controversial music theatre piece *The Decision* (1930) is another example. Written as a learning play for German communists agitating for revolution in the last years of the Weimar Republic, it reads today like a historical curiosity from a vanished time. But the scale of Brecht's liturgical conception and the sheer power of Hanns Eisler's Bach-like choruses make it an exhilarating parable of commitment in the face of impossible odds. It's a manual for anyone involved in illegal opposition to a regime, in the name of a cause he knows to be right: revolutionaries, freedom fighters and political activists of all kinds.

Let Cassius have the last word on the changing relevance of political drama:

> How many ages hence
> Shall this our lofty scene be acted over
> In states unborn and accents yet unknown.[15]

The important thing is to recognize that while the actions may seem superficially similar, their expression and meaning is continually changing.

Universal meaning?

It's perhaps inevitable that the best works of art are hailed as 'universal' in their reach and importance.

The notion of the 'universal genius' has its roots in the Renaissance idea of the 'world spirit', the classical figure – Plato, Socrates, Aristotle, Virgil, Homer and Ovid are the chief contenders – who are able to speak for all humanity. In the late eighteenth century this idea was appropriated by the Romantics, who believed in the great poets whose words could reach beyond the superficial features of their time and describe something deep within the human soul – 'the unacknowledged legislators of the world', as Shelley called them.[16]

---

15   *Julius Caesar* (3.1)

16   Percy Bysshe Shelley *In Defence of Poetry* (1821)

Ben Jonson declared that Shakespeare was 'not of an age but for all time'[17] and adherents of the notion of the 'universal genius' often echo this early judgment. They claim that the plays are so great that they speak to all of humanity and can be understood by everyone, regardless of background, culture, age, religion, language or period. They believe that human beings are fundamentally the same, whatever their circumstances, and that 'human nature' does not change.

In the twentieth century, claims for Shakespeare's universality were mostly associated with a conservative, even nationalist position, which implied that the greatest product of English culture must have a universal appeal because Englishness itself is universal. In recent years, ironically, the same view has gathered support from multi-culturalists who dismiss all claims that Shakespeare's writing might be culturally specific as exclusive or even racist.

The universalist position takes support from an undeniable fact: the ability of the plays to entertain audiences throughout the world, and their adaptability to wildly different contexts, from college students on the South Side of Chicago to peasants in Kazakhstan. The pursuit of universalism has often been liberating in the theatre, and given houseroom to many different approaches: an Icelandic *Romeo and Juliet* with actors suspended from trapezes, a Zulu *Macbeth*, a *Richard III* set in the Third Reich, and hundreds of others. Nor should we ignore the way that the plays reveal themselves in new contexts: as the world changes different elements come to the fore.

Unfortunately, champions of the universalist approach tend to ignore several obstinate facts. The first is that the plays have their roots in popular material: folk tales, classical legends, Italian novellas, religious stories and national history. The fusion of these diverse elements is fundamental, but it's a mistake to ascribe Shakespeare's popularity solely to his own powers of invention: he was writing for a commercial theatre and a great part of his success derived

---

17   Ben Jonson 'To the memory of my beloved, the author Master William Shakespeare, and what he hath left us.'

from the way that he used existing popular conventions for his own ends.

Furthermore, many of the claims made for Shakespeare's universal appeal are based on the plays being presented in translation. Although no translator can reproduce the ambiguities, references and overall linguistic cunning of the original, the plays can spring to life with an immediacy that is impossible in four hundred year old English. In other words, the advantages of translation shouldn't be taken as evidence of universality.

Finally, we shouldn't forget the irregular and often antiquated surfaces of the writing itself. These are sometimes dismissed as insignificant details which obscure the 'secret Shakespeare' lurking beneath: the unchanging human dramas which, commentators say, are handed down from generation to generation across the world. But while it's true that Shakespeare used every means possible to convey depth and three-dimensionality and that his plays boast an unprecedented range of cultural cross-references, an approach that neglects the particular way in which he wrote can only be superficial itself.

The limits of theatrical interpretation

People who work in the theatre often claim that the best way to understand a play is to see it performed – and I've made the case for it throughout. But the same people then often argue that the theatre – and playwriting for that matter – can only be kept alive by a continuous process of re-interpretation and conceptual intervention, in other words by the involvement of the director as *auteur*.

At this point a caveat should be offered. Not only is a bad production the best way to kill a play stone dead, the current trend for directorial interpretation results in highly partial readings. Thus, a production of *King Lear* set in a police state, of *Macbeth* that takes place in an abattoir or of *Julius Caesar* set in post-invasion Iraq, are all in danger of simplifying the contradictory texture of the original. Conceptual productions are most admired by people who know the play well, but often render it obscure for people seeing it for the first time. They replace the idiosyncratic nature of the play with an alien vision: in stressing novel interpretations, they distort the lively, if often awkward, shapes of the original.

Speaking about the reaction against what he called 'the ghastly boredom of traditional productions', Brecht observed that:

> Actors and producers, many of them talented, set out to remedy this by thinking up new and hitherto unknown sensational effects, which are however of a purely formalist kind: that is to say, they are forcibly imposed on the work, on its content and on its message, so that even worse damage results than with traditional-style productions, for in this case message and content are not merely dulled or flattened out but absolutely distorted. Formalist 'revival' of the classics is the answer to stuffy tradition, and it is the wrong one. It is as if a piece of meat had gone off and were only made palatable by saucing and spicing it up.[18]

In other words, when we see a play in the theatre we need to remember that we're watching a partial account. And when we read a play and try to elucidate its deeper meanings, we should, above all, attend to the original text in front of us.

That's certainly essential if we are to answer the most elusive question of all: is it any good?

---

18   See 'Classical Status as an Inhibiting Factor' (1954) in *Brecht on Theatre*, edited by John Willett (1977)

11. Is it any good?

VALUE JUDGMENTS ARE NOTORIOUSLY subjective: one reader's masterpiece strikes another as a failure. There is a long-running debate about whether it's possible to judge a work of art definitively, and the criteria are so varied that it's sometimes difficult to distinguish between the excellent and the merely fashionable, the bad and the unjustly ignored.

So let's approach the problem indirectly, by asking the kinds of questions a director or literary manager has to answer every day.

Is it dramatic?

When we say a play is 'dramatic' we usually mean that it features a clash between two opposing forces, in which something important is at stake – a life, a piece of property, a country, an idea even – and that we find the result exciting to watch.

This collision of forces, both across society and within the individual, is perhaps the single most important characteristic of the greatest classical plays: *The Oresteia*, *Hamlet*, *The Cherry Orchard*, *Hedda Gabler* and *Life of Galileo* all describe the crisis caused when different ways of being come into conflict with each other. And the same can be said of the best contemporary plays: Lorraine Hansberry's *A Raisin in the Sun* (1959), David Hare's *Skylight* (1995) and Sarah Kane's *Blasted* (1995) all dramatise the clash between different values and insist that we come to our own judgments.

It's important that these conflicts aren't presented as abstractions and that the contrasting positions are embodied in fully rounded and plausible individuals. And so we need to ask: has the playwright understood his characters? Do we believe in them? Do we understand what drives them? We require something more than simply the playwright's ability to capture individual psychologies: we want to understand the way that his characters have been moulded by the circumstances and times in which they live. Without such credibility, the dramatic conflict will be superficial, at best.

And this conflict needs to be dramatised in a compelling story which should engage us quickly and hold our attention throughout. And so in asking whether a play is dramatic we need to ask ourselves some fundamental questions: Are we gripped? Does the writer make us care about what happens next? Does his play build to a convincing climax and does that climax, in some subtle way, change our perception of the world and of our fellow human beings? If the answer to all these questions is not a resounding 'yes', it's unlikely that the play will be truly interesting.

But, of course, in using the word 'dramatic' as a universal criterion of value, we need to realise its limits: Beckett's *Waiting for Godot* (1953) is hailed by many as the most remarkable play of the twentieth century, but it's hardly dramatic in any conventional sense. It's evident that other questions have to be asked.

Is it theatrical?

The word 'theatricality' describes the extent to which a play understands and exploits the particular qualities of the live theatre. Some plays go out of their way to do this: Peter Weiss's *Marat/Sade* (1963);[1] Hélène Cixous's epic *Sihanouk* (1985);[2] Robert Lepage's production of his own piece, *The Seven Streams of the River Ota* (1994); or the adaptation of Michael Morpurgo's *War Horse* (2007) at the National Theatre. All of these – and many more – have made for thrilling theatrical events, communicating as much through image, light, music and sound, as they do through spoken language, character or argument.

---

1   The full title is *The Persecution and Assassination of Jean-Paul Marat as Performed by the Inmates of the Asylum of Charenton under the Direction of the Marquis de Sade* (1963). Peter Brook directed a famous production for the RSC.

2   The full title is *The Terrible but Unfinished Story of Norodom Sihanouk, King of Cambodia* (1985). Ariane Mnouchkine directed it for the Théâtre du Soleil.

But theatricality doesn't necessarily mean special effects. A play can be theatrical if it has a vivid, sensual life. David Storey's naturalistic plays are richly theatrical: the steaming hot showers and banging locker doors in *The Changing Room* (1972); the gradual erection of a marquee in *The Contractor* (1969); or the two forgetful old men sat under gathering clouds talking about a vanished England in *Home* (1970). The same, of course, can be said for any number of naturalist plays: for all their restraint, Chekhov, Ibsen, Lawrence, O'Casey and Arthur Miller theatricalise – sometimes even render sacramental – the human figure.

Brecht had an astonishing knack of providing a simple but highly theatrical image through which his meaning could be expressed: Mother Courage's cart, one moment laden with supplies, the next ragged and torn, being hauled around the empty, brilliantly lit stage; the circle in chalk that Azdak draws on the floor for his reworking of the judgment of Solomon; and Galileo sticking a match in an apple and carrying Andrea around the room on a chair to give a practical demonstration of the laws of gravity and the rotation of the earth around the sun. This use of visual and physical metaphor lies at the heart of all good theatrical drama.

But we need to be careful about theatricality. Brecht once joked that 'the Nuremberg Rallies were good theatre': he was warning us against work that is theatrically impressive but serves pernicious ends. It's easy for a dramatist – or a director and designer, more likely – to insist on a wall of twenty-four television screens tuned to different channels and it'll probably be hailed as 'innovative'. But the danger of the 'immediate theatre', as Peter Brook dubbed it, is that theatricality becomes a substitute for content and staging a play becomes an exercise in theatrical technique, not an attempt to reflect life.

Does it provide a truthful image of life?

Hamlet is clear in his advice to the players about the purpose of the theatre:

Suit the action to the word, the word to the action, with this special purpose that you overstep not the modesty of nature. For anything so overdone is from the purpose of playing, whose end, both at the first and now, was and is, to hold, as twere, the mirror up to nature, to show virtue her own feature, scorn her own image, and the very age and body of the time his form and pressure.[3]

Of course, Hamlet's view of mimesis shouldn't be taken as an expression of Shakespeare's own views, let alone gospel truth; but it does provide a valuable template against which to assess the value of drama and offers us as good a set of criteria as any.

Good drama depicts reality. It shows us human experience in all its contradictions: love and hate, hope and despair, folly and wisdom, courage and fear, strength and frailty. By holding 'a mirror up to nature', by showing us how human beings think and behave, the best plays help us understand our own experience. And so one of the best criteria for judgment is whether we believe that this reflection is a true one.

Shakespeare's *Much Ado About Nothing* is a good example. The play explores the nature of sexual attraction within a complex society and does so in a three-dimensional fashion. It offers an image of the heartfelt seriousness of young love in Hero and Claudio, but it also explores the role of irony, wit and sarcasm in another, more mature couple, Beatrice and Benedick. What's more, it dramatises the dangerous destructiveness of aristocratic passion in the melancholic Don John, and demonstrates the limits of the state's power in the antics of Dogberry, Verges and the Watch. The combination of these perspectives makes the play a truthful reflection of the relationship between *eros* and society.

One of the intriguing features of Hamlet's 'Advice to the Players' is how quickly holding 'a mirror up to nature' gives way to the need for moral and social improvement – showing 'virtue her own feature, scorn her own image, and the very age and body of the time his form and pressure'. Thus in praising a playwright for

---

3   *Hamlet* (3.2)

his ability to present reality, we will inevitably conclude that his work is also rich with suggestions as to how that reality could be improved. When, finally, Benedick promises 'brave punishments' for the villainous (and anti-social) Don John, we are confident that not just the society of the play, but the audience watching it, will be improved as a result.

However, even in praising Shakespeare for his extraordinary talent for controlled objectivity, we need to be careful about the kind of moderation that the scrupulously intelligent and moral Hamlet is calling for. Drama needs to take sides as well as be objective, it should be both Dionsyiac and Apollonian. Jimmy Porter in *Look Back in Anger* offers us a dire warning:

> One day when I'm no longer running a sweet-stall, I may write a book about us all. It's all here. Written in flames a mile high. And it won't be recollected in tranquillity either, picking daffodils with Auntie Wordsworth. It'll be recollected in fire, and blood. My blood.[4]

Drama needs such passion: an Olympian commitment to objectivity isn't always enough.

Does it succeed on its own terms?

It's important that we try to judge a play on its own terms. It's absurd to criticise a Feydeau farce by the standards of *Hedda Gabler*, not because one is better than the other, but because there are radically different reasons why the two exist.

Our approach to Brecht's *Fear and Misery of the Third Reich* (1935-8) is a case in point. In writing a cycle of largely realistic short plays about the conditions of everyday life in mid-1930s Nazi Germany, Brecht wanted to show his émigré audiences the truth about Fascism, and give them a sense of how it could be opposed. The problem for the modern reader is that the plays were eclipsed by events (as Brecht himself said, 'writers cannot write as rapidly

---

4   John Osborne *Look Back in Anger* (1956)

as governments can make war, because writing demands hard thought') and can look quaint in retrospect. What's more, by largely ignoring anti-Semitism – with the notable exception of *The Jewish Wife* – and exaggerating the strength of the working class opposition to Hitler, the plays strike us as a rather limited and partisan account. But it's unfair to criticise Brecht for not doing something that he never attempted and his achievements were more remarkable than his shortcomings: we should heed EP Thompson's warning about the 'enormous condescension of posterity' and avoid the luxury of hindsight.

Critics have sometimes accused classical writers of being insufficiently radical in their attitude to social and economic injustice. Shakespeare is criticised for not letting the mob – the 'people' – triumph in *Coriolanus*; Ben Jonson is attacked for not showing up the crimes of capitalism in *Volpone*; and Farquhar is charged with not condemning the tactics of recruiting officers who bully farm boys into taking the king's shilling. What these critics forget is that the very existence of these controversial subjects in the plays is remarkable and they should refrain from attacking the playwrights for being insufficiently like them.

Even the finest classical playwrights have been lambasted for their unenlightened views on racial and gender questions. *The Merchant of Venice* raises awkward questions, but the fact that Jews were outlawed in Elizabethan England should make us realise Shakespeare's courage in writing Shylock's great speech 'Hath not a Jew eyes?'. Similarly, Ibsen has been accused of misogyny in *Ghosts*,[5] but Mrs Alving's acceptance of her own complicity in her husband's depravity should be seen as a great stroke of dramatic realism.

New plays by young writers are often criticised for not being as good as the classics, usually by theatre directors who prefer the creative freedom offered by revivals. But the question should be turned on its head: why are people so obsessed by material that is the product of an alien world, when we are surrounded by living

---

5   See Joan Templeton *Ibsen's Women* (2001). In conversation, the actress Diana Quick countered Templeton's argument that Ibsen blames Mrs Alving for her husband's dissipation with a succinct 'It takes two to tango'.

playwrights desperate to write about contemporary life? The standard answer refers to the 'universal' relevance of the classics. But, as I've argued elsewhere, 'universality' is a problematic concept and we should ask instead whether the obsession with the classics is, in fact, an escape from the challenge of championing plays about today.

Does it say anything useful about the world?

The theatre has always strived to be a place that engages with the world in which its audience lives and the best playwrights dramatise the conflicts and contradictions of their time.

John Osborne's *Look Back in Anger* (1956) was written in reaction to a specific world: the narrow-minded and deferential nature of English society in the early 1950s. Many young people came to feel that the change promised by the post-war settlement had been betrayed and that the old order had been reasserted by *force majeur*. The play locates these emotions in a young man living in a small flat in an unnamed town in the Midlands with his best friend and his young wife.

Caryl Churchill's *Top Girls* (1982) likewise emerged at a particular moment in British history and dramatised the new energies unlocked by Mrs Thatcher's political and social revolution. As well as satirising the new breed of 1980s feminists – tough young women who wanted to get ahead, make money and be independent – Churchill asked what would happen to those at the bottom, who failed to thrive in the free enterprise, dog-eat-dog world that had been created. I saw the play at its premiere at the Royal Court and it struck me as an important warning; seeing a revival ten years later, it seemed like an elegy for a lost world.

But we need to be careful about definitions of social relevance. A play steeped in references to newsworthy events is not necessarily 'contemporary' in any meaningful sense of the word. And if it's badly written, or based on a shallow understanding of those events, it's worse than useless. A brilliantly written play that catches the particular features of modern life without any reference to current affairs may well have much more to say. Relevance is as complex a concept when applied to new plays as it is to old ones.

What does it say about the past?

As I've argued throughout, old plays should be read historically. If we do this we notice two things. First we see the way society and behaviour has changed. As Walter Benjamin wrote 'There is no document of civilization which is not at the same time a document of barbarism,'[6] and a historical reading of an old play will help us understand that civilisation, however barbaric. By comparing the past with the present, we can gain a clearer understanding of the road travelled to where we are today.

Secondly, we come to understand the historical processes at work. We see the dialectics of history, the way that different forces propose different solutions and that through conflict change is enacted. In an important passage in *The Messingkauf Dialogues* (1940), Brecht spoke about what he called:

Those useful junction points, where the new ... collided with the old. We too are at one and the same time fathers of a new period and sons of an old one. We understand a great deal of the remote past and can still share once overwhelming feelings which were stimulated on a grand scale... All the same there is a lot in these works [Shakespeare's plays] that is dead, distorted and empty. This can continue to be printed; for all we know it may be shamming dead, and may anyway explain other aspects of the period. I would almost sooner draw your attention to the wealth of living elements still to be found in such works at apparently dead junctures. An infinitesimal addition, and they spring to life, specifically now, specifically not till now. What really matters is to play these old works historically, which means setting them in powerful contrast to our own time. For it is only against the background of our time that their shape emerges as an

---

6   Walter Benjamin *Theses on the Philosophy of History* (1940)

old shape, and without this background I doubt if they could
have any shape at all.[7]

This sense of the historical clash of different systems, held up in
contrast to our own world, provides us with a dynamic way of
approaching drama from the past.

Plays are not intended as historical documents. But they do
tell us an enormous amount about the way people lived in different ages. Without a historical perspective we look at plays down
the wrong end of the telescope. With it, however, we notice that
Theseus, who at the outset was persuaded by his councillor Egeus
to uphold the law of Athens, eventually comes to overrule him; we
see that Nora, by being exposed to the real world of money-lending,
forged signatures and blackmail, discovers her own identity; and
we observe how Mother Courage's fortunes improve rapidly when
war is raging, but decline catastrophically when 'peace has broken
out'.

In other words, if we read the classical playwrights with some
historical perspective, we can learn an enormous amount about
their times. But so also, by extension, can we understand our own.

Is it enjoyable?

In one of his many deliberately provocative statements Brecht
wrote:

> Let us therefore cause universal dismay by revoking our
> decision to emigrate from the realm of the merely enjoyable,
> and even more general dismay by announcing our decision
> to take up lodging there. Let us treat the theatre as a place of
> entertainment, as is proper to its aesthetic discussion, and
> try to discover which type of entertainment suits us best...
> Nothing needs less justification than pleasure.[8]

---

7   Bertolt Brecht *The Messingkauf Dialogues* (1940)

8   Bertolt Brecht 'A Short Organum for the Theatre' translated John Willett in *Brecht on Theatre* (1977)

There are few universal constants that can be applied to all theatre cultures, but the most significant is that they try to be enjoyable.

But there can be no accounting for taste: 'De gustibus non est disputandum', as the Latin tag has it. And so when we come to ask the hardest question of all – is it enjoyable? – we can only fall back on personal preferences. The fact is that there are many different pleasures offered by a good play: laughter, intellectual challenge, aesthetic pleasure, shock, provocation and tears. The problem with much of the modern critical debate is the way that mass-market entertainment is privileged as the only kind of pleasure available. It's as meaningless as the argument that only the incomprehensible and difficult can be valuable. In other words, there are many different ways to be entertained.

How does it leave us feeling?

The last question is how will the audience feel when it leaves the theatre.

Aristotle said that tragedy induced a combination of pity and terror, and that this leads to a purgation of the worst elements in the individual and the reformation of society as a whole. This defence of drama usually appears in societies where there is a belief in the perfectibility of the human being, whether on religious grounds or through political and social reform.

Of course, the religious often object to drama: the church authorities of Shakespeare's England argued that the theatre – with its lies, its impertinence and its bawdiness, not to mention its tendency for subversive questioning and political demystification – could do nothing to improve society or the individual, and should be carefully controlled. And political regimes of every hue have looked upon the performing arts with similar disdain.

There is a growing argument that the arts have no real worth at all. This is set out in John Carey's admirable *What Use Are the Arts?*[9] which dismisses all notions of quantifiable value. This is a compre-

---

9   John Carey *What Use Are the Arts?* (2005)

hensive rejection of some of the leading cultural thinkers of the last 150 years: from Matthew Arnold's emphasis on the civilising effect of great art to FR Leavis's idea of moral discrimination and Lord Reith's commitment to the widest possible social benefit. The Arts Council struggles with conflicting criteria for funding, from artistic excellence on the one hand, to instrumental social value on the other, but finds it hard to come to any conclusions.

It's certainly possible that seeing a play in the modern theatre has only the most limited value: it warms our hearts, tickles our fancy, sparks our imagination and refreshes our eyes. But by inducing strong feelings a play helps us feel, and by showing the truth, it helps us understand. This potent combination of emotion and judgment, empathy and criticism, love and analysis, makes the theatre – and all the arts – invaluable. So long as we don't imagine that plays can solve society's problems – let alone substitute for effective hospitals, good schools or decent housing – they will remain unquantifiable in their value, unsure in their social function, unpredictable in their impact, but fundamental to the way that society sees itself, and individuals face up to the truth of their lives.

12. What's Next?

I SOMETIMES WONDER ABOUT THE future of playwriting. What are the conditions under which modern playwrights are working? What opportunities exist for young dramatists and what's next for this most ancient of artistic activities?

The role of the classics

In Britain, at least, the mainstream theatre is dominated by revivals of the classics. There are many reasons for this, above all a widespread recognition of the power and quality of the best drama from the past. But there are financial considerations too: most commercial producers regard plays with an established track record as safer bets than new ones. And many critics and theatre people argue that only the classical playwright can feed our appetite for drama of ambition and scope. They criticize the modern playwright for a failure of imagination and a lack of self-confidence.

Of course, it's not an either/or. Modern playwrights can learn from their predecessors, and the presentation of great old plays is an important part of the service that the theatre can offer culture as a whole. But it's also true that the dominance of classical drama can be detrimental to the cause of making the theatre a living forum for the discussion of contemporary life.

A moratorium on Shakespeare?

No playwright is more dominant than Shakespeare and the director Matthew Warchus has provocatively suggested that the British theatre should impose a ten-year moratorium on the revival of his plays. This would encourage us to explore the rest of the repertoire with a more open mind and would open up a space that could be taken by the new and the different. What's more, it would help us approach Shakespeare with a new level of inquiry and open-mindedness once we came to stage his plays again. Of course, far too much is invested in Shakespeare – money, talent, education, and so on – for this to become a reality, but the suggestion alone could help us look at Shakespeare's dominance with greater scepticism.

The important thing is to try to answer that hardest of questions: what is it about Shakespeare that is so good and why does he still matter? If we can't come up with a satisfactory answer to these questions – and to the supplementary one, how do we stage them in the theatre? – then we should perhaps take a step back and leave his work alone for a while.

The dominance of Europe and the United States

Kenneth Tynan's list of plays for the National Theatre (See *Why Read a Play?*) is impressively international: it features writers from all over the world, with large contingents from Africa, Japan and the Far East. And several British theatres are doing what they can to broaden the geographical scope of what is seen, especially in London. Nevertheless, the theatrical repertoire is still dominated by Europe, European Russia and America.

One of the most important developments in recent years has been the number of black writers, mostly from America, but also Europe and Africa, who have had their work produced. But this hasn't been the case with playwrights from Asia, and it'll be interesting to see whether the newly globalised world – and the many challenges that come in its wake – will provoke work that can filter through into the mainstream repertoire.

It's essential that the modern theatre is as international and cosmopolitan as society itself. Modern communication grants us immediate access to many different cultures and we should seize the opportunity to engage with them with both hands. But an understanding and celebration of the values of individual cultures is important too, and we need to be wary of creating a theatrical mush, lacking in tone or distinction, which smoothes over idiosyncrasies and cultural particularity.

The challenge of modernity

There is a potent argument that the bewildering complexities of modern life cannot be adequately expressed with the modest means available in the theatre. Think for a moment of the 9/11 attacks. We have seen dramatisations of the suffering of the relatives of those who died, and plays like *Stuff Happens* (2004) and *Guantanamo* (2004) have tried to show the West's reactions to these events. But nobody, as far as I know, has dramatised its causes or successfully placed on stage the dark side of our globalised world.

The objection is an obvious one: 9/11 was such a cataclysmic event, played out live on television screens across the world, that the theatre – or any art form – could never adequately describe it; indeed that the great events of the modern world cannot be represented on the stage. Adorno claimed that lyric poetry was impossible after Auschwitz.[1] There's hardly a decent play on the subject – with the notable exception of Peter Weiss' *The Investigation* (1965) – and we may have to accept that the theatre is too primitive an art form to be able to represent the terrifying dramas of modern life. Are certain aspects of modern experience so bizarre that, to quote Fabian in *Twelfth Night*, 'if this were played upon a stage now I could condemn it as an improbable fiction'?[2] If so, we may need to bow to film and television in our desire to create a kind of drama that reflects our very peculiar time.

New forms for a new world?

Let's lower the bar for a moment, however, and ask whether the modern theatre succeeds in representing other, less dramatic, but no less modern experiences successfully: the bewildering impact of rapid travel, mass tourism, information technology and so on.

There are a handful of interesting twentieth-century plays about science: the most striking are Michael Frayn's *Copenhagen* (1998), Tom Stoppard's *Arcadia* (1993) and supremely, Brecht's *Life*

---

1   Theodor Adorno *Negative Dialectics* (1966)

2   *Twelfth Night* (3.4)

of Galileo (1938-9, 1945-7). Although Patrick Marber's *Closer* (1997) features an hilarious sequence of two men talking to each other on their computers (see *What Do They Say?* above), the impact of modern communication technology on everyday life has not – as far as I'm aware – been adequately dramatised.

Climate change presents the playwright with an even bigger challenge. There is a growing tendency among many of the most innovative theatre makers to use modern technology to tackle this kind of material and audio-visual equipment, projectors, complex sound effects, high-tech scenery all play their part. This certainly creates a compelling illusion of modernity and, when allied to credible characterisation and dramatic action, can catch a peculiarly modern sense of alienation and individuality.

But there's the rub: good plays require conflict and interaction if they're to do more than provide a series of static images. Drama at its best explores and expresses the individual's relationship with his society. But the modern world offers few shared locations, places where people can meet, interact and try to change each other, and so contemporary drama often finds it hard to represent anything more dynamic than mere facts and experiences. The search is on for a location in which the contradictions and conflicts of modern life can be dramatised.

Popular television drama, especially soap opera, has solved this problem: hospitals, pubs, police stations, schools, are all places where people meet each other, where much is at stake, and where the stuff of everyday life can be played out. What's proving more difficult is to use this open-ended, essentially naturalistic and popular form to explore and comment on the most specifically modern – and profoundly contradictory – of experiences.

One of the most notable features of Brecht's work is the way that he pillaged and changed existing theatrical structures and forms to fit the new content that he was eager to dramatise. The important lesson for modern writers is to let formal innovation follow new content and not the other way around.

Verbatim theatre

Recent years have seen a flowering of documentary drama, particularly 'verbatim theatre' where the drama consists of actors impersonating real figures and using the words originally spoken in the real-life situation. This is partly a response to a culture of secrecy surrounding high profile cases, but it's also a way of creating political drama with authority and credibility.

The Tricycle Theatre in Kilburn has produced several verbatim plays, often researched and compiled by the journalist Richard Norton-Taylor: probably the best regarded are *Half the Picture* (1994), a dramatisation of the Arms to Iraq Inquiry; *The Colour of Justice* (1999), a reconstruction of The Stephen Lawrence Inquiry; and *Justifying War – Scenes from the Hutton Inquiry* (2003). Audiences have mixed responses: some are mesmerised, while others wonder whether they've been given anything that cannot be gathered by a careful reading of the newspapers.

Verbatim theatre isn't new. Peter Weiss' *The Investigation* (1965) consists of chilling transcripts of the trials of 22 Auschwitz guards and SS officials in Frankfurt. And the flowering of British political theatre in the 1970s and 1980s often used real material: two of the finest examples were Louise Page's *Falkland Sound/Voces de Malvinas* (1983) and *The Garden of England* (1985), a piece presented by the National Theatre Studio about the 1984-6 miners strike. I remember being sat in the Cottesloe surrounded by striking miners and their families: it was one of the most powerful evenings I've spent in the theatre. Shortly afterwards I suggested to the Intendant of the famously left-wing Schauspielhaus in Bochum that he should commission a piece of verbatim theatre about the experience of the Turkish *gastarbeiters*. He dismissed the idea: it would not be 'künstlerisch' (artistic), he said, and I understood something about different notions of political theatre.

Devised plays

Devised theatre is not a recent development. The *commedia dell'arte* placed improvisation at its heart and it's impossible to know the nature and extent of the collaboration between the Elizabethan dramatists and their actors. The folksy image of Shakespeare piecing together *Hamlet* with his friends over a glass or two in the Mermaid Tavern is surely far-fetched, but it's striking that Shakespeare's fellow actors are given pride of place in the First Folio, acknowledging, at the very least, their contribution to the playwright's own success.

In 1945 Joan Littlewood and her husband Ewan MacColl founded Theatre Workshop, an ensemble company dedicated to a theatre that involved cast and audience. In 1953, they secured a lease on the crumbling Theatre Royal, Stratford East, where they produced their greatest hit, *Oh! What A Lovely War!* (1963), a richly theatrical devised play about the First World War. The text has none of the sinewy strength of *Mother Courage*, let alone the poetical power of O'Casey's *The Silver Tassie* (1927); but the production was an extraordinarily moving event whose impact derived from its deathly white Pierrot figures, fiercely cheerful music-hall patter and documentary photographs of the First World War.

In 1974 a group of directors and writers set up the Joint Stock Theatre Group. They developed a unique way of working: the directors would gather a group of actors and a playwright, and 'workshop' an idea for several weeks. The writer would then go away and write a play, and the actors would be re-engaged to rehearse it. Described by one of the actors as a 'directorial dictatorship', the Joint Stock method resulted in some of the most interesting plays of the 1970s: David Hare's *Fanshen* (1975), Howard Brenton's *Epsom Downs* (1977), Stephen Lowe's *The Ragged Trousered Philanthropists* (1978) and Caryl Churchill's *Cloud Nine* (1979). What they lack in literary quality they make up for in theatrical confidence, political rigour and sharp dialogue: all direct results of the workshop process.

Performance art

Twentieth-century theatre had three main strands: premieres of new plays, revivals of classics, and productions that don't have a playwright attached. Such performance art has the power to move and provoke like the most radical of plays.

Performance art has its roots in the theatrical experiments of Vsevolod Meyerhold in Revolutionary Russia. Working with the filmmaker Sergei Eisenstein and the writer Vladimir Mayakovsky, Meyerhold wanted to dissolve all notions of cultural property and hierarchy. His productions saw 'text' as only one part of a much wider theatrical project. He had an enormous influence on the radical directors of post-war European theatre, including Peter Brook, whose remarkable productions have relied on a whole range of theatrical effects, quite separate from the text.

Brook also borrowed from the Polish director, Jerzy Grotowski, whose 'Poor Theatre' attempted a new intimacy between actor and spectator. Another Pole, Taduesz Kantor, was responsible for some of the masterpieces of performance art, including the astounding *The Dead Class* (1975). American performance artists of the 1960s staged a number of 'happenings' and the New York based Wooster Group has kept many of these ideals alive in their radical reworkings of classical texts. Several companies devoted to performance art have emerged in Britain in recent years.

Performance art is difficult, however, and requires all the intellectual and artistic discipline of the twentieth century avant-garde. Modern audiences are sometimes offered a shallow imitation of what in its heyday was a strikingly powerful theatrical form.

Discovering new playwrights and new voices

The modern theatre has a responsibility for the development of the next generation of playwrights. One of the striking features of the British theatre is the range and strength of its young writers. Whereas in France and Germany playwrights tend to be over 40, in Britain new plays by young playwrights are produced all the time.

There are many reasons for this, but the most important is a peculiarly British attitude to new drama.

At its best, the British theatre embraces the emerging writer and is unfazed that he lacks the philosophical and intellectual depth of the classical dramatists. A number of theatres go out of their way to celebrate the authentic voices of those traditionally neglected – whether it's the working class, the immigrant or racial minorities – and try to develop further the range of subjects and worlds that drama can describe. The danger lies in the over-promotion of new writers simply because they're young or from outside the white middle classes. But there is wisdom in the argument that we can never do too much for the young or excluded, and we should accept that an occasionally craven attitude to new writers is at least well intentioned.

George Devine saw the Royal Court as a writer's theatre and established a commitment and way of working that has held good for fifty years. One of the most astonishing young writers to have emerged from the Court was Andrea Dunbar. A poorly educated working class girl from a housing estate near Leeds, who died tragically young of a brain haemorrhage, Dunbar wrote her first play, *The Arbor* (1977), at the age of 15. Encouraged by a school teacher, she sent it the Royal Court, where it was staged by Max Stafford Clark in 1980, won various awards and played in New York. Described by Shelagh Delaney as a 'genius from the slums', Dunbar's subsequent plays were *Rita, Sue and Bob Too* (1982, made into a film by Alan Parker in 1986), and *Shirley* (1986). One test for any theatre interested in presenting new writing today might be this: would it discover and champion the teenage Andrea Dunbar if the handwritten manuscript of *The Arbor* arrived one day in a tatty brown envelope in the post?

Dramaturgs and workshops

In 1767 the German poet and playwright Gotthold Lessing wrote the *Hamburgischer Dramaturgie*, one of the key works of the German Enlightenment and a fundamental text in the development of theatrical appreciation. Dramaturgy has been central ever since, with many of the best playwrights contributing to the theory that is so important to German culture. Every German theatre has its own in-house dramaturg (sometimes several) and if a director decides to revive a classical play, he examines the various translations available, provides an academic and historical context, writes the programme notes and helps the director articulate his interpretations. Many dramaturgs hold academic positions and are playwrights in their own right; some even play a role in marketing.

The British tradition is very different. For a start, the British theatre is much more pragmatic – and commercial – in its orientation and pays less respect to an intellectual approach. What's more, it places the playwright and the actor, not the director and the academic, at the centre of the theatrical experience. Finally, as a rule, the British theatre is more interested in developing the new writer than in reappraising the writer of the past and, when it does do so, is usually content to provide as faithful a reading as possible without too much interpretation. And so the British theatre has been traditionally happier with the 'literary manager' – a title held by a number of remarkable figures including, of course, that doyen of the trade, Kenneth Tynan at Laurence Olivier's National Theatre.

In recent years, however, the British theatre has embraced dramaturgs. This is not just a matter of semantics: the dramaturg does a very different job. Whereas the literary manager is content to read plays (both old and new) and recommend them for production, the dramaturg provides novel interpretation and adaptation of old works, and happily involves himself in the rewriting, restructuring and wide-scale alteration that he believes is necessary. With the new interest in conceptualisation and interpretation, his role is increasingly important.

One of the key roles of both dramaturg and literary manager is to give advice to the writer about rewrites. These are sometimes considerable: 'Act One doesn't work and you need to think about what happens to your heroine'. They are sometimes simply technical: 'We're not told the characters' names early enough'. Such observations can be helpful and many writers are happy to acknowledge the contributions made by such critical friends. Indeed, when plays have been commissioned the incorporation of some of these comments will often be a condition for performance.

In considering the 'final draft' for performance, directors and theatre managements often find it useful to arrange a rehearsed reading. Even Alan Bennett's astonishingly successful play, *The History Boys* (2004), was given a private reading at the National Theatre Studio before the final decision was made to stage it. Sometimes directors will want to 'workshop' a play for a week or two before deciding to produce it. A writer often finds it useful to see his ideas acted out and a well-managed workshop can clarify the problems with a play and point to solutions which he has been struggling with for months.

Invaluable as such workshops can be, theatres need to be careful not to treat them as a substitute for performance. More importantly, they should resist the temptation for their new plays to be written by committee. A good play, like any work of art, is the product of an individual vision, and artistic directors must ensure that well-meaning contributions don't diffuse the writer's voice and obscure his original vision.

The question is a simple one: are we prepared to grant the playwright – living or dead – his pivotal role at the heart of the theatre? The literary manager usually stands up for the status quo; the dramaturg, however, eager for a more creative role, helps the ambitious director dislodge the playwright from his central position. The British theatre should be careful not to give either of them too much power.

The dramatist under threat?

We live in changing times. Written drama – 'text-based theatre', as it's sometimes (and usually contemptuously) called – is being challenged on all sides: by musicals, physical theatre, devised work, multi-media events, and so on. We're told that an image says more than a thousand words, and that it's time to create a new form of theatre for the modern world. We're also reminded that modern audiences are blessed with visual literacy but cursed with a short attention span, and that old plays are the product of an alien world and need to be reinterpreted if they're to have any currency in the modern world.

This questioning of the primacy of the written word is increasingly played out in the way that the theatre is put together. There is a growing desire to do without a playwright, or at best relegate him to a minor role. In some theatres, the director has become the key figure and his work, along with the designer's, is at the heart of the experience. The result is a new kind of theatre: an event that communicates through a whole range of means, of which the spoken word is sometimes the least important.

In the world of reality television, FaceBook and text messages, the lonely playwright working away in his attic may seem a quaint figure. I'm convinced, however, that people still go to the theatre to listen to a play, and that, whatever directors and designers may say, the writer is still the primary creative figure. And I fear that the emphasis on theatricality is detrimental to the fundamental contract between playwright and audience.

I think Hamlet is wrong: it's not the actors, it's the playwrights who hold 'a mirror up to nature, show virtue her own feature, scorn her own image, and the very age and body of the time his form and pressure.' If so, let's extend Hamlet's advice to Polonius to include the playwrights of today:

> Let them be well used, for they are the abstract and brief chronicles of the time. After your death you were better have a bad epitaph than their ill report while you live.

POLONIUS

> My lord, I will use them according to their desert.

HAMLET

> God's bodykins, man, much better. Use every man after his desert, and who should scape whipping? Use them

> after your own honour and dignity. The less they deserve,
> the more merit is in your bounty.[3]

Playwrights aren't just responsible for some of the greatest works of art of the past: they're the key to the long-term survival of the theatre in the future. If we turn our backs on them, the theatre and our culture as a whole will wither on the vine. Playwrights tell us the stories that make sense of our lives. They show us how other people live and open our minds to new ways of thinking. They are creating the shapes of the future. We would be crazy to ignore them.

---

3   *Hamlet* (2.2)

APPENDIX: 250 PLAYWRIGHTS

READING LISTS ARE OUT of fashion: it's presumed that the modern student will know what to read without external authority. Perversely, I've decided to end my book with a list of two hundred and fifty of the best-known playwrights, along with the titles of their most famous plays. Inevitably such a list is partial: perhaps the only answer is to read them all and make up your own mind.

Arthur Adamov (1908–70) *Professor Taranne*

Aeschylus (c525–456 BC) *The Persians, The Oresteia, Prometheus Bound*

Edward Albee (born 1928) *Who's Afraid of Virginia Woolf?*

Anonymous *The York, Chester, Wakefield* and *Coventry Cycles*

Jean Anouilh (1910–87) *The Lark, Becket*

John Arden (born 1930) *Sergeant Musgrave's Dance, Live Like Pigs, Armstrong's Last Goodnight, The Island of the Mighty*

Aristophanes (c456–c386 BC) *The Frogs, Lysistrata*

Antonin Artaud (1896–1948) *Spurt of Blood*

W H Auden (1907–73) *The Ascent of F6*

Alan Ayckbourn (born 1939) *Absurd Person Singular, Seasons Greetings, The Norman Conquests*

James Baldwin (1927–87) *The Amen Corner, Blues for Mr Charlie*

Howard Barker (born 1946) *The Love of a Good Man*

James Barrie (1860–1937) *Peter Pan*

Richard Bean (born 1956) *Under the Whaleback, Honeymoon Suite*

Pierre de Beaumarchais (1732–99) *The Barber of Seville, The Marriage of Figaro*

Samuel Beckett (1906–89) *Waiting for Godot, Endgame, Krapp's Last Tape, Happy Days, A Piece of Monologue*

Henri Becque (1837–99) *The Vultures*

Brendan Behan (1923–64) *The Quare Fellow*

Aphra Behn (1640–89) *The Rover*

David Belasco (1853–1931) *The Girl of the Golden West*

Alan Bennett (born 1934) *Forty Years On, Habeas Corpus, Single Spies, The History Boys*

Simon Bent (born 1956) *Elling*

Thomas Bernhard (1931–89) *Over All the Mountain Tops*

Steven Berkoff (born 1937) *East*

Bjørnstjerne Bjørnson (1832–1910) *Beyond Human Might*

Robert Bolt (1924–95) *A Man for All Seasons*

Edward Bond (born 1934) *Saved, The Pope's Wedding, Lear, The Bundle, Bingo, The Sea*

Wolfgang Borchert (1921–47) *Outside the Door*

Dion Boucicault (1820–90) *The Shaughraun*

Bertolt Brecht (1898–1956) *The Threepenny Opera, The Mother, Fear and Misery of the Third Reich, Mother Courage and Her Children, Life of Galileo, The Caucasian Chalk Circle*

Howard Brenton (born 1942) *Weapons of Happiness, The Romans in Britain, Pravda*

Eugène Brieux (1858–1932) *Damaged Goods*

Harold Brighouse (1882–1958) *Hobson's Choice*

Ferdinand Bruckner (1891–1958) *Pains of Youth*

Georg Büchner (1813–37) *Woyzeck*

Mikhail Bulgakov (1891–1940) *Flight, Moliere*

John Byrne (born 1940) *The Slab Boys*

Pedro Calderón de la Barca (1600–81) *Life is a Dream, The Great Theatre of the World*

Albert Camus (1913–60) *Caligula*

Karel Čapek (1890–1938) *R.U.R.*

Agatha Christie (1890–1976) *The Mousetrap*

Anton Chekhov (1860–1904) *The Seagull, Uncle Vanya, Three Sisters, The Cherry Orchard*

Caryl Churchill (born 1938) *Cloud Nine, Top Girls, Serious Money*

Hélène Cixous (born 1937) *The Terrible but Unfinished Story of Norodom Sihanouk, King of Cambodia*

Jean Cocteau (1889–1963) *Les Enfants Terribles*

William Congreve (1637–1708) *The Double Dealer, Love for Love, The Way of the World*

Copi (1939–87) *The Fridge*

Pierre Corneille (1606–84) *Le Cid*

Noel Coward (1899–1973) *The Vortex, Design for Living, Private Lives, Present Laughter, Blithe Spirit*

Martin Crimp (born 1956) *Attempts on Her Life*

Shelagh Delaney (born 1939) *A Taste of Honey*

Lope de Vega (1562–1635) *Fuente Ovejuna*

Tankred Dorst (born 1925) *Merlin*

Alexandre Dumas (1824–95) *La Dame aux Camélias*

Andrea Dunbar (1961–90) *The Arbour, Rita, Sue and Bob Too*

Marguerite Duras (1914–66) *La Musica*

Friedrich Dürrenmatt (1921–90) *The Visit, The Physicists*

TS Eliot (1888–1965) *Murder in the Cathedral*

George Etherege (1635?–92) *She Would if She Could, The Man of Mode*

Euripides (c.480–406 BC) *Medea, The Trojan Women, Iphigenia in Tauris, Orestes, Electra*

George Farquhar (1678–1707) *The Recruiting Officer, The Beaux' Stratagem*

Eduardo de Filippo (1900–84) *Filumena Marturano*

Georges Feydeau (1862–1921) *A Flea in Her Ear*

Peter Flannery (born 1951) *Our Friends in the North*

Marieluise Fleisser (1901–74) *Pioneers in Ingolstadt*

Dario Fo (born 1926) *Accidental Death of an Anarchist*

John Ford (1586–1640) *Tis Pity She's a Whore*

María Irene Fornés (born 1930) *Sarita*

Michael Frayn (born 1933) *Noises Off, Copenhagen*

Brian Friel (born 1929) *Translations*

Max Frisch (1911–91) *The Fire Raisers, Andorra*

Christopher Fry (1907–2005) *Venus Observed*

Athol Fugard (born 1932) *The Island, Sizwe Bansi is Dead, Master Harold… and the Boys, My Children! My Africa!, Statements after an Arrest under the Immorality Act*

John Gay (1685–1732) *The Beggars' Opera*

John Galsworthy (1867–1933) *The Skin Game, Justice, Strife*

Pam Gems (born 1925) *Piaf*

Jean Genet (1910–86) *The Maids, The Balcony, The Blacks*

W.S. Gilbert (1836–1911) *The Mikado*

Peter Gill (born 1939) *Kick for Touch, Small Change, Cardiff East, The York Realist*

Jean Giraudoux (1882–1944) *The Trojan War Will Not Take Place*

Johann Wolfgang von Goethe (1749–1832) *Faust I and II, Torquato Tasso, Iphigeneia in Aulis*

Nikolai Gogol (1809–52) *The Government Inspector*

Oliver Goldsmith (1730–74) *She Stoops to Conquer*

Carlo Goldoni (1707–93) *The Servant of Two Masters*

Witold Gombrowicz (1904–69) *Princess Ivona, The Wedding*

Maxim Gorky (1868–1936) *Summerfolk, The Lower Depths*

Carlo Gozzi (1720–1826) *The Love for Three Oranges*

Harley Granville Barker (1877–1946) *The Voysey Inheritance, Waste, The Madras House*

Günter Grass (born 1927) *The Plebeians Rehearse the Uprising*

Simon Gray (1936–2008) *The Common Pursuit*

Debbie Tucker Green *Stoning Mary*

Graham Greene (1904–91) *The Return of A.J. Raffles*

Trevor Griffiths (born 1935) *Comedians*

Sydney Grundy (1848–1914) *The Degenerates*

John Guare (born 1938) *The House of Blue Leaves, Six Degrees of Separation*

Václav Havel (born 1936) *The Memorandum, Largo Desolato*

Patrick Hamilton (1904–62) *Gaslight*

Peter Handke (born 1942) *Kaspar, The Ride Across Lake Constance, They Are Dying Out*

St John Hankin (1869–1909) *The Return of the Prodigal*

Christopher Hampton (born 1946) *The Philanthropist, Les Liaisons Dangereuses*

Lorraine Hansberry (1930–65) *A Raisin in the Sun*

David Hare (born 1947) *Plenty, The Secret Rapture, Skylight*

Jonathan Harvey (born 1968) *Beautiful Thing*

Ronald Harwood (born 1934) *The Dresser*

David Harrower (born 1966) *Blackbird*

Tony Harrison (born 1937) *The Trackers of Oxyrynchthus*

Stanley Houghton (1881–1913) *Hindle Wakes*

Lilian Hellman (1905–84) *The Children's Hour*

Thomas Heywood (c1570–1641) *A Woman Killed With Kindness*

Rolf Hochhüth (born 1931) *The Representative*

Lodvig Holberg (1684–1754) *Jeppe of the Hill*

Ödön von Horváth (1901–38) *Tales from the Vienna Woods, Casimir and Caroline*

Hugo von Hofmannsthal (1874–1929) *Everyman*

Langston Hughes (1902–67) *Black Nativity*

Victor Hugo (1802–85) *Hernani*

David Henry Hwang (born 1957) *M. Butterfly*

Henrik Ibsen (1828–1906) *Brand, Peer Gynt, A Doll's House, Ghosts, The Enemy of the People, Hedda Gabler, The Wild Duck, Rosmersholm, The Master Builder, John Gabriel Borkman*

Eugène Ionesco (1909–94) *Rhinoceros, The Chairs*

Alfred Jarry (1873–1907) *Ubu the King*

Terry Johnson (born 1955) *Insignificance*

Ben Jonson (1572–1637) *Volpone, The Alchemist, Bartholomew Fair*

Henry Arthur Jones (1851–1929) *Saints and Sinners*

James Joyce (1882–1941) *Exiles*

Georg Kaiser (1875–1945) *The Burgers of Calais, The Raft of the Medusa*

Ayub Khan–Din (born 1961) *East is East*

Bernard–Marie Koltès (1948–89) *The Night Just Before the Forests, Roberto Zucco*

Franz Xaver Kroetz (born 1946) *The Nest, Through the Leaves*

Sarah Kane (1971–99) *Blasted*

Karl Kraus (1874–1936) *The Last Days of Mankind*

Tony Kushner (born 1956) *Angels in America*

Thomas Kyd (1558–94) *The Spanish Tragedy*

Heinrich von Kleist (1777–1811) *The Broken Jug, Amphitryon, Penthesilea, Katie of Heilbronn, The Prince of Homburg*

Neil LaBute (born 1963) *Bash: Latter–Day Plays*

Eugène Labiche (1815–88) *The Italian Straw Hat*

David Lan (born 1952) *Serjeant Ola and His Followers*

DH Lawrence (1885–1930) *The Daughter in Law, The Widowing of Mrs Holroyd, A Collier's Friday Night*

Mike Leigh (born 1943) *Abigail's Party*

Jakob Lenz (1751–92) *The Tutor*

Gotthold Ephraim Lessing (1721–89) *Emilia Galotti, Nathan the Wise*

Federico García Lorca (1898–1936) *Blood Wedding, Yerma, The House of Bernarda Alba*

Doug Lucie (born 1953) *Fashion*

Patrick Marber (born 1964) *Closer*

John Masefield (1878–1967) *Nan*

Somerset Maugham (1874–1965) *The Letter, The Circle*

David Mamet (born 1947) *American Buffalo, Glengarry Glen Ross*

Maurice Maeterlinck (1862–1949) *Pelléas and Mélisande*

Pierre de Marivaux (1688–1763) *The Game of Love and Chance, The Island*

Christopher Marlowe (1564–93) *Doctor Faustus, Tamburlaine the Great, I and II*

John Marston (1576–1634) *The Malcontent*

Philip Massinger (1583–1640) *A New Way to Pay Old Debts*

Vladimir Mayakovsky (1883–1930) *The Bedbug*

Conor McPherson (born 1971) *The Weir*

Frank McGuinness (born 1953) *Observe the Sons of Ulster Marching to the Somme*

Menander (c342–391 BC) *The Girl from Samos*

Adam Mickiewicz (1798–1855) *Forefathers' Eve*

Arthur Miller (1915–2005) *All My Sons, Death of a Salesman, The Crucible, View from the Bridge*

Thomas Middleton (1580–1627) *A Chaste Maid in Cheapside, Women Beware Women, The Changeling, A Game of Chess*

Ferenc Molnár (1878–1952) *Liliom, The Guardsman*

Tirso de Molina (1571?–1642) *The Trickster of Seville*

John Mortimer (1923–2009) *Voyage Round My Father*

Jean Baptiste de Molière (1622–73) *The Misanthrope, Tartuffe, The School for Wives, The Hypochondriac, Don Juan*

Heiner Müller (1929–95) *Hamletmachine*

Phyllis Nagy (born 1960) *Butterfly Kiss*

Johann Nestroy (1801–62) *On the Razzle, The Talisman*

Peter Nichols (born 1927) *A Day in the Death of Joe Egg*

Sean O'Casey (1880–1964) *Juno and the Paycock, The Plough and the Stars, The Shadow of a Gunman*

Clifford Odets (1906–63) *Waiting for Lefty, Rocket to the Moon*

Eugene O'Neill (1888–1953) *Long Day's Journey into Night*

Joe Orton (1933–67) *Loot, What the Butler Saw*

Alexandr Ostrovsky (1823–86) *The Storm*

John Osborne (1929–94) *Look Back in Anger, The Entertainer*

Thomas Otway (1652–85) *Venice Preserv'd*

Joe Penhall (born 1967) *Blue/Orange*

Harold Pinter (1930–2008) *The Caretaker, The Birthday Party, The Homecoming, Betrayal*

Luigi Pirandello (1867–1936) *Six Characters in Search of an Author*

Arthur Wing Pinero (1855–1930) *The Magistrate, The Second Mrs Tanqueray, Trelawney of the 'Wells'*

Winsome Pinnock (born 1961) *Leave Taking*

Plautus (254–184 BC) *The Rope*

Roger Planchon (born 1931) *Old Man Winter, Fragile Forest*

JB Priestley (1894–1984) *An Inspector Calls*

Alexander Pushkin (1799–1837) *The Little Tragedies*

TW Robertson (1829–71) *Caste*

Terence Rattigan (1911–77) *French Without Tears, The Winslow Boy, The Deep Blue Sea, Separate Tables*

Mark Ravenhill (born 1966) *Shopping and Fucking*

Jean Racine (1639–99) *Phèdre, Britannicus, Andromache*

Philip Ridley (born 1967) *The Pitchfork Disney*

Elizabeth Robins (1862–1952) and **Florence Bell** (1851–1930) *Alan's Wife*

Romain Rolland (1866–1954) *Georges Danton*

Edmund Rostand (1868–1918) *Cyrano de Bergerac*

David Rudkin (born 1936) *Afore Night Come*

Willy Russell (born 1947) *Educating Rita*

Victorien Sardou (1831–1908) *Fédora*

William Saroyan (1908–81) *The Time of Your Life*

Jean–Paul Sartre (1905–80) *Huis Clos*

NF Simpson (born 1919) *One Way Pendulum*

Carl Sternheim (1878–1942) *Die Hose*

George Bernard Shaw (1856–1950) *Pygmalion, Mrs Warren's Profession, Saint Joan, Arms and the Man, Heartbreak House*

Seneca the Younger (c4 BC–AD 65) *Medea, Thyestes*

Githa Sowerby (1876–1970) *Rutherford and Son*

Wole Soyinka (born 1934) *The Lion and the Jewel, Death and the King's Horseman*

Friedrich Schiller (1759–1809) *The Robbers, Intrigue and Love, Don Carlos, Wallenstein Trilogy, Mary Stuart*

Arthur Schnitzler (1862–1931) *Anatol, La Ronde, Professor Bernhardi*

William Shakespeare (1564–1616) *The Comedy of Errors, Richard III, As You Like It, Much Ado About Nothing, Julius Caesar, Henry V, Richard II, Twelfth Night, Measure for Measure, Hamlet, King Lear, Henry IV parts I and II, Macbeth, Othello, Antony and Cleopatra, The Tempest*

Anthony Shaffer (1926–2001) *Sleuth*

Peter Shaffer (born 1926) *Equus, Amadeus*

Ntozake Shange (born 1948) *For Colored girls who have Considered Suicide when the Rainbow is Enuf*

Richard Brinsley Sheridan (1751–1816) *The Rivals, The School for Scandal*

Sam Shepard (born 1943) *Buried Child, Fool for Love*

RC Sherriff (1896–1975) *Journey's End*

Neil Simon (born 1927) *Barefoot in the Park, The Odd Couple, Brighton Beach Memoirs*

Sophocles (c495–406 BC) *Antigone, Oedipus in Colonus, Oedipus the King, Ajax, Electra, Philoctetes*

Simon Stephens (born 1971) *On the Shore of the Wide World*

Ena Lamont Stewart (born 1912) *Men Should Weep*

Tom Stoppard (born 1937) *Rosencrantz And Guildenstern are Dead, Jumpers, Travesties, The Real Thing, Arcadia, The Coast of Utopia*

David Storey (born 1933) *Home, The Changing Room*

Botho Strauß (born 1944) *The Park, Big and Little*

August Strindberg (1849–1912) *The Father, Miss Julie, The Dance of Death, A Dream Play, The Ghost Sonata*

JM Synge (1871–1909) *The Shadow of the Glen, Riders to the Sea, The Playboy of the Western World*

Rabindranath Tagore (1861–1941) *Red Oleanders*

CP Taylor (1929–81) *Good*

Terence (c185–159 BC) *The Eunuch*

Dylan Thomas (1914–53) *Under Milk Wood*

Leo Tolstoy (1828–1910) *The Power of Darkness, The Fruits of the Enlightenment*

Ernst Toller (1893–1939) *Hoppla, We're Alive!*

Cyril Tourneur (1575–1626) *The Revenger's Tragedy*

Ben Travers (1886–1980) *Rookery Nook*

Sophie Treadwell (1885–1970) *Machinal*

Michel Tremblay (born 1942) *Les Belles Soeurs*

John Vanburgh (1664–1726) *The Relapse, The Provoked Wife*

Michel Vinaver (born 1927) *Situation Vacant*

Vsevelod Vishnevskiy (1900–51) *The Optimistic Tragedy*

Derek Walcott (born 1930) *Odyssey*

Frank Wedekind (1864–1918) *Spring Awakening*

John Webster (1580–1634) *The White Devil, The Duchess of Malfi*

Peter Weiss (1916–82) *Marat/Sade, The Investigation*

Timberlake Wertenbaker (born 1956) *Our Country's Good*

Arnold Wesker (born 1932) *Roots, Chicken Soup with Barley, The Kitchen*

Peter Whelan (born 1931) *The Herbal Bed*

Thornton Wilder (1897–1962) *Our Town, The Skin of Our Teeth*

Oscar Wilde (1854–1900) *Lady Windermere's Fan, A Woman of No Importance, An Ideal Husband, The Importance of Being Earnest*

August Wilson (1945–2005) *The Piano Lesson, Fences*

Emlyn Williams (1905–87) *Night Must Fall*

David Williamson (born 1942) *Up for Grabs*

Tennessee Williams (1911–83) *The Glass Menagerie, A Streetcar Named Desire, Cat on a Hot Tin Roof*

Charles Wood (born 1932) *Dingo*

Nicholas Wright (born 1940) *Mrs Klein*

William Wycherley (1640–1716) *The Country Wife, The Plain Dealer*

WB Yeats (1865–1939) *Cathleen Ní Houlihan*

Carl Zuckmayer (1896–1977) *The Captain of Köpenick*

Émile Zola (1840–1902) *Thérèse Raquin*

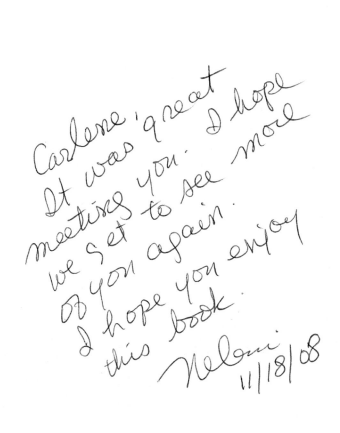

Carlene, great
It was great
meeting you. I hope
we get to see more
of you again.
I hope you enjoy
this book.
Nelomi
11/18/08

"Angels in Training"

by

Nelani A. Nettrour

Illustrated by:

Heather D. Nettrour

Third Millennium Publishing

**A Cooperative of Online Writers
and Resources on the INTERNET**

http://3mpub.com

ISBN 1-932657-57-6

114 pages

Michael McCollum
Proprietor
Third Millennium Publishing
1931 East Libra Drive
Tempe, AZ 85283
mccollum@scifi-az.com

"Angels in Training"

Dedicated to all who choose right over
wrong, good over evil. Never give up!

Author's Note: This book is written and illustrated with the utmost
respect to the true entities of Angels.   Though told in childlike
simplicity and rhyme the message is an ageless one that I hope will
be shared by both parent and child.   Illustrations of both good and
evil represent this unseen battle.   But the Bible tells us that if our
spiritual eyes were opened we would be able to see the unseen battle
that goes on around us.

If you could see beyond the eyes,
And see with your soul and your heart,
You would see that what you see,
Is only just a part.

And beyond what can be heard,
Beyond what can be felt,
Beyond what can be touched,
Beyond what can be smelt.

Is a world between today and tomorrow,
A world in eternity's space,
It can't be entered by normal ways.
But can only be entered by grace.

And in this eternal place,
Immortal angels live,
And sometimes come amongst us,
When they have a message to give.

And angels are sent as Guardians,
To those who will belong to God someday,
To watch over and protect them,
And shield them along the way.

This I know from the Bible,
This I know for sure.
But this story I'm about to tell,
Is what if and what were.

What if angels were trained,
And had to start oh so small,
And learn before given a big job,
If they were to learn at all?

What do you suppose would be their task,
If no one their bodies could see,
And if their whispers were to your heart,
Not to your ears clearly?

Nelani Nettrour

If angels did have helpers,
I think dogs they would choose,
They are so faithful and true,
With a dog you hardly can lose.

And on the other side of this world,
Away from where the angels abide,
In a place away from God,
Is where the Devil and demons reside.

They are those who turned from God,
Who turned from paradise's gate.
Instead chose evil and darkness,
And want others to copy their hate.

Then they would also do their best,
To trip you up when they could,
Creating a life filled with chaos,
To keep you from doing what's good.

The Devil is called the Father of Lies,
And there's a good reason for that,
He'll trick you up any way that he can,
And lead you to doom with a wink and a pat.

Demons won't always be easy to spot,
Or easy to tell from the rest,
For deception is a thing they do,
A thing they do the best.

Imitating the angels of light,
With beauty and wit they tie up their lies,
If you search for truth you'll know,
Don't be fooled by your eyes.

Their disguises may fool many,
It's their attempt to cover the evil inside,
But they will be revealed by their actions,
Some things they just cannot hide.

So imagine a fight going on around you,
Where good and evil take a stand,
Each trying to make you theirs,
Each trying to change the land.

If angels could talk to you
Their advice would be greater than a sage,
Listen closely to some advice,
Written on each page.

To be selfish, spiteful and mean,
Is to give your allegiance to evil's side,
Do you really want demons to cheer you on,
And the faces of angels to hide?

The way of wrong seems easier,
And seems to bear less grief,
But this is as much a lie,
As the excuses of a thief.

Angels in Training

It might be harder to tell the truth,
And your punishment to take,
Than to lie and think you're off the hook,
But that would be a big mistake.

For just because you think no one saw,
Doesn't mean that you weren't seen,
Bad decisions can become a habit,
And before you know it you're mean.

Do you think that a bully was born that way?
That he had no choice in who he'd be?
It was little steps of choosing wrong,
And ignoring the angels' plea.

When you are stubborn,
In things that are wrong,
You become a slave,
You become weak instead of strong.

Soon thoughts not even your own,
Will be guiding you,
Leading you down a path of darkness,
And you'll no longer know what is true.

If you've done something wrong,
And you are sorry through and through,
Ask forgiveness and be forgiven,
Don't let guilt eat at you.

The Devil is also called The Accuser,
For a good reason this I know,
Don't let something in the past,
Make you always feel so low.

Instead try to learn from your past,
Everyone will make mistakes as they grow.
Learn to choose what brings true happiness,
And your heart will feel the warm glow.

Nelani Nettrour

Sometimes what it takes to help,
Is very easy to see,
To lend a hand when someone falls,
Or just a friend to be.

Someone who is a true friend,
Took helpful steps along the way,
Doing good at every chance,
Bringing gladness to a day.

Nelani Nettrour

When you do what is right,
An angel gives a cheer,
The next good turn is easier,
And His footsteps ahead are clear.

Nelani Nettrour

Angels in training are there for you,
That is their job after all,
So remember that when you are blue,
Or you are feeling small.

When you have trouble sleeping,
And it seems hardships tug at your life,
Remember it only takes a prayer,
To put an end to the strife.

The peace of angels can be yours,
They will guard your sleep,
And keep you in their shelter,
Through the dark and through the deep.

When you're sick and weak,
And pain fills your head,
Think of the angels surrounding you,
Giving comfort instead.

Even when people aren't around,
Angels have plenty to do,
Though you may not see their actions,
The results are a help to you.

Look at things with an open heart,
Surprised you just might be,
How often you can see an angel,
In what you can actually see.

You are never truly alone,
With an angel by your side,
Imagination is always sparked,
When with angels you abide.

And even as you grow older,
Don't forget this way to see,
For it will help you be the person,
You were born to be.

The side of goodness may seem quiet,
It hardly makes a fuss,
But goes on doing what is right,
No matter what the muss.

For goodness connects to the Creator,
The Maker of us all,
And even where cell phones can't reach,
He always hears your call.

Nelani Nettrour

Darkness can never hide His light,
If you call He will always hear,
And send the help you need,
In the meantime He'll hold you near.

You can call out anytime,
Even if you are lost,
He will hear and answer,
For He has paid the cost.

In little things and little steps,
What we choose and what we do,
Makes it easier to be one way,
Makes it easier to be false or true.

Just because you are a child,
Doesn't mean your choices don't count,
Choices you make have a consequence,
And that is true without a doubt.

For you were born with a conscience,
Though it may be quiet at the start,
It is there to be your guide,
If you listen with your heart.

Don't put yourself above others,
Don't neglect to do what is right,
Follow what leads to good,
And you'll be following the light.

Angels in Training

Think how you want to be treated,
And treat others that way,
And angels will be smiling,
And helping you on that path to stay.

And when you're tempted to do wrong,
Tell those demons to "get out of here!"
Call the angels to your side,
And demons will run away in fear.

Don't make excuses or blame others,
For something that you have done,
Take responsibility for your actions,
And from the truth don't run.

Don't give demons power over you,
By doing the wrong they suggest,
They cannot force you to do anything,
They tempt, but you do the rest.

So in your time of choosing,
Put a face to the choices you make,
Would an angel smile at your decision?
Or would you see a demon's smile so fake?

Books by Nelani A. Nettrour
(More are always in the works)

Check out the website: www.3mpub.com/nettrour

Adult fantasy (just in case your parents want to read something)

Soaring Free (Book One of the Soaring Free Trilogy)

Arcan's Revenge (Book Two of the Soaring Free Trilogy)

A Fatal Blow (Book Three of the Soaring Free Trilogy)

Chantra's Awakening (Book One of the Awakening Trilogy) (starts where A Fatal Blow left off and continues on the series)

Poetry (Also available on Audio CD)

Steps (Poetry, Musings and the Short Story, A Trespass in Time) (with b+w illustrations by Autumn I. Nettrour and Barry E. Nettrour)

Pathways (Poetry, Musings and the Short Story, *The Forgotten Void*) (with contributions from some family members and color artwork.)

Children's Books, (and for those who've never lost their child's heart) (Also available on Audio CD) Full Color Illustrations

(Illustrated by Heather D. Nettrour or Autumn I. Nettrour)

Tales of Lamac—the world of Lamac, in the newness of creation, the world introduced in the Soaring Free Trilogy, but with enchanting color illustrations to show the world, the people and the creatures with children in mind. Also great background for those who want to know more of the ancestors and creatures of Lamac, the world of Lamac, and the worlds that have dealings with Lamac.

Anara Arrives—Book One (the first princess of Lamac to be born) H.D.N.

Birth of Takaira—Book Two (at home on Flittaf, before Takaira found Anara) A.I.N.

Calastapeas' Gathering—Book Three (Who are these calastapeas?)A.I.N.

Other children's books:

Nunkey's Adventures—Book One (introduces Nunkey the draget and his world in rhyme.)A.I.N.

Nunkey's Adventures—Book Two—*Birth of Reekey* (In rhyme tells the story of Nunkey the draget and his new baby sister Reekey) A.I.N.

The Dragon Lands—Book One—*The Ripple* (two children from Earth caught up in an other-worldly adventure. Will they ever make it back home?) H.D.N.

The Dragon Lands—Book Two—*Banshees* (continuing adventures of William and Dusty, and their new friends of Dragon Lands, this time an encounter with Banshees.)H.D.N.

The Dragon Lands—Book Three—*The Village* (What do William and Dusty learn when they finally reach Usa's village?) H.D.N.

The Imagynairs of Jemmidar—Book One (through rhyme introduces some of the creatures of Jemmidar) A.I.N.

The Imagynairs of Jemmidar—Book A—*Andree, Alleeo and Alpeeka* (through rhyme tell more of the Andree, Alleeo and Alpeeka) A.I. N.

Cow's Milk (my interpretation of why we started drinking cow's milk in the first place) H.D.N.

Dog Tails—Book One—*Welcoming Garcon* (the first week in a new home from the dog's point of view, in this case, Garcon) H.D.N.

Dog Tails—Book Two—*All About Krammer* (see the world through the eyes of Krammer, the Nettrours' feisty Boston Terrier) H.D.N.

Jodi's Bugs (through rhyme introduces Jodi, whose love of bugs—the ones with the dots especially—enlightens her friends to the joys of nature around them.) H.D.N.

Jodi and the Seasons (through rhyme Jodi, her family and friends enjoy the diversity of the seasons.) H.D.N.

Dragon Guardians—Book One—Meeshu's Keep (Meeshu is given a new life and along with it a task for his life and the charge of a dragon's egg.) Not intended for small children. Animated injuries depicted. H.D.N.

Angels in Training (the unseen struggle between good and evil is depicted and the story told through rhyme.) H.D.N.

Illustrated by Tina R. Lesnick:

Dragonfly Flight (through rhyme follow a dragonfly on his flight around the Northwoods.)T.R.L.

Angels in Training

Biography: Nelani

Nelani lives in Northern Wisconsin with her husband Barry and their five children, Josh, Jasmine, Sam, Heather and Autumn. With Sam's marriage in 2004 Jamie has joined their family. The members of the family continue to contribute their artistic talents to complement Nelani's writing. Krammer, their feisty Boston Terrier, has been joined by Winry and The Cuteness, Boston Terrier/Toy Poodle Mix.

Nelani is the 4th child of 9. She has 5 brothers, Kirk, Devan, Keith, Patrick and Marc, and 3 sisters Moana, Simone and Karen.

The family enjoys the great outdoors and the multitude of activities it affords. Among some of their favorites are: Stargazing, Iridology, Herbal Healing, Biking, Hiking, Swimming and Gardening.

Angels in Training is Nelani's 24th book, her 18th children's book. She also writes adult fantasy and poetry.

Nelani records audio CDs of her children's books and books of poetry. With the help of her woodworking husband they have turned many of Nelani's poems into framed Canvas Prints. The poetry is printed superimposed on background pictures Nelani has taken of the Northwoods area.

In the winter of 2006, to keep her fans informed on the progress of upcoming books, book signings, contests and events Nelani along with Heather and Autumn have started their own newsletter called *Creature Companion News*.

Nelani Nettrour

Biography: Heather

Heather was born May 19, 1982. She is the 4th child of 5, the second girl.

Angels in Training is the 11th children's book she has illustrated. The others are: *Tales of Lamac, Book One, Anara Arrives: Cow's Milk: Dog Tails, Book One, Welcoming Garcon: Dog Tails, Book Two, All About Krammer: The Dragon Lands Book One, The Ripple: The Dragon Lands, Book Two, Banshees: The Dragon Lands, Book Three, The Village: Jodi's Bugs, Jodi and the Seasons and Dragon Guardians, Book One, Meeshu's Keep.* She also has poetry, musings and artwork in a section of *Pathways*.

On the CD versions of *The Dragon Lands Book One, Two, and Three* she wrote and sang a short song. *For Dog Tails, Book Two, All About Krammer*, she also wrote and sang a short song for Krammer. She also created the music and sang the story of *Jodi's Bugs* on its CD. Heather is in the process of illustrating more children's books.

Last year Heather became an apprentice dog groomer. She is learning from the ground up and finds it also helps her with the characterizations of the dogs and other creatures she draws.

Some of Heather's favorite activities include, illustrating, writing, playing all kinds of flutes and ocarinas, walking, biking, hiking, playing video games, swimming, stargazing and gardening.

She also enjoys taking care of children. The children that Heather has been babysitting over the years have made their way into her contributions in *Pathways* and *All About Krammer*. Many have also become characters in other books she illustrates, or have posed for some of the characters.

Heather's new puppy Winry (full name Winry Inu Nettrour), a Boston/Terrier toy poodle mix has added a new joy to Heather's life and more inspiration. She's even crept into this book (along with her sister The Cuteness—Autumn's dog and Krammer.)